Essential GWT

Developer's Library Series

Visit **developers-library.com** for a complete list of available products

---

The **Developer's Library Series** from Addison-Wesley provides practicing programmers with unique, high-quality references and tutorials on the latest programming languages and technologies they use in their daily work. All books in the Developer's Library are written by expert technology practitioners who are exceptionally skilled at organizing and presenting information in a way that's useful for other programmers.

Developer's Library books cover a wide range of topics, from open-source programming languages and databases, Linux programming, Microsoft, and Java, to Web development, social networking platforms, Mac/iPhone programming, and Android programming.

Essential GWT

Building for the Web with Google Web Toolkit 2

Federico Kereki

✦✦ Addison-Wesley

Upper Saddle River, NJ • Boston • Indianapolis • San Francisco
New York • Toronto • Montreal • London • Munich • Paris • Madrid
Capetown • Sydney • Tokyo • Singapore • Mexico City

Many of the designations used by manufacturers and sellers to distinguish their products are claimed as trademarks. Where those designations appear in this book, and the publisher was aware of a trademark claim, the designations have been printed with initial capital letters or in all capitals.

The author and publisher have taken care in the preparation of this book, but make no expressed or implied warranty of any kind and assume no responsibility for errors or omissions. No liability is assumed for incidental or consequential damages in connection with or arising out of the use of the information or programs contained herein.

The publisher offers excellent discounts on this book when ordered in quantity for bulk purchases or special sales, which may include electronic versions and/or custom covers and content particular to your business, training goals, marketing focus, and branding interests. For more information, please contact:

U.S. Corporate and Government Sales
(800) 382-3419
corpsales@pearsontechgroup.com

For sales outside the United States please contact:

International Sales
international@pearson.com

Visit us on the Web: informit.com/aw

Library of Congress Cataloging-in-Publication Data

Kereki, Federico, 1960-
  Essential GWT : building for the web with Google Web toolkit 2 / Federico Kereki.
       p. cm.
  Includes index.
  ISBN-13: 978-0-321-70514-3 (pbk. : alk. paper)
  ISBN-10: 0-321-70514-9 (pbk. : alk. paper)
1. Ajax (Web site development technology) 2. Java (Computer program language)
3. Google Web toolkit. 4. Application software–Development. I. Title.
  TK5105.8885.A52K47 2011
  006.7'6–dc22
                                                              2010018606

ISBN-13: 978-0-321-70514-3
ISBN-10:   0-321-70514-9
Text printed in the United States on recycled paper at RR Donnelley in Crawfordsville, IN.
First printing, July 2010

Editor-in-Chief
Mark Taub

Acquisitions Editor
Trina MacDonald

Development Editor
Songlin Qiu

Managing Editor
John Fuller

Project Editor
Anna Popick

Copy Editor
Apostrophe Editing Services

Indexer
Jack Lewis

Proofreader
Linda Begley

Editorial Assistant
Olivia Basegio

Technical Reviewers
Jason Essington
Jim Hathaway
Daniel Wellman

Cover Designer
Gary Adair

Compositor
Rob Mauhar

To my parents, Eugenio Kereki and Susana Guerrero, who got me started on my way, and always stood by me, and to my wife, Sylvia Tosar, who had to bear without a husband while I wrote the book, who nevertheless kept the family and home going on, and without whom I wouldn't want to go anywhere.

Contents at a Glance

Contents

x   Contents

Preface

Developing modern, interactive, complex web sites has become a harder task since users' expectations are higher today. The bar has been raised by the current crop of applications such as Gmail or Google Maps, and developers are expected to work up to that level and provide similarly powerful new web sites. The style, speed, and interaction levels of modern sites practically rival those of classical desktop installed applications, and of course users don't want to go back. How do you develop such sites?

It can be said that the usage of Ajax was what started the trend toward such distinctive applications, but even given that technique, the rest of the development of web pages was the same, tools were the same, testing methods were the same, and the whole result was that the programmers' jobs had gotten much harder than needed.

(Personally, I should confess that I really never liked classic-style web development: Building large-sized applications was harder than it needed to be, JavaScript was—and still is—missing constructs geared to complex systems, the click-wait-click-wait again cycle was inevitably slow and not very interactive, and, to top it all, unless you were quite careful with your testing, your design was prone to fail on this or that browser in unexpected ways.)

GWT, in just a very few years, has grown into a powerful tool by harnessing the power of Java and its considerable programming environment and many development tools, and producing efficient and consistent output, despite the too-many and well-known incompatibilities between browsers.

Getting started with GWT isn't that hard—documentation is reasonably good, the development environment can be Eclipse or several other equally powerful IDEs, and programming is quite similar to old-fashioned Java Swing coding—so you can have your first short application up and running in a short time.

Creating production-quality, secure, internationally compliant, high-level code can be, however, a bit more complex. You need to take many factors into account, from the initial setup of your project and development of the user interface, to the final compile and deployment of your application.

Similarly, we'll also have to focus on methodologies and on software design patterns, so we can go forth in a safer, more organized way toward the complete application. For example, we'll consider how the model-view-presenter (MVP) pattern can not only enhance the design of the application, but also help run fully automatic tests, in modern Agile programming style, to attain higher quality, better tested software.

We'll be working with the latest tools and versions; not only GWT's (2.0.3 just now), but also Eclipse, Subversion, Tomcat, Apache, MySQL, and so on. Because all these tools are open source, we can support the notion that an appropriate software stack can be built starting with GWT and ending with a full open web solution.

After my earlier confession on my dislike of classic web development strategies, I should now aver that GWT did change that for me. Working in a high-level setting, with plenty of tools, and practically forgetting about browser quirks, HTML, CSS, and JavaScript, while gaining in clarity, maintainability, and performance, has made web application creation an enjoyable task again!

The Structure of This Book

Chapters 1 through 3 deal with the basic setup for working with GWT. After considering the main reasons and objectives for using GWT, we'll study what other tools are required for serious code development, the methodology to use, and the internal aspects of projects.

Chapters 4 and 5 are the backbone for the book, for they deal with the basic design patterns that we use for building the User Interface. The code style and idioms developed here will be used throughout the rest of the book.

Chapters 6 and 7 deal with communications with servers, either through RPC (to connect with servlets) or through direct Ajax (to communicate with remote services).

Chapters 8 and 9 study how to add both JavaScript coding and third-party APIs to your application. Together with the previous two chapters, everything that's needed for mashing up services and getting information from different sources will have been covered.

Chapters 10 and 11 have to do with common server related problems, such as security aspects, and file upload and download.

Chapter 12 deals with developing GWT applications that will be used worldwide and covers both internationalization and localization.

Finally, Chapters 13 through 15 consider general themes such as testing GWT applications, optimizing their performance, and finally deploying them.

Who Should Read This Book

This book goes beyond "just learn GWT," and is targeted to programmers who already have a basis of GWT programming and want to encompass other web applications, services, APIs, and standards as well, to produce Web 2.0-compliant Rich Internet Applications (RIAs). A previous experience with web development, possibly in a J2EE environment, will come in handy.

Having read this book through, the reader should not only be able to develop a RIA on his own by just using GWT, but he will also have a reference book to help solve the common problems that arise in such applications. Complete source code is given for all examples, so getting started is quicker.

Web Resources for This Book

The Google Web Toolkit site at http://code.google.com/webtoolkit/ is a mandatory reference, and so is the forum at http://groups.google.com/group/google-web-toolkit.

The code examples for this book are available on the book's web site at www.informit.com/title/9780321705143.

Acknowledgments

Writing a book can be a daunting task (and I should know because the idea really frightened me at the beginning) and without the collaboration of many people, it would probably become almost impossible.

I would like to thank the Addison-Wesley team, led by Trina MacDonald, who first had the idea for this book and then followed it through all the way, helping me deal with the many stages and norms of the book writing process, answering myriad questions, and giving shape to the book from an initial basic plan to its final structure. The fact that I live "down below" in Montevideo, Uruguay, with five hours' difference in time with regard to the location of her office, also surely added an extra bit of complexity to the whole experience!

I would also like to thank Songlin Qiu, the development editor, and Jason Essington, Jim Hathaway, and Daniel Wellman, the three technical editors, who had the task of sifting through all my code and text, endeavoring to make the book clearer, better organized, correctly formatted, well structured, and more easily understood. Reading other people's code is never easy, and doing that with a critic's eye, seeking to make it clearer, checking if it's well commented and explained, and endeavoring to make the whole more pedagogic and comprehensible obviously adds a lot to the job to be done.

I would also like to highlight and thank the contributions of Gabriel Ledesma, Enrique Rodríguez, Miguel Trías, and Rodolfo Vázquez, who through many discussions (with or without an eventual agreement!) on Java, design patterns, web development techniques, usability, and teaching, helped shape many of the chapters in the book.

Finally, I would also like to thank the mostly nameless Google people who made GWT possible, who roam the GWT forums helping everybody in need of aid, who write documentation, examples, and tutorials, and who constantly seek to make GWT even better and more powerful.

About the Author

Federico Kereki is a Uruguayan systems engineer, with more than twenty years' experience as a consultant, system developer, university professor, and writer. He has been applying and teaching GWT since 2007. He has taught several computer science courses at the Universidad de la República, Universidad ORT Uruguay, and the Instituto Universitario Autónomo del Sur. He has written texts for some of these courses, and several articles—on GWT and other open source topics—for magazines such as *Linux Journal* and *LinuxPro Magazine* in the United States, *Linux+* and *Mundo Linux* in Europe, and for web sites such as linux.com and IBM Developer Works. Kereki gave talks on GWT in public conferences organized by Microsoft and TCS in 2008 and 2009, and he has used GWT to develop several companywide Internet systems for businesses in Uruguay. His current interests tend toward software quality and software engineering—with Agile Methodologies topmost—while on the practical side he is working with tools such as GWT and Java, Ajax, SOA, and PHP. He has been working with Open Source Software (FLOSS) for more than ten years, with both Windows and Linux. He resides, works, and teaches in Uruguay.

Developing Your Application

Why would you use GWT? What can you develop with it and how? Before delving into specifics (as we'll be doing in the rest of the book) let's consider the answers to these questions, so you'll know what to focus on.

Developing applications with GWT can be seen as a straightforward job, but you should ask some interesting questions to unlock the way to powerful, distinct, applications. What kind of applications should you develop with GWT? (And, given the current push for Cloud Computing, you can even add "Where would you deploy your application?") How can you go about it? And, why would you use GWT?

Let's consider all these questions in sequence to start you on your way through this book, knowing your goal and the road to it.

Rich Internet Applications

When you start reading about Rich Internet Applications (RIAs), your JAB (Jargon, Acronyms, and Buzzwords) warning should go off because there are many words that are bandied about, without necessarily a good, solid definition or a clear delimitation of their meanings.

Basically, what we build are web applications that have the look and feel of classic desktop applications but that are delivered (and "installed") over the web. Many tools have been used for this purpose, such as Java (through applets), Adobe Flash, and more recently, Microsoft Silverlight, but used in this way, all these tools are beaten, in terms of practicality, by simple HTML-based systems.

The RIAs that we will be developing are based on JavaScript and Ajax and just require an appropriate browser to run. Classic web applications were developed with a different set of tools, subjected the user to frequent waits (the hourglass cursor was often seen), and had severe restrictions as to usability, with a much clunkier feel to them than desktop installed programs.

Although some people distinguish between RIAs and the kind of interactive web applications we build, the frontiers are getting blurrier and blurrier. You could argue that Flash or Silverlight require preinstalled plugins, or that development runs along different lines, but in terms of the final result (which is what the user experiences) differences are not so marked, and well-designed HTML/JavaScript/Ajax applications can compete for equality with applications developed with the other tools. (Also, some people opine that HTML 5 can seriously challenge Flash, up to the point of making it obsolete, but that's still to come.[1]) There used to be obvious differences—the ability to store local data at the user's machine was the biggest one—but tools such as Google Gears or current developments in HTML 5 have provided this feature to web applications.[2]

Given its ubiquity (from desktops to netbooks, and from cell phones to tablet PCs) the browser can be considered a universal tool, and Ajax provides the best way for the creation of highly interactive applications. Of course, a few years ago there weren't many tools for doing this (GWT itself appeared in 2006) and creating heavy-lifting interactive code with just JavaScript wasn't (and still isn't) an appealing idea.[3]

Furthermore, given that users have been subjected for many years to web applications, and are familiar with their idioms, you are a bit ahead in terms of user interface design by keeping to a reasonable standard.

As for the language itself, using Java as a tool—even if it gets compiled into JavaScript, as GWT does—provides both a way around JavaScript's deficiencies and introduces a widely used language with plenty of development tools, which has been used over and over for all kinds of applications and has been proved to scale to large-sized applications.[4]

Web 2.0

Web 2.0 is another expression that has been bandied about a lot since its invention in 2004. Though there are way too many definitions for it, most seem to agree on the idea of using the "Web as Platform," where all applications run in a browser instead of being preinstalled on your desktop. Furthermore, the idea of allowing users to produce their own contents (à la Wikipedia) is also included, highlighting the collaborative aspect of work, and thus bringing into the fold all kind of community and social networking sites (think Facebook or YouTube). Finally (and that's what actually works for us) the concept of *mashing* together different data sources (probably from many web services) is also included.

1. See www.ibm.com/developerworks/web/library/wa-html5webapp/ for an article of some HTML 5 features already available in current browsers.

2. Google Gears' development was practically stopped (other than support for currently available versions) by the end of 2009 because of the upcoming HTML 5 features for local storage.

3. It might be said that developing large applications with, say, Flash, isn't a walk in the park either, for different reasons to be sure, but complicating the programmer's job in any case.

4. It should be remarked that GWT isn't the only such compile-to-JavaScript solution; for example, the Python-based Pyjamas project (http://code.google.com/p/pyjamas/) provides Python-to-JavaScript translation, and there are many more similar tools.

GWT applications can obviously be used for producing highly interactive people sites, but they can also link together information from different origins, consuming web services with no difficulty, either connecting directly to the server or by means of proxy-based solutions. Various data formats are also not a problem; if you cannot work with such standards as XML or JSON, you can include external libraries (or roll out your own) through JSNI or Java programming. (We cover this in Chapter 8, "Mixing in JavaScript," and Chapter 9, "Adding APIs.")

In this context, the phrase Service-Oriented Architectures (SOA) frequently pops up. Instead of developing tightly integrated, almost monolithic, applications, SOA proposes basing your systems on a loosely integrated group of services. These services are general in purpose and can be used in the context of different applications—and, as previously mentioned, GWT is perfectly suited to "consuming" such services, dealing with different protocols and standards. (We'll cover this in Chapter 6, "Communicating with Your Server," and Chapter 7, "Communicating with Other Servers.") If your company is centered on an SOA strategy, your GWT-developed applications will fit perfectly well.

Cloud Computing

Next to the idea of using the browser as the basis for the user's experience, the most current term related to modern application development is *Cloud Computing*. This idea reflects the concept of sharing resources over the web, on demand, instead of each user having a private, limited pool of resources. In this view, software is considered a "service" (the acronym SAAS, which stands for "Software as a Service," is often used) and a resource similar to more "tangible" ones as hardware.

(As an aside, the vulnerability of some operating systems, most notably Windows, to viruses, worms, and similar attacks, has given a push to the idea of using a simple, secure, machine and storing everything "on the web," letting the cloud administrators deal with hackers and program infections.)

For many, this concept is yet another cycle going from centralized resources (think mainframes) to distributed processing (PCs, possibly in client/server configurations) and now to having the web as your provider. The main requirements for such an architecture involve reliable services and software, delivered through specific data centers, and running on unspecified servers; for the user, the web provides an access to a cloud of resources.

For GWT applications, your applications are basically destined from the ground up to be used "in the cloud" because of the standard restrictions imposed by browsers. Distributing an application over the web, accessing it from anywhere, and having your data stored in a basically unknown place are all characteristics of any applications you might write.[5]

---

5. With current (or forthcoming) standards, you might also resort to storing data locally, or to using your own private, dedicated, resources, but that's not original and more often associated with classic desktop applications.

The "Death of the Desktop"

The trend toward Cloud Computing has even spawned a new concept: the "Death of the Desktop." This presents rather starkly the problem of going overboard, to the limit: From the appearance of mini netbooks (with flash-based disks, slow processors, not much RAM) and iPhone-look-alike cell phones, some have reached the conclusion that desktop applications (and even desktop computers!) are on their way out. If this were true, it could be great for GWT developers, but things are a bit different.

Despite several impressive opinions and pronouncements from people all over the industry, the trend toward more powerful machines, with CPUs, memory, and I/O facilities that put to shame the supercomputers of just a few years ago, doesn't seem to be slowing down. Even if you are enamored with the latest netbooks or high-powered cellphones, you should accept that working all the time with minimal screens isn't the way that things can get done at a company. (And for gaming or graphic-intense usages, small machines aren't so hot either; they may do, however, for business-oriented applications.) In any case, GWT can help you because you can use its layout facilities and CSS styling to produce applications for just about any device out there.

Also, remove the rosy glasses for an instant. Cloud computing offers several advantages (and GWT applications can be considered to be right in the middle of that concept) but also presents problems, so you need to plan accordingly. Aside from the obvious difficulty of dealing with possibly flaky web connections, security and compatibility can be stumbling blocks. (On the other hand, scalability is well handled; there are plenty of large sites, with hundreds or thousands of servers, proving that web applications can scale well.) The important point is, with or without desktops, GWT provides some ways around these kind of problems, and we'll study this in upcoming chapters.[6]

Advantages of GWT

Why would you develop with GWT? Shouldn't directly using JavaScript make more sense? How do you manage with browser quirks? Let's consider the reasons for GWT.

HTML Ubiquity and Browser Differences

The first reason for GWT applications is the ubiquity of HTML. Even if some time ago browsers for, say, cell phones, weren't as capable as their desktop brethren, nowadays you can basically find the exact same capabilities in both. In terms of GWT, this is a boon because it means that a well-designed application can run and look pretty in devices from 3 inches to 25 inches.[7]

---

6. And, of course, these inconveniences haven't stopped anyone from developing HTML-based applications!

7. Don't expect to get the screen design right the first time; managing to build clear, small screen browser applications is more an art than a science.

This availability is somehow tempered because today's browsers are not created equal—but you certainly knew that if you designed web pages on your own! When Microsoft's Internet Explorer ruled the roost, having practically 100% of the browser market, this wasn't a noticeable problem. However, today browser usage statistics point to a different status quo: Mozilla Firefox and Safari, among others, have started carving larger and larger niches in the market, and in some countries (mostly European) they have out-numbered Internet Explorer. The current trend is toward applying web standards, and that bodes well for web developers. In any case, GWT is quite adept at solving browser quirks and differences, so the point may be considered moot for the time being.

JavaScript Deficiencies

Even assuming fully standard-compliant browsers, the fact remains that JavaScript, no matter how powerful, isn't a good language from the specific point of view of software engineering. Because this isn't a book on JavaScript, we won't delve in its main problems, but using it for large-sized application development can be, to say the least, a bit complicated.

This language isn't well adapted either to development by large groups of people, and the tools it provides for system development aren't that adequate, so the programmer must add extra code to bridge the distance between a modern object-oriented design and its actual implementation.

One solution that has been applied is the usage of different libraries that provide a higher-level way of using the language.[8] GWT solves this problem in a radically different way, by enabling the use of the higher level Java language, for which there are plenty of modern development, testing, and documentation tools.

Software Methodologies to Apply

For classic application development, many well-known methodologies exist, but in the context of modern web development, you should definitely use some techniques.

Classic Development Problems

If you learned to develop systems years ago, you were surely exposed to the Waterfall Model or some other methodologies directly based on it. In this model for the development process, progress is seen as flowing like a waterfall from stage to stage, through

---

8. You could consider Google's "Closure" library (see http://code.google.com/closure/) used for Gmail's development, or Yahoo!'s YUI library (see http://developer.yahoo.com/yui/), jQuery (http://jquery.com/), Dojo (www.dojotoolkit.org/), Prototype (www.prototypejs.org/), MooTools (http://mootools.net/), and many others. The functionality of these libraries isn't always the same, but there's considerable overlap between them, showing the problems they set out to solve are real and well known.

well-defined phases (see Figure 1.1) starting with the Analysis of Requirements, following with the Design of the Solution and its Implementation, then to Testing (or Quality Assurance), and finally to Installation and future Maintenance.

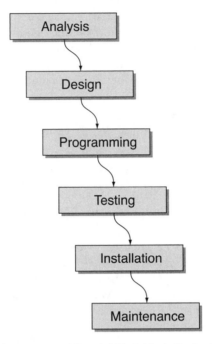

Figure 1.1 The classic Waterfall Model isn't the best possible
for GWT development.

This model is flawed in several ways (and of course, there are some fixes for that) but its main problem is its orientation to highly regimented industries such as Construction, in which late changes can be quite costly to implement, usually requiring tearing down what was done and practically starting anew.

Another point—and an important one—is that you cannot expect users to be fully aware of what they require; it is sometimes said "Users don't know what they want, but they know what they don't want."[9] Classical methodologies do not take this into consideration, and might thus incur important costs, because newly discovered or determined requirements can invalidate a previous design.

Finally, it's difficult to predict where difficulties will occur; problems with functionality are usually found "on the go," and if going back to change something to help future development is too costly, you can face a dilemma: Spend money and time revising your

9. "I'll know it when I see it" is another way of expressing this.

design, or keep your substandard design, and spend money and time later trying to make your software do tasks it wasn't well designed to do.

It has been said that the Waterfall Model, and similar ones, are based on the old "Measure Twice, Cut Once" saw, but you cannot actually apply this when you don't actually know what's being measured! (And, furthermore, what happens if requirements change along the way, and by the time you finish with development, the problem has actually changed?) Modern, agile technologies try to take this into account and work in a radically different way, and that's the way you should use with GWT.

Agile Methodologies

Several software development methodologies seek to reduce the time between the requirement analysis phase and the development phase to develop at least parts of the system in shorter times, using possibly an iterative method to advance to the final application. Prototypes are frequently used to bridge the distance between the user and the developer, helping both to understand what's actually required. Instead of attempting to do a whole system at once, development is parceled in smaller subsystems. The user is involved all the time, instead of providing his input (in the form of requirements) only at the beginning and then dealing with the system after its installation.

All these suggestions are currently applied in Agile Software Methodologies (born in 2001) that emphasize collective (i.e., users plus programmers) development of systems, in highly iterative steps, with frequent verification and (if needed) adaptation of the written code.

Agile Methodologies usually break a complex system into several short stages, substituting short, easily measured and controlled iterations, for long-term (and hard to do) planning. Each iteration (usually shorter than a month) involves a mini development cycle that includes all the stages associated with a Waterfall Model but finishes with giving the users a working product with increasing functionality that serves not only as a measure of advance, but also as an aid to determine if changes are needed. The delivered software is used as the main measurement for progress, instead of depending on a Gantt chart or other documents.

GWT is perfectly suited to such methodologies, because it can offer iterative development, rapid prototyping (and here tools such as UiBinder, which we will study, can help quickly develop appropriate interfaces), and automated testing. The latter point is particularly important: Given that development can (and will) go back and forth, and code used in a previous iteration can be modified several times along the complete development process, it's important to check whether old functionality hasn't been lost and whether bugs have been introduced. GWT has tools that provide for both unit testing (at the lowest level) and acceptance testing (at the user level).

Forever Beta?

As a side effect of the iterative development process, it's usually hard to define what constitutes a "version" of the final system. Because practically every iteration produces new functionality, and the final goal isn't as well defined as with classic methodologies (in which the complete roadmap is laid out at the beginning and then preferably left unchanged) with iterative development, you deliver the system in many small steps, rather than in large ones.

In this context, it's not unknown for systems to be considered in "perpetual beta"; beta testing refers to the tests done by actual users with a system that is close to the full product but not necessarily complete. (An extreme case of this is Google's Gmail, which was considered to be at beta level from 2004 to 2009!) With GWT, you can provide functionality increases in short steps, and the web model enables for easy distribution of the updated code.[10]

Summary

We touched upon several considerations that impact web application development. In the rest of the book, we will be elaborating on them and provide specific techniques to help you develop company-sized RIAs with the expected levels of quality and functionality.

10. This could be said, of course, of any web-based application not necessarily written with GWT; the point is that GWT helps you work this way.

Getting Started with GWT 2

Why use GWT 2? What are its advantages and disadvantages? What is required to take advantage of this tool? How should you plan your work? In this chapter we consider the whys, whats, and hows of GWT development; why you and your company should consider its usage, what components are included in its framework, and how—with which tools—you should do your development.

Why Use GWT?

Since its introduction at the JavaOne conference in May 2006, GWT has been evolving, going from version 1.0 through 1.7 and up to the current 2.0.3, but the question is still asked frequently: Why would you code web applications with GWT? Why not stay with JavaScript? What advantages does GWT bring? Is it a complete framework for web development? Even if you are already comfortable with GWT, these questions bear consideration: Why would you recommend using GWT at your job?

Let's start by defining what GWT is: It's a tool that enables you to develop client-side code, working with Java, and compiling your code into JavaScript, which is then executed at the client's browser. The final product is a web application with almost desktop-application levels of interactivity, which executes client-side with minimal needs of server-side code or interaction. Compiling into JavaScript provides an extra touch of speed, and the final code is optimized and as good, or better, than human written code. And, most important, you won't need to (Okay, almost never will; see Chapter 4, "Working with Browsers," for specific cases in which you may want or have to) worry about browser differences and quirks because GWT generates appropriate code for each specific browser.[1]

---

1. The idea of compiling to JavaScript isn't a GWT exclusive: Several other tools, such as Pyjamas (see http://code.google.com/p/pyjamas/) or OpenLaszlo (see www.openlaszlo.org/) also work this way.

Why Java?

The usage of Java is quite relevant. For starters, there's a wealth of Java-experienced pro-grammers, and the learning curve for GWT isn't as hard as for other frameworks.[2] On the other hand, JavaScript development is as yet still far from mature, with little support from IDEs, and too basic debugging methods—`alert(...)` calls are still probably the most commonly used tool! Of course, if Java isn't good enough, or if you have some special-case-coding situation, you can resort to JavaScript code that can call and be called from your Java code. Another plus is debugging your code by using Java debuggers.

Java also is well suited for Agile Development Methodologies, such as XP or Scrum. TDD (Test Driven Development) is highly encouraged, with support for JUnit testing, both for client- and server-side code. (In Chapter 13, "Testing Your GWT Application," we'll go over the topic of GWT code testing.)

Web development also becomes easier; you can develop the presentation layer by either using Swing-like techniques (as in common Java desktop programming), an HTML-based approach, or the recent UIBinder declarative technique. (We will cover this ground in Chapter 5, "Programming the User Interface.") If you want a better look, you can integrate widget or effects libraries to enhance the look of your application.

Some Actual Disadvantages

So, what's not to like? To be fair, let's consider some of the (real or imagined) disadvan-tages of GWT. Despite all we have said, which are good reasons for using GWT, you should also mind some negative points.

For starters, GWT web pages aren't indexable by search engines. Because the applica-tion is generated dynamically, search engines cannot index its contents. Some solutions, such as *cloaking,* exist (having two sets of pages and presenting one to common users and other with different content to search engine spiders) but they are difficult to apply with GWT and might even fall afoul of indexing engines. If your business model somehow depends on Search Engine Optimization (SEO) considerations, GWT might not be fully adequate for you.

Also, GWT pages do not "gracefully degrade" in the presence of older browsers; either the application will or won't run, but there's no middle ground with limited func-tionality or restricted scope.[3] Techniques such as *progressive enhancement* can be applied (meaning, deploy a most basic site, which enables extra functionality if and only if the browser supports it) but would demand duplicate coding, because if the user's browser

---

2. The GWT team explains that they didn't just want to develop technology for the sake of doing so, and Java already had many available tools. See http://code.google.com/webtoolkit/makinggwtbetter.html for more details.

3. The current attitude is "just upgrade," which tends to ignore valid reasons why users would want or have to use older versions of more modern browsers.

doesn't match GWT's requirements, the application most surely will fail. You can apply some workarounds for a few problems (such as using `iframes` to simulate Ajax calls) but an inappropriate browser is usually a stumbling block. Happily, this objection is slowly fading away, and in time you won't need to worry about this. However, if you require, for example, using your application with cell phones, you might find out that many users will be locked out because of inadequacies in their browsers.[4]

For security, GWT applications are just as prone to attacks as any JavaScript application. (We will consider security aspects in Chapter 10, "Working with Servers.") Using GWT won't allow you to just ignore security. There are, however, some security-related enhancements coming up (to avoid some of the more common attacks) but for the time being, you should just take the same precautions as for web applications developed with any other tools.[5]

Developers may complain that compiling and deploying is slower than with straight JavaScript. This is probably trivially true (*no* compilation beats *any* compilation!) but the point here is that writing the code is slower and more bug prone with JavaScript than with Java. There are fewer tools for JavaScript coding, browsers have many quirks, and your program will be full of `if (isIE8)...` tests. A solution is to use libraries such as jQuery, prototype, Dojo, or ExtJS, which wrap some of those differences internally... but in this case, why not use GWT that enables you to fully forget those differences?[6]

Similar notions are proposed by others who simply suggest that to develop rich Internet applications, you should be directly working with JavaScript, because that's "what real programmers do," and forget any alternatives! This conclusion is supported by the notion that the Java-to-JavaScript conversion should necessarily be poor (because of the differences between both languages) and that the generated code will be bulky and slow. Apart from the unwarranted latter objections, the key point here is that JavaScript isn't the only problem; the differing implementations across browsers are the other big problem. Real browser-independent code is quite hard to write (and larger, too) and it's difficult to ensure the application of the required discipline; you end up spending more time, and writing more code, to achieve the same results as with a few lines of Java.[7]

---

4. Android cell phones and iPhone tend to work well out-of-the-box, but that's not the rule for all current cell phones.

5. In any case, note that GWT applications are neither more nor less prone to attacks than any other JavaScript website, so this shouldn't be considered a GWT-specific disadvantage but rather a "fact of life" as pertaining to web development.

6. For more on this, read the "Reveling in Constraints" article by one of GWT creators, Bruce Johnson, at http://queue.acm.org/detail.cfm?id=1572457.

7. If you worry about what happens when a new browser version is released, check the answer to "Will my app break when a new browser comes out?" in the GWT FAQ at http://code.google.com/webtoolkit/doc/latest/FAQ_GettingStarted.html.

The GWT Components

In this section we will discuss the three basic components of GWT: the high-quality Java-to-JavaScript compiler, the Java Runtime Environment (JRE) Emulation library, and the User Interface (UI) library. If you were used to previous versions of GWT (up to 1.7) you may be missing the "hosted browser" that enabled you to try out code in hosted mode, but GWT now uses "in browser development" (and development mode) that enables you to directly test your application on your own browser, as we'll see in Chapter 3, "Understanding Projects and Development."[8]

Compiler

The first and most important component of GWT is the Java-to-JavaScript compiler. It takes your Java 1.5 code and produces distinct equivalent JavaScript versions that can be run on all supported browsers: At the time of writing, all versions of Safari and Firefox, Opera (at least up to versions 9.x), and versions 6 to 8 of Internet Explorer—Google Chrome, being based on the same layout engine (WebKit) as Safari, is also supported and runs Safari's code.[9] (Actually, the number of generated versions of the JavaScript code can be far larger, if your application uses i18n—internationalization—as we'll study in Chapter 12, "Internationalization and Localization.") Code can be minimized for size, for faster downloads; there are also facilities for *code splitting*, which lets you download the required JavaScript code in smaller pieces, on a when-required basis; see Chapter 15, "Deploying Your Application," for more on this.

The compiler does several code optimizing tasks during the compilation run, with the stated goal of producing high-quality code, ideally besting code developed by hand by experienced programmers. (Usually, code is obfuscated, but you can also ask for "Pretty" or even "Detailed" output to better understand what the compiler does. The desired option can be chosen when compiling, as we'll see in Chapter 15.) Among the many optimizations applied, the following are most significant:[10]

- **Dead Code Elimination:** Code that never gets called isn't included in the output file. If you develop a class with ten methods, but only use a couple of them, the compiler won't generate code for the rest of them. Similarly, if you inherit a module with several dozen methods, output code will be generated only for the actually required methods; you won't incur in any size penalty because of methods you don't need.

---

8. This "in browser" mode was, at least for a while, called OOPHM, standing for Out Of Process Hosted Mode.

9. There are many other browsers (some for cell phones) that are also based on WebKit and thus could run GWT applications; check http://webkit.org/ for more details.

10. See http://code.google.com/p/google-web-toolkit/wiki/AdvancedCompilerOptimizations for planned future optimizations.

- **Constant Folding:** When the value of an expression can be known at compile time, the expression is calculated beforehand, and the result will be directly used. For example, if you write something such as `Window.alert("Hello "+"World")` the generated JavaScript code will be something such as `$wnd.alert("Hello World")`; note that this executes a bit faster because the needed string concatenation is already done.

- **Copy Propagation:** An extension of Constant Folding, it lets you carry forward the value of a variable if it can be known at compilation time. For example, given the code `int a=15; int b= a*a+5;` the second line will be compiled as if it read `int b=230`.

- **String Interning:** To avoid creating the same strings over and over again, each distinct string is created once (and assigned to a variable with a name such as `$intern_22`, for example) and used everywhere.[11]

- **Code Inlining:** For short, simple methods, GWT substitutes the actual method code for the original call.

All these optimizations mean that the final code will be quite good. On the negative side, GWT won't do partial compilations; whenever you want to compile your code, GWT looks at the whole of it and does a monolithic compilation to maximize the number of possible optimizations. This was a conscious design decision by the Google development team; you lose such advantages as reusing previously compiled modules, but you gain a greater performance. If you were to compile a piece of code in advance, you couldn't do dead code optimization, for example, because you couldn't predict if a certain method would be required.[12]

There are some other snags you need to be aware of:

- JavaScript doesn't have a 64-bit integer numeric type, so GWT emulates `long` variables with a pair of 32-bit integers. This works properly but is noticeably slower. Also, when you use JSNI, you cannot pass these variables to JavaScript routines.

- For floating point numbers, JavaScript provides only a 64-bit (double) type, which implies that overflows and result precision in arithmetic operations won't be exactly the same as in Java. Also, the `strictfp` keyword is disregarded.

- Exceptions are also handled differently. In JavaScript, most of the Java produced exceptions (such as `NullPointerException` or `MemoryOverflowException`) are replaced by a `JavaScriptException`. This causes a problem: When running in development mode, a `NullPointerException` will be thrown, and you need to `catch (NullPointerException e)` but in compiled mode, you need to `catch`

---

11. Yes, having variables start with "$" makes you think somebody in the GWT group must really miss his PHP coding days...

12. Also, note that while in "development mode," GWT doesn't require (or do) a complete compile/deployment process because it actually executes Java code.

(`JavaScriptException e`) and you duplicate your exception handling code. Another option, of course, is just to `catch (Exception e)` and then check for the class of the exception.

- JavaScript provides no multithreading, so all thread-related functions will either be ignored or rejected.

JRE Emulation Library

While in common Java you can use a prepackaged library without further concerns; because of the way the GWT compiler works, it requires access to actual source code for any class you might want to use. This requirement extends to the JRE, and GWT provides a partial implementation of it called the JRE Emulation Library.[13]

There are only four packages: `java.io` (sorely restricted!), `java.lang`, `java.sql` (also quite limited), and `java.util`, but you can find some missing classes or methods. (This is logical: For example, because JavaScript cannot use files, most of the classes in `java.io` just wouldn't work when compiled into JavaScript.)

Going into details, the `java.io` package is most limited, including just the `Serializable` interface, which RPC considers a synonym for `isSerializable`. (We'll get to this in Chapter 6, "Communicating with Your Server.") The reason for this limitation is simple: The GWT-produced JavaScript code is executed in a browser sandbox and cannot access any local files or printers. This might change (a little) with some HTML 5 features, but for now there's nothing you can do.

More interesting, `java.lang` includes exceptions, classes, general utility methods, and some interfaces.

Exceptions

ArithmeticException	IndexOutOfBoundsException
ArrayIndexOutofBoundsException	NegativeArraySizeException
ArrayStoreException	NullPointerException
AssertionError	NumberFormatException
ClassCastException	RuntimeException
Error	StringIndexOutOfBoundsException
Exception	Throwable
IllegalArgumentException	UnsupportedOperationException
IllegalStateException	

Classes

Boolean	Character
Byte	Class

---

13. Check http://code.google.com/webtoolkit/doc/1.6/RefJreEmulation.html for details.

Double	Object
Float	Short
Integer	String
Long	StringBuffer
Number	StringBuilder

Utility:

Math	System[a]

Interfaces:

Appendable	Comparable
CharSequence	Iterable
Cloneable	Runnable[b]

a. Note that `system.err` and `system.out` won't work in web mode, unless you use the `System.setErr(...)` and `System.setOut(...)` calls.

b. Because JavaScript provides no multithreading, `runnable` won't run in a separate thread as in standard Java.

The `java.sql` package includes three classes useful for date/time processing but nothing else. And of course, from a security point of view, you wouldn't want to try to connect directly to a SQL database from your client, would you?

Classes

Date	TimeStamp
Time	

Finally, `java.util` includes the following exceptions.

Exceptions

ConcurrentModificationException	NoSuchElementException
EmptyStackException	TooManyListenersException
MissingResourceException	

Classes

AbstractCollection	EventObject
AbstractHashMap	HashMap
AbstractList	HashSet
AbstractMapEntry	IdentityHashMap
AbstractMap	LinkedHashMap
AbstractQueue	LinkedHashSet

Classes

AbstractSequentialList	LinkedList
AbstractSet	MapEntryImpl
ArrayList	PriorityQueue
Arrays	Stack
Collections	TreeMap
Date	TreeSet
EnumMap	Vector
EnumSet	

Interfaces

Collection	Map
Comparator	Queue
Enumeration	RandomAccess
EventListener	Set
Iterator	SortedMap
ListIterator	SortedSet
List	

You can also look for certain GWT packages that provide extra functionality that Java programmers take for granted:

- `com.google.gwt.i18n.client.DateTimeFormat` and `com.google.gwt.i18n.client.NumberFormat` provide formatting functions.
- `com.google.gwt.core.client.Duration` can be used for timing purposes. (See Chapter 14, "Optimizing for Application Speed," for more on benchmarking and performance aspects.) The returned values are `double`, so performance is better than with the `long` Timer. (See the discussion at the end of the previous section about `long` emulation in GWT.)
- `com.google.gwt.user.client.Random` provides a substitute for `java.util.Random`.
- `com.google.gwt.user.client.Timer` can be used instead of `java.util.Timer`.

As a general advice, before relying on any specific class or exception, check whether it's actually implemented, or just a placeholder needed for JRE compatibility, or a trimmed down, limited, version of the usual JRE version. (You need to check GWT's own source code to do this check; yes, not very simple or friendly…)

On the other hand, don't think that Java programming will become near to impossible with GWT. As we saw, in some cases there are alternative classes, and in others, you can usually get by with JavaScript (JSNI) or any open source library.

UI Library

GWT provides a large, standard set of widgets (such as buttons or text input fields) and panels. Using widgets is quite similar to Swing, so Java programmers can feel at home; however, note that there are no layout managers (discussed next) and panels or CSS are used instead for positioning objects.

Widgets are usually mapped into browser objects (think Heavyweight objects in Swing) so they'll share the visual aspect of whatever browser the user adopts. Styling can be done on an object-per-object basis, or more generically by applying CSS, which is the preferred solution. Some composite objects, more often associated with rich desktop applications, are also included, such as a `DatePicker` for date input, `SuggestBox` for real-time suggestions based on whatever the user has typed, `RichTextArea` for formatted text input, and more.[14]

Panels are containers for widgets or other panels. Panels also do double-duty as layout managers; for example, `FlowPanel` uses standard HTML flow rules (or Swing's `FlowLayout`'s), whereas `VerticalPanel` stacks its elements vertically. We'll go into more detail about creating the user interface in Chapter 5.

Setting Up GWT

To develop a basic GWT application, you can make do with just about any text editor and a few command line utilities, but for more serious work you need several other tools. (And as we saw, the Google developers thought that a good reason for using Java was the quantity of available tools for that language, so why skimp?) In this section, we'll consider several tools and plugins you should use for better GWT development.

Writing Code

Though you can develop GWT applications with just a text editor, Java, and a few scripts, you should get Eclipse (at www.eclipse.org/), which is the Google-suggested IDE for GWT. You should go for the JEE version, the most complete version for Java development. All the examples in this book were developed with Eclipse 3.5, Galileo. You can also give NetBeans (at http://netbeans.org/) with Gwt4nb (see https://gwt4nb.dev.java.net/) a try, or go for Intellij IDEA (at www.jetbrains.com/idea/). I know programmers who swear by each of these alternatives, so take your pick!

If you go with Eclipse, the Google Plugin for Eclipse (at http://code.google.com/eclipse/) is practically mandatory; functions you usually had to do with shell commands (such as creating a new project) can now be done within Eclipse. (See Figure 2.1.) Installation is the same as for any plugin: Open Eclipse, go to Help, Install New Software, add the Google Plugin URL, and it downloads and installs the rest of GWT.

---

14. See http://gwt.google.com/samples/Showcase/Showcase.html for samples of most available widgets and panels.

(We'll go over the usage of the plugin in Chapter 3.) The plugin also provides other features; for example, it can help you work with UiBinder (as we'll be doing in Chapter 5), or with JSNI (as in Chapter 8).

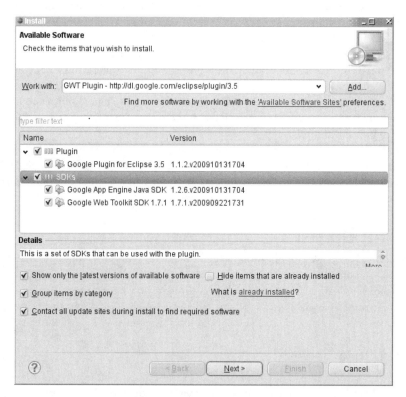

Figure 2.1 The Google Plugin for Eclipse is a must, and it simplifies creating both common web and Google App Engine applications.

(As an aside, Cypal Studio for GWT [at http://code.google.com/p/cypal-studio/] was an alternative to the Google plugin, but for GWT 2, it's in alpha version just now. As an extra advantage, it simplified creating remote services [we'll get to this in Chapter 6] and deploying your application [see Chapter 15], but in its current alpha status, I wouldn't recommend it and suggest waiting for a release version.)

Lastly, all developers should follow the same standards. CheckStyle (at http://checkstyle.sourceforge.net/) is a tool that enforces whatever rules you decide to follow; by default, Sun's Eclipse-CS (at http://eclipse-cs.sourceforge.net) is a suitable plugin for Eclipse; after installing it the standard way, a new option will be added to your project menu (CheckStyle), and after running it, all nonstandard lines will be marked.

Version Control Management

For version control management, I work with Subversion; therefore, I suggest using Subclipse (at http://subclipse.tigris.org/), which is an Eclipse plugin, currently at version 1.6.5. Installation is similar to the Google Plugin's; to be on the safe side, pick all packages and let Eclipse request any missing packages. I have also worked with Subversive (at http://community.polarion.com/), another Eclipse plugin, and had no problems; pick whichever suits you best.[15]

As for Subversion servers, which is beyond this book, but you can either install your own server (see http://subversion.tigris.org/ for details) or use any of several public free or paid servers; google a bit for this. (An appropriate venue could be Google's own Project Hosting at http://code.google.com/hosting/)

Testing

One of GWT's greatest advantages is testing, and you have to install JUnit (from www.junit.org/). The latest version, currently 4.8, can possibly be installed directly through your distribution package manager (that was the case with OpenSUSE) or by following the installation instructions at http://junit.sourceforge.net/README.html#Installation. You need to add JUnit4 to the list of libraries; right-click on your project, click Properties, Java Build Path, Libraries, and add JUnit4.

For testing coverage metrics, add EclEmma (at www.eclemma.org/). This plugin adds a new launch mode (coverage) which, after running your test suite, produces a marked up listing of your source code showing, which lines were or weren't exercised by the test. (See Chapter 13 for more on testing.) Installation is the usual one for Eclipse plugins.

Finally, for unit testing, EasyMock (at http://easymock.org/) is a valuable tool. Added to the GUI patterns that we apply (see Chapter 5 for a discussion of the MVP design pattern as applied to GWT) it will simplify writing our automatic tests. You need to install both EasyMock (currently at version 2.5.2) and the EasyMock Class Extension (at version 2.4), and add both jars to the build path. See Figure 2.2 on the next page for a finished installation.

Running and Deploying

You should also have Firefox (at www.mozilla.com/en-US/). Actually, about any browser could do, but Firefox has lots of great plugins for development, such as FireBug (a debugger and inspector) and FireCookie (an extension that lets you examine cookies).[16]

---

15. Of course, version control is part of all development projects, and not really GWT-specific, but I wanted to include everything that you would be likely to require for serious application development.

16. If you are running Linux, ironically you won't be able to use Google's own Chrome for development, since a required plugin isn't expected to be available until at least version 5 of the browser.

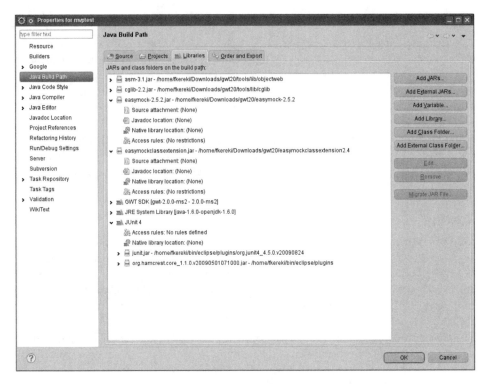

Figure 2.2 A nicely filled out set of libraries for development and testing

When you start developing with GWT and testing your applications with your own browser (we'll get started with this in Chapter 3) you will be required to install an appropriate plugin; follow onscreen instructions, depending on what browser you use. Also, you should also get Selenium (at http://seleniumhq.org/), which is a great tool for acceptance tests, and the Selenium IDE (a good help for setting up the tests) is provided as a Firefox extension.

To finish, to deploy the actual application, you need some servlet container (such as Tomcat, Jetty, or Glassfish, among many possibilities) or if your server side isn't Java based, a web server (Apache or Lighttpd come to mind). We won't be covering how to install and set up these programs in this book.

Summary

We analyzed why you should use GWT (and even some reasons against it, which aren't that weighty, in our opinion), what GWT is in terms of its components, and which tools you need to get the most out of your development. Now, let's get started with actual GWT development, from the initial setup to the final deployment of your application.

3

Understanding Projects and Development

In this chapter we'll create a project, study its structure, configure its modules, and show how development works with GWT. Since GWT 1.0, this whole process has evolved significantly; now it's more streamlined, with a plugin for easier project creation and OOPHM for faster, simpler development and testing.

Creating a Project

First, let's start by creating a project—a "Hello World" application if you will—though we won't use it to showcase GWT, but rather to study the structure of a project. (And we will throw some criticism at this simple application in Chapter 5, "Programming the User Interface.") We won't do any coding because GWT can generate such code by itself, and it's good enough for our purposes. And, by the way, the simplest way to create your own project and make certain that it was created correctly is by deleting Google's standard code and start writing your own.

You can create a GWT project in at least three ways: by means of the Google Plugin for Eclipse, by using a shell script, or even directly by hand, file per file—though of course there isn't much going for the latter option, so we'll avoid it.[1]

Using the Google Plugin for Eclipse

Originally, GWT provided some scripts to create a project with all required files and directories (and we'll look at this next) but using the Google Plugin for Eclipse (which we installed in Chapter 2, "Getting Started with GWT 2") is by far the simplest way.

1. In Eclipse, go to File, New, Other, Google, Web Application Project.

2. Give the project a name. (I inspiredly chose sampleproject.)

---

1. For just a single example of other ways to create a project, Maven users could utilize the CodeHaus plugin at http://mojo.codehaus.org/gwt-maven-plugin/, and it's likely that sooner or later you'll find plugins for just about any development environment.

3. Specify which package should be created. (I went with `com.fkereki.sample`.)

4. Check Use Google Web Toolkit and Use Default SDK. It is possible to install several versions of the SDK at the same time; for example, for testing purposes, or for building GWT projects created with older versions.

5. Because we aren't going to deploy this project to Google App Engine, uncheck Use Google App Engine.

6. Click Finish.

That's all there is to creating a project with the Google Plugin for Eclipse; a certainly simple process.

Using the GWT Shell Script

If you aren't using Eclipse, you can use the `webAppCreator` shell script to generate all needed directories and files. Note that before GWT 1.6 you had to use two scripts, `projectCreator` and `applicationCreator`, to accomplish the same result.

You need to specify the module name, and you can also include several parameters:

- `-overwrite` means all existing files will be overwritten.

- `-ignore` means existing files will be left as-is and not overwritten. Note that `-ignore` and `-overwrite` are mutually exclusive; you cannot specify them both.

- `-out someDirectory` specifies the output directory; by default, the current one.

- `-XnoEclipse` implies no Eclipse-specific files will be created; you would use this if you plan to use other IDE instead.

- `-XonlyEclipse` on the contrary means the script will generate only those files needed for Eclipse; you can import this project into Eclipse.

The following is the (slightly abridged for legibility) result of a project creation run:

```
> cd work
> md secondsample
> sh webAppCreator com.kereki.secondsample
Created directory /home/fkereki/work/src
Created directory /home/fkereki/work/war
Created directory /home/fkereki/work/war/WEB-INF
Created directory /home/fkereki/work/war/WEB-INF/lib
Created directory /home/fkereki/work/src/com/kereki
Created directory /home/fkereki/work/src/com/kereki/client
Created directory /home/fkereki/work/src/com/kereki/server
Created file /home/fkereki/work/src/com/kereki/secondsample.gwt.xml
Created file /home/fkereki/work/war/secondsample.html
Created file /home/fkereki/work/war/secondsample.css
Created file /home/fkereki/work/war/WEB-INF/web.xml
Created file /home/fkereki/work/src/com/kereki/client/secondsample.java
```

```
Created file /... /work/src/com/kereki/client/GreetingService.java
Created file /... /work/src/com/kereki/client/GreetingServiceAsync.java
Created file /... /work/src/com/kereki/server/GreetingServiceImpl.java
Created file /home/fkereki/work/build.xml
Created file /home/fkereki/work/README.txt
Created file /home/fkereki/work/.project
Created file /home/fkereki/work/.classpath
Created file /home/fkereki/work/secondsample.launch
Created file /home/fkereki/work/war/WEB-INF/lib/gwt-servlet.jar
```

After creating the project, you can import it into Eclipse with these steps:[2]

1. Go to File, Import, General, Existing Projects into Workspace.

2. Browse to the directory with the new project and select it.

3. Uncheck Copy Projects into Workspace, so Eclipse uses the directory you chose.

4. Click Finish.

We'll study the files layout in the next section.

Project Structure

Let's now get into the project structure. (See Figure 3.1 on the next page.)
You need several directories:

- Your production Java code goes in the `src` directory, which is further divided into `client` (code that runs at the user's browser), `shared` (a post-GWT-2.0 addition for code used both at the client and the server) and `server` (code that runs server-side).[3] You can further create any subpackages within these three directories. You can have other directories for client-side code but need to include them with the `<source>` element. On the other hand, server-side code must reside within `server`; you cannot specify other directories for it. If you want to share classes in client and server-side code, you should include them in the shared directory, because they need translation into JavaScript; this automatically implies that all client-side code limitations apply to those classes.

- For testing, you may have `test` and `gwttest` directories (for JUnit and GWTTestCase automatic tests) as we see in Chapter 13, "Testing Your GWT Application."[4]

---

2. An equally valid alternative would be importing it into Netbeans and working with the GWT4NB plugin, as we mentioned in Chapter 1, "Developing Your Application."

3. Note that in standard Java fashion, `com.kereki.sample.client` actually stands for the `com/kereki/sample/client` subdirectory.

4. The testing directories are actually optional but skipping automatic tests would go against the idea of GWT development.

Figure 3.1 The basic structure for a recently created project. This
structure is missing the directories for your automatic test code.

- Your output code will be produced in the **war** folder. This directory is in the
  appropriate format for Java web servers such as Tomcat or Jetty, so you can directly
  deploy your application. (We see more on this in Chapter 15, "Deploying Your
  Application.") Within it, you can find the files that form the client-side application
  (static ones such as CSS or HTML, plus the compiler-generated JavaScript files)
  and the Jar files and servlet configuration files for your server-side code.

The basic units in GWT are modules. You use modules both for the actual client-side
application and for libraries that you want to reuse across several projects. The module
definition goes in the project root and has a **gwt.xml** extension. A most basic module
description for our recently created project could contain

```
<?xml version="1.0" encoding="UTF-8"?>
<module rename-to='sampleproject'>
  <inherits name='com.google.gwt.user.User'/>
  <inherits name='com.google.gwt.user.theme.standard.Standard'/>
  <entry-point class='com.kereki.sample.client.Sampleproject'/>
  <source path='client'/>
</module>
```

Let's first examine this example and then move on to a fuller description of available elements and attributes.

- The optional `rename-to` attribute in the `<module>` element lets you change the generated application name from `com.kereki.sample.client` to the far friend-lier, simpler `sampleproject`.

- The `<inherits>` elements include the contents of other modules; in this case, we import basic GWT functionality (`com.google.gwt.user.User`) and a default style for widgets (`com.google.gwt.user.theme.standard.Standard`).

- The `<entry-point>` element shows the starting class for the application.

- The `<source>` element defines which directories will or won't be included for code generation; here, we just include the standard `client` directory.

For a simple project, you don't need more than this, but several elements let you add further capabilities to your project; let's now go into more detail.

- The root element for the gwt.xml file is `<module>`. You can define only a single module per `gwt.xml` file, but you can have several differently named modules within the same project. This would allow having, for example, a production mod-ule definition (used for deployment, as we see in Chapter 15) and a development module definition, which could be compiled more quickly, just for a single browser and language.

- You can use the `<rename-to>` attribute to rename a module (as we previously did) to give the compiled application a simpler name; otherwise, instead of going to http://yourwebsite.com/sample, the user would have to browse to http://yourwebsite.com/com.fkereki.sample.Sample, which isn't so friendly.

  If you were having a production module and a development module as previously described, you could use this attribute so both modules produce an identically named application. For example, we could have `development.gwt.xml`, whose compilation would just produce a Safari version of the code; we'll see more of this in Chapter 15.

```
<?xml version="1.0" encoding="UTF-8"?>
<module rename-to='sampleproject'>

  ...same as earlier...

  <set-property name="user.agent" value="safari" />
</module>
```

- The `<source>` element lets you `include` (the default action) or exclude specific directories and file patterns. The default source path is `client` and not including any source elements is equivalent to just including `<source path='client'/>`. You can also include or exclude files or patterns; see the following `<public>` ele-ment description.

- The `<entry-point>` element lets you specify an entry point class for your application (i.e., a class that `implements EntryPoint`) as in `<entry-point class='com.kereki.sample.client.Sampleproject'/>`. If you have several entry point classes, their `onModuleLoad` methods will be executed sequentially, in the same order as in the module file.

- The `<script>` and `<stylesheet>` elements let you automatically include external JavaScript and CSS files with your module. Syntax is similar: `<script src='someJavaScriptFileUrl'/>` and `<stylesheet src='someCssFileUrl'/>`. JavaScript files will be loaded before calling any of your entry point classes. CSS files will be loaded in the given order. If the URLs are absolute, they will be used as given; if not, they will be taken as relative to the URL of your project, meaning its default public path.

  Why would you include files this way, instead of using `<script>` and `<link>` tags within the HTML file for your application? It would be particularly apt if you were writing a module that depends on specific scripts or CSS files; any users of your module would automatically require those files without having to remember to include them.

- The `<public>` element also fulfills a similar objective. If you add `<public path='some/path/at/your/project'/>` to the module specification, all the corresponding files in that path will be copied to the output directory. Again, the main reason for using this would be forcing any user of your module to include the desired files; otherwise you could just make do by directly copying the files to wherever you wanted them in the web directory.[5] The standard placement for the `public` directory is at the same level as the `client` and `server` directories.

  The `<source>` and `<public>` elements support some extra attributes, to further limit what files will be included or excluded. All files in the path are included by default, unless you specify one or more patterns with `includes="somePattern"` (to include only those files) or `excludes="otherPattern,anotherOne, yetEvenAnother"` (include everything except these files).

  Even more, if you want to include or exclude many specific files or patterns, you can use the `<include name='aListOfPatterns'>` and `<exclude name= 'otherPatterns'>` elements.[6]

---

5. This is used, for example, to include some Internet Explorer 6 files in your `war/yourModule/ gwt/standard/images/ie6` directory when you inherit a widget style module.

6. By default, several patterns are excluded, including backup files, CVS and SVN files, and more. You can suppress this exclusion by adding `defaultexcludes=no` but it isn't likely you will want to do so; check http://ant.apache.org/manual/dirtasks.html#defaultexcludes for more on this. You can also set filename matching not to be case-sensitive by adding `casesensitive=false`.

```
<public path='public'  includes='*gif,*png'>
  <include name='ubuntu*'/>
  <include name='opensuse*'/>
  <exclude name='install.gif'/>
</public>
```

- If your application uses RPC (we'll work with RPC in Chapter 6, "Communicating with Your Server,"), you need to configure the called servlets in the `war/WEB_INF/web.xml` file. (We'll consider how to deploy an application, servlets included, in Chapter 15.) However, and only for GWTTestCase testing, you need to include `<servlet path="url" class="className"/>`. The given classname should be fully qualified as in `com.kereki.sample.server.AnyServlet` and the URL should be an absolute path, such as `/AnyServlet`; of course, these values should coincide with the `web.xml` values.

There are some compiler-specific element you will rarely want to mess with, such as `define-linker` and `add-linker` that define which linker class will do the final JavaScript packaging, at the end of the compilation; we won't be using them.

Finally, and for completeness' sake, let's also list in advance several tags used for deferred binding, which we'll examine in Chapter 4, "Working with Browsers." Managing properties is done with `define-property`, `set-property`,[7] `extend-property`, and `property-provider`.

You can set specific properties for generators with `define-configuration-property`, `set-configuration-property`, `clear-configuration-property`, and `extend-configuration-property`.

There are also several predicates such as `when-property-is`, `when-type-assignable`, `when-type-is`, `all`, `any`, and `none`, which are used with the `replace-with` and `generate-with` deferred binding directives.

Running Your Application: Development Mode

The most important change in GWT 2 was the introduction of OOPHM (Out Of Process Hosted Mode) that meant you will try your code in your own browser. (Another change is that the old Hosted mode is now called Development mode; the old name was prone to generate confusion.) Running code in Development mode is essential to developing a GWT application: It lets you use Java debugging tools, while you see the effects of your code in a production browser.

The previous Hosted mode used an old Mozilla-based browser, which didn't enable useful extensions or plugins (such as Firebug) to work. Also, you were limited to testing your code in the development machine's environment; you couldn't connect to your

---

7. We already used this element when defining a development module, to specify that code should be generated only for a specific browser, as in `<set-property name="user.agent" value="safari" />`.

Linux machine from a Windows machine in the same network and try to run the code with Internet Explorer.

To try Development mode, right-click on your project, select Run As, and Web Application. A GWT Development Mode window appears with a message Waiting for Browser Connection To; open your favorite browser, and point it to the given URL. (See Figure 3.2.)

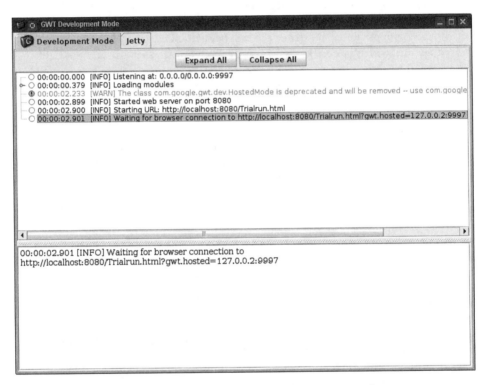

Figure 3.2 Trying out your code in Development mode

Running in your own browser needs a special plugin that manages the connection between your browser and the development environment. If you haven't installed it yet, instead of your running application, you get a warning about the lack of the plugin, as shown in Figure 3.3.

Clicking on the given link redirects you to a page that enables you to download and install the plugin. (See Figure 3.4.)

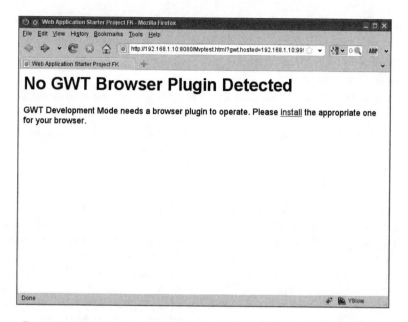

Figure 3.3 GWT's new Development Mode needs a special plugin so that your browser can communicate with the development environment.

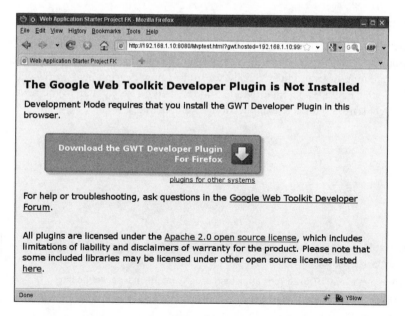

Figure 3.4 The first time you run an application in Development Mode, you need to install the appropriate version of the GWT Developer Plugin for your browser.

Simply follow the onscreen instructions, install the plugin, and you can run the application.[8] If you were used to the old GWT Hosted Mode, you notice some differences:

- There is no special Refresh button; just use F5, and the client application will be recompiled and reloaded.
- If you need to make some changes in the server side of your application, click the Jetty button at the GWT Development Mode window and then Restart Server.[9]
- When the application runs, you see a third tab for your application console. You can display messages here by using `GWT.log("some message",null)` in your code. You don't need to worry about leaving these calls in your production code; they will be optimized out by the compiler.[10]

There's something that hasn't changed; the first time you run your application in Development mode you'll have a short wait, the same as in the old Web mode. However, refreshing your application is quite fast, so you'll soon get in the run-test-modify-rerun cycle, leaving the Development mode window open all the time.

Finally, note that you can as easily debug your application; right-click on your project, select Debug as and Web Application. The rest will be exactly as running your program, but you will have full access to Eclipse's debugging tools, meaning you can set breakpoints, examine variables, and so on. We won't be delving into this because it's pure Java debugging; you can forget about GWT, JavaScript, compilation, translation, and everything else, and just work with the Java code.

Summary

We saw how to create a project, both by using the GWT Plugin for Eclipse and the `webAppCreator` shell script, and then went over the internal structure of a project and the configuration of its modules. Finally, we studied how development works with GWT, tried its new Development Mode, and touched on debugging. In the next chapter, we'll get started with actual application development.

---

8. Note that for some browsers—notably Google's own Chrome—you need to do some extra steps beyond the plugin's installation.

9. Earlier versions of GWT used Tomcat instead of Jetty for internal servlet hosting.

10. You could also consider using project GWT-log at http://code.google.com/p/gwt-log/ for extra logging features.

## 4

Working with Browsers

Even if generating browser-independent code is one of GWT's main selling points, there still remain some details you need to be aware of—hopefully without having to go all the way to producing browser-specific code!

First, you need to pay special attention in case the user wants to go back to a previous screen by using the Alt+Backspace combo or the Back button in his browser. Because GWT applications run in a single screen, that action will probably log the user out of your program.

Then, in some cases (such as deciding whether to show a video by using HTML 5's tags) you might need to be aware of the specific version of the user browser; we'll see two solutions for that, a classic one you surely already know, and a better GWT-specific one taking advantage of deferred binding. Deferred binding will also pave the way for automatic code generation, which we shall use to automate the production of part of our application.

And, finally, you might need to deal with old browsers (yes, there still are IE 5 browsers around) and users who have disabled JavaScript—all of which are certain show-stoppers for GWT applications.

So, in this chapter we will mainly deal with these kind of browser details you always must take care of, and, as a welcome side effect, bring into being a general launcher infrastructure that can help building menus and linking parts of your application, and see some more about deferred binding and the inner workings of the GWT compiler.

The Back Button Problem

GWT applications (as most other Ajax-based applications, too) usually run in a single page, which is dynamically created and regenerated as needed. This mode of work creates the Back Button or Alt+Backspace problem: If the user tries to go back to a previous screen in your application, results will be unexpected. Instead of going back as desired, he will get kicked out of your application, landing in whichever page he had been before visiting yours. Of course, the user cannot expect that your application won't behave like any other web application, so this behavior would be, to say the least, aggravating. You have no way of inhibiting the Alt+Backspace combo and the browser's own Back command, but fortunately GWT provides a simple way out, with the History class.

It should be noted that at the 2009 Google I/O conference, the first point in Ray Ryan's "GWT App Architecture Best Practices" was "Get browser history right, and get it right early."[1] The rationale for this is that you will find it far easier to get it right at the beginning than to retrofit at a later point. So, let's get into this right now, before starting to develop any other code; what we shall see here will be complemented by the MVP pattern discussion in the next chapter.

Setting Up Your HTML Page

The History class is GWT's answer to the Alt+Backspace problem. It enables you to easily deal with Back and Forward commands, in a way that will be totally transparent to the user. However, before starting with the actual details of this class, let's add some required code to your basic HTML page. Within its `<body>` add the following script:

```
<iframe src="javascript:''"
    id="__gwt_historyFrame"
    tabIndex='-1'
    style="position: absolute; width: 0;
        height: 0; border: 0">
</iframe>
```

Be careful with the double underscore at the beginning of `__gwt_historyFrame`. If you try using the `History` class without having included the preceding code, when running in Development mode, you get the following warning in the log:

```
Unable to initialize the history subsystem; did you
include the history frame in your host page? Try
<iframe src=\"javascript:''\" id='__gwt_historyFrame'
style='position:absolute; width:0; height:0;
border:0'></iframe>
```

Note, however, that this message will only appear if you use Internet Explorer 6 and 7 browsers, which lack the necessary `onhashchange` event.[2] (Of course, you might opt for another solution, and kick the user out if his browser isn't adequate. We will see ways to do this later in this chapter, but it certainly wouldn't be too friendly!) Other browsers, such as Firefox or Safari, can run even without this script. The latest Internet Explorer 8 added support for this event with its Ajax Navigations feature.[3]

---

1. Check http://code.google.com/events/io/2009/sessions/GoogleWebToolkitBestPractices.html for the conference video and presentation.

2. And neither does Internet Explorer 8, when in Compatibility mode; see www.microsoft.com/windows/internet-explorer/features/easier.aspx for a description of this mode.

3. Read http://msdn.microsoft.com/en-us/library/cc891506(VS.85).aspx for more on this.

The History Class

The `History` class manages Back and Forward events, letting you provide a handler that will deal with each command. You can find this class in the `com.google.gwt.user` `.client` package. All its methods are static (so you use them without creating a History object) and some are even `native` JavaScript code.

Whenever the users goes to a different part of your application, the URL changes:[4] instead of being, say, `www.yoursite.com/yourapp`, it will become something like `www.yoursite.com/yourapp#sales`—and "`sales`," the string after the hash mark, would be a token your application should recognize and use to identify some module of your site. Your handler should decide what content to show depending on its value.[5]

What's a token? In short, just about any string you can recognize and associate to a given state in your program. Note that GWT's documentation doesn't specify a token's maximum length, but you shouldn't assume it can be of any length, and rather keep it to, say, about 100 bytes long.

To process `History` events, you first need to add a handler by using `History.addValueChangeHandler(...)` and pass it an object that implements the `ValueChangeHandler<String>` interface; your `EntryPoint` class will be the obvious candidate to implement it. The handler will be called on every `History` change event, and give you the chance to react and show the correct page.[6]

Note, however, that the first time your application is loaded you won't be getting any change event; browsers do not consider the first page load a hash change event for performance reasons. Thus, you need to get the initial token on your own, by using the `History.getToken()` method, followed by the `History.newItem(...)` call, so the token will get processed instead of just pushed into the history stack.

Your initialization code will end up being something like the following—but careful, there are some problems with the code, which we shall point out and fix quite soon.

```
import com.google.gwt.user.client.History;
import com.google.gwt.core.client.EntryPoint;
import com.google.gwt.event.logical.shared.ValueChangeEvent;
import com.google.gwt.event.logical.shared.ValueChangeHandler;

//more imports...

public class Mvptest implements EntryPoint,
    ValueChangeHandler<String> {
```

4. For more on hashes and parameters, check www.w3.org/TR/hash-in-uri/.

5. Tokens look very much like HTML anchors, but there's an important difference. In the case of browsers, they navigate to anchors (which are just a sort of bookmark in the page) by just scrolling the text of the currently displayed page. On the other hand, your GWT application will have to create and show the appropriate page.

6. Earlier versions of GWT used a Listener instead, but that's deprecated now.

```
public void onModuleLoad() {
  // do all kinds of initializing...

  String startingToken = History.getToken();
  History.addValueChangeHandler(this);
  History.newItem(startingToken, true);
}

@Override
  public void onValueChange(ValueChangeEvent<String> event) {
    String token = event.getValue();

    // depending on the value of token, do whatever you need

    if (token.isEmpty()) {
      // show the initial screen or menu
    } else if (token.equals("login")) {
      // show a login form
    } else if (token.equals("some")) {
      // show some form
    } else if (token.equals("other")) {
      // show other form
    } else if (...) {
      // ...more checks for other token values...
    } else {
      Window.alert("Unrecognized token=" + token);
    }
  }
}
```

Starting Your Application

Given the preceding code, it can be seen that an easy way to get a part of your program
to run at the beginning (such as a login form, for instance) is by just pushing a certain
token and letting the history mechanism take care of it. However, this also represents a
security fault. (See Figure 4.1 for a simple login form.) Think about what would happen
if the user had bookmarked a URL with a token in it and now opted to visit it. The
token would be processed, and the user would end up directly going to the desired part
of the application, without having ever logged in; not very safe or secure!

We can handle this with a bit of care. First, right at the beginning we check whether
there's already a token in the URL, and if so, we store it for later, but otherwise ignore
it. Then, we go about priming the history stack with the login token, so the user will
need to log in before starting to use the application. And finally, when the login process
is done (more on this later) we can process the original token, and jump to wherever the
user wanted to go. Of course, we also need to clear the saved token, because otherwise
we will keep going back to it whenever the user goes back to the main screen.

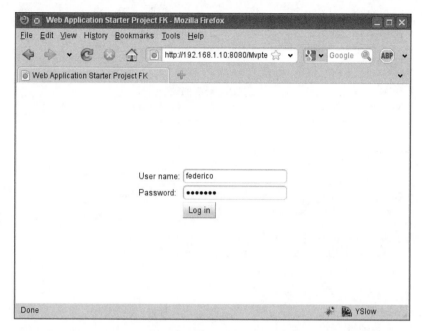

Figure 4.1 A login screen must be shown, even if the user bookmarked an inner page of your application. After the user successfully logs in, he may be sent to the page he asked for.

As a result, we honor the user's request, but in a safe way, without bypassing the login procedure. Given all this, a better startup code would be something like the one shown next.

(A little advance warning: In the preceding code, we used hard-coded strings to stand for the tokens, as in `token.equals("login")`. It's far better to use constants [nothing new here] and in our form design [which we'll see in Chapter 5, "Programming the User Interface"] we shall include a PLACE named constant in every screen; for example, we would have

```
static final String PLACE="login";
```

We are getting just a bit ahead of ourselves, but you'll agree that including hard-coded constants is not usually considered good design and that we had to change it anyway.)

```
public class Mvptest implements EntryPoint,
    ValueChangeHandler<String> {

  String startingToken = "";

  public void onModuleLoad() {
    // initialize everything...
```

```
  /*
   * If the application is called with a token, we cannot
   * just jump to it; we need go past the login form
   * first.
   *
   * After the user has logged in, the showMainMenu(...)
   * method --called in the login callback-- will take
   * care of jumping to the appropriate place.
   */
  startingToken = History.getToken();

  /*
   * Set up the history management, and start by showing
   * the login form.
   */
  History.addValueChangeHandler(this);
  History.newItem(LoginPresenter.PLACE, true);
}


void showLogin() {
  // show login form
  // after a valid user has logged in
}


void showMainMenu() {
  // Use user information for menu configuration
  // and create the main screen and menu

  /*
   * If the application was started with a token, now that
   * the user is logged in, it's time to show it.
   *
   * Don't forget to clear startingToken, or after a
   * logout/login, we will go back again to the token.
   */
  if (!startingToken.isEmpty()) {
    History.newItem(startingToken, true);
    startingToken = "";
  }
}


@Override
public void onValueChange(ValueChangeEvent<String> event) {
```

```
  // as above...
 }
}
```

For extra safety, you should include tests (in the `OnValueChange(...)` method) to check whether the current user is allowed to go to where the token points; the current user might not be the one who originally saved the bookmark, or might be keying in the URL by hand as an experiment to get into parts of your application that would otherwise be forbidden to him.

This, however, isn't yet perfectly safe; the user might use some browser debugging tool, and cheat by changing, after having been logged in, the stored information for him to gain admission to other parts of the system. As we'll see in Chapter 10, "Working with Servers," you'll require more secure methods for a safer application.

Showing Forms in Pop-Ups

The preceding code in the `onValueChange(...)` method can be enhanced; let's get to the final version. There are two details we might want to consider. As it is, it does two functions: It processes the change event and also launches a form. Because we might want to launch a form without going through the history mechanism (for example, in a `PopupPanel`) we should think about separating both functions.

Also, because in the latter case we wouldn't want to show the new form on the main screen, we need to pass a parameter: the panel where the new form should be shown. This refactoring leads us to the following version; note that the `show(...)` methods now receive a panel parameter.

```
@Override
public void onValueChange(ValueChangeEvent<String> event) {
  executeInPanel(RootPanel.get(), event.getValue());
}


public void executeInPanel(Panel myPanel, String token) {
  if (myPanel==null) {
    myPanel = RootPanel.get();
  }
  myPanel.clear();
  if (token.isEmpty()) {
    // no need to do anything...
  } else if (token.equals(LoginPresenter.PLACE)) {
    // show login in panel myPanel
  } else if (token.equals(someForm.PLACE)) {
    // show some form in panel myPanel
  } // etc.
}
```

With this refactoring, if a form needs to show other forms in a pop-up, the logic will become something like: (1) create the `PanelPopup` object, (2) `show(...)` it, and (3) invoke the `executeInPanel(...)` method, giving it the panel, so the new form can go in there. (See Figure 4.2 for a instance of a searcher form shown on top of the main form application.) This kind of code will surely be required in several points of our application, and in Chapter 5 we'll decide we should move it into the `Environment` object, a good place for all kinds of general code and constants, which we haven't yet met.

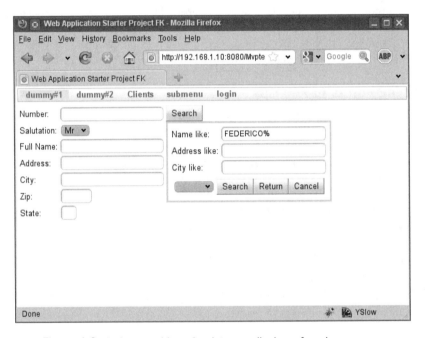

Figure 4.2 An improved launcher lets you display a form in a pop-up panel. The form itself isn't aware of whether it's displayed on the main screen or in a lesser panel.

So far, we have managed to show a form either on the main window or in a specific panel, and we know how to perform that from a menu. The only thing we are missing is the possibility of passing starting parameters to a form because it's not always the case that you want to start with an empty, cleared form, but rather with some preloaded data.

Passing Parameters

When using normal anchors, URLs can include parameters, but they will appear before the hash mark, as in `www.somemoviesite.com?film=123#synopsis` that won't work in our case. Whenever the part before the hash changes, a page is loaded, so passing parameters in this way would mean that the whole application would get reloaded, losing its state.

So, if you want to pass parameters to a form, you need to include them after the corresponding token, in the classic style `?key1=value1&key2=value2...` but then you need to do the parsing on your own because the GWT `Window.Location.getParameter(...)` and `Window.Location.getParameterMap(...)` methods do not apply to hashes.

Note, if you want to be picky, that since tokens are any string you want, you do not need to use any particular style, and you can invent your own notation and standard, but why bother? Simple code like the following one can extract the parameters, which you can provide to a form's presenter as an extra parameter, so it can do whatever it needs.

```
public void executeInPanel(Panel ppp, String token) {
  String args = "";
  int question = token.indexOf("?");
  if (question != -1) {
    args = token.substring(question + 1);
    token = token.substring(0, question);
  }
  // rest of the code, as before, but
  // remember to provide whatever form is
  // launched with the "args" parameter string
```

Note that if some parameters could include a question mark, it is up to you to encode/decode them appropriately; the use of GWT's URL `encode(...)` and `decode(...)` methods (similar to PHP's `urlencode(...)` and `urldecode(...)` functions, for example) comes to mind.

Having each form parse the parameter string on its own, to get the keys and values, would be a bad design. We can do better by adding some code that will do that job and construct some kind of hash map with the actual parameters. We can get the string with the parameters and use a `KeyValueMap` (an extension of `HashMap<String,String>`) to store the extracted values. Let's first write that class.

```
public class KeyValueMap extends HashMap<String, String> {
  /**
   * KeyValueMap: a short way of specifying a class that
   * will be used to pass parameters to forms.
   */
  private static final long serialVersionUID = 5225712868559413562L;


  /**
   * Standard constructor; produces an empty KeyValueMap.
   */
  public KeyValueMap() {
    this("");
  }
```

```
/**
 * Create a KeyValueMap, and initialize it with the params
 * string.
 *
 * @param params
 *         A string with URL-like parameters (see below)
 */
public KeyValueMap(final String params) {
  initializeWithString(params);
}
```

The `initializeWithString(...)` method loads the hash map with the keys and values included in the string. We must be careful to do the right thing if the string is empty (meaning, create an empty hash map) or if some value is missing (and then we'll just assume the corresponding value is an empty string).

```
/**
 * Initialize a KeyValueMap with a parameters URL-like
 * string.
 *
 * @param params
 *         A string formatted like
 *         param1=value1&param2=value2&... It is assumed
 *         that the value has been appropriately escaped.
 */
void initializeWithString(String params) {
  clear();
  if ((params != null) && !params.isEmpty()) {
    String[] args = params.split("&");
    for (String element : args) {
      int equalIndex = element.indexOf("=");
      if (equalIndex == -1) {
        put(element, "");
      } else {
        put(element.substring(0, equalIndex), element
          .substring(equalIndex + 1));
      }
    }
  }
}
```

Having a `toString(...)` method isn't actually required for our application, but it's quite good in terms of debugging and following standard practices.

```
@Override
public String toString() {
  String result = "";
  String separator = "";
```

```
    for (String key : keySet()) {
      result += separator + key + "=" + get(key);
      separator = "\n";
    }
    return result;
  }
}
```

We'll get back to this class in Chapter 13, when we'll write some automatic tests for it, and in Chapter 15, where we build an independent module out of it.

Creating a Menu

The same mechanism we used for history management can be used to build a menu. (Think about common bar-styled menus, with drop-down options, as seen in most desktop applications; that's our goal here.) GWT's implementation of menus require `Command` objects, and because we always want to go to a part of our application, it makes sense creating an appropriate class. Because all launching code goes in the Environment class, our new class also goes there.

```
protected class HistoryCommand implements Command {
  String historyToken;


  public HistoryCommand(final String newToken) {
    historyToken = newToken;
  }


  public void execute() {
    launch(historyToken);
  }
}
```

In case we want to do something that doesn't fit this pattern, we can just use a simple `Command` object, as in the following example.

```
Command sorry = new Command() {
  @Override
  public void execute() {
    showAlert("Sorry, this isn't ready yet.");
  }
};
```

Building the menu is standard fare; you could create a specific version for each user if you want. (Because this kind of code is quite suitable for automatic generation, we shall be writing an appropriate code generator later in this chapter when we consider deferred binding and code generators.) The first part of our code just creates the bar on top of the screen and a panel below it (where forms will be shown) and then goes on to check whether an initial token was provided; if so, the correct form is launched. We use a Grid object to place objects onscreen; you could also work with CSS if you prefer designing screens in that way.

```
final Grid rootDisplay = new Grid(2, 1);
final MenuBar runMenuBar = new MenuBar();
final VerticalPanel runPanel = new VerticalPanel();

private void showMainMenu() {
  // TODO Use user information for menu configuration

  runMenuBar.clearItems();
  runMenuBar.setWidth("100%");
  createMenu(runMenuBar);

  rootDisplay.setWidth("100%");
  rootDisplay.setWidget(0, 0, runMenuBar);
  rootDisplay.setWidget(1, 0, runPanel);

  RootPanel.get().clear();
  RootPanel.get().add(rootDisplay);

  /*
   * If the application was started with a token, now that
   * the user is logged in, it's time to show it.
   *
   * Don't forget to clear startingToken, or after a
   * logout/login, we will go back again to it.
   */
  if (!startingToken.isEmpty()) {
    launch(startingToken);
    startingToken = "";
  }
}
```

Creating the menu by hand isn't complicated; only sort of boring. We are dealing with a single menu here; a more complex application could build different menus depending on a user type parameter.

```
private void createMenu(MenuBar mb) {
  // TODO Add user type parameter, for specific menu
  // generation

  mb.addItem("dummy#1", new HistoryCommand(
    DummyOnePresenter.PLACE + "?parameter=value"));
  mb.addItem("dummy#2", new HistoryCommand(
    DummyTwoPresenter.PLACE));
```

```
MenuBar mb2 = new MenuBar(true);
mb2.addItem("subitem1", sorry);
mb2.addItem("subitem2", sorry);
mb2.addItem("subitem3", sorry);
mb2.addItem("subitem4", sorry);

mb.addItem("submenu", mb2);

mb.addItem("login", new HistoryCommand(
  LoginPresenter.PLACE));
}
```

GWT also provides `Hyperlink` widgets, which work with the History mechanism. We could let the user open any desired form, and even pass parameters to it, by writing something along the lines of

```
new Hyperlink("Go to Dummy #1",
  DummyOnePresenter.PLACE+"?parameter=value");
```

Detecting the User's Browser

Though GWT does a good job of detecting your browser type (and generating code that best suits it) you might want to generate different code depending on what kind of browser the user has. We will examine a classic way of doing this—similar to the ways you may do this in JavaScript—and a GWT-ish way of accomplishing the same task, by using deferred bindings.

By the way, if you need a reason for doing this (and it'd better be good, because you are doing away with one of GWT strengths!) you might think about generating HTML 5 tags for video watching, or dealing with the different tags required for Flash playback in Firefox and IE? (Think the now-deprecated <EMBED> tag in opposition to the modern <OBJECT> tag.) However, it can be argued that these concerns are becoming moot because all modern browsers are converging toward actual standards compliance. In any case, doing this kind of job will let us learn a bit more about deferred binding replacement, a most powerful device.

If you are not totally convinced that generating HTML code on your own will be a great idea, you might really be satisfied with simply excluding older Internet Explorer browsers from being used. So, in this section we'll see different methods of detecting your user's browser and react accordingly.

The Classic Way

Browser detection is old hat for web developers, who have long known the need for "special" handling of the differences between supposedly equal implementations of the HTML standard. We can achieve this in two different ways: at run time—something you have probably already done on your own—or at compile time, which is a special characteristic of GWT. Let's analyze first the classic way and then move on.

GWT provides JSNI (JavaScript Native Interface) to mix Java and JavaScript code, and we'll see more of it in Chapter 8, "Mixing in JavaScript." However, let's get ahead of ourselves, because using a `native` (i.e., JavaScript) method is the easiest way to get at the user agent. For example, the following code (the `/*-{` and `}-*/` delimiters are part of the JSNI "magic"; we'll explain it later) does just that in an economical way. Note that producing the result in lowercase helps writing further tests.

```
public static native String getUserAgent() /*-{
    return navigator.userAgent.toLowerCase();
  }-*/;
```

Given this code, you may write code such as

```
if (getUserAgent().contains("gecko"))...
```

and act accordingly. This test will be done, however, at run time, and your generated application will have to include code for all possible agents you want to consider. (Do you really want to include Firefox-optimum code for IE users? And what about Opera, Safari, or Chrome users; do they also need that baggage?) So, although this method works, and is easy to understand, you probably want to move on to more advanced ways and do things in GWT's own way.[7]

The Deferred Binding Way

The other way to recognize the browser type is far subtler and uses GWT's deferred binding replacement technique. In server-side Java, you have dynamic binding that lets you, at runtime, select the appropriate subclass and create an instance of it. However, GWT doesn't support reflection but provides deferred binding instead: Think "dynamic class loading at compile time."

When your source code is compiled, the GWT compiler produces a different version of your code for each specific configuration it finds; this is how separate versions of your application are created for Firefox, IE, and so on, and for each language. (We see more on internationalization in Chapter 12, "Internationalization and Localization.")

How could you use this? Let's work out a simple example, by writing a greeter that will work differently for IE and for other browsers. First, let's set up a general class, which we can use everywhere we need it. (This allows hiding the special `GWT.create(...)` idiom from the rest of the application.)

---

7. By the way, if you want to detect the operating system in use, you could use JSNI to get the value of navigator.userAgent and then analyze its contents to determine the operating system. There are plenty of such routines online; google for `javascript detection os OR "operating system"` and you'll get plenty of appropriate hits.

```
public class HelloBrowser {
  HelloBrowserStdImpl helloImpl = GWT.create(HelloBrowserStdImpl.class);


  public void salute() {
    helloImpl.sayHello();
  }
}
```

Note that the class doesn't do anything on its own; it delegates the work to the `helloImpl` object, which was created by GWT. We have different classes for IE and for other browsers. For the latter:

```
public class HelloBrowserStdImpl {
  public void sayHello() {
    Window.alert("You don't have IE.");
  }
}
```

And for IE:

```
public class HelloBrowserIEImpl extends HelloBrowserStdImpl {
  @Override
  public void sayHello() {
    Window.alert("If you are seeing this, you have IE.");
  }
}
```

If we run the code as is, it will always show a standard hello message; we need to tell GWT about both implementations of the class and when to use it. In the XML file for your project, add, before the final `</module>` line:

```
<replace-with class="com.fkereki.mvptest.client.HelloBrowserIEImpl">
  <when-type-is class="com.fkereki.mvptest.client.HelloBrowserStdImpl"/>
    <any>
      <when-property-is name="user.agent" value="ie6"/>
      <when-property-is name="user.agent" value="ie8"/>
    </any>
</replace-with>
```

Note the `<any>...</any>` construct, which lets you test for any of several agents at the same time. You can also use `<all>...</all>` (which requires that all conditions must be satisfied) or `<none>...</none>` (which requires that no conditions are satisfied) as alternatives. Of course, if you just want to check a single condition (say, for `ie6`) you could have written more simply:

```
<replace-with class="com.fkereki.mvptest.client.HelloBrowserIEImpl">
  <when-type-is class="com.fkereki.mvptest.client.HelloBrowserStdImpl"/>
  <when-property-is name="user.agent" value="ie6"/>
</replace-with>
```

At runtime, the GWT-created `user.agent` property will be one of `ie6`, `ie8`, `gecko`, `gecko1_8`, `safari`, or `opera`.[8] (Yes, there is no `ie7`.) The code we added in the XML file says to the compiler that when the `user.agent` property is any of `ie6` and `ie8`, class `HelloBrowserIEImpl` should substitute class `HelloBrowserStdImpl`.[9]

When the user downloads the application code, IE users get a version that has `HelloBrowserIEImpl` built in; other users get `HelloBrowserStdImpl` instead. (See Figure 4.3 to see this code in action.)

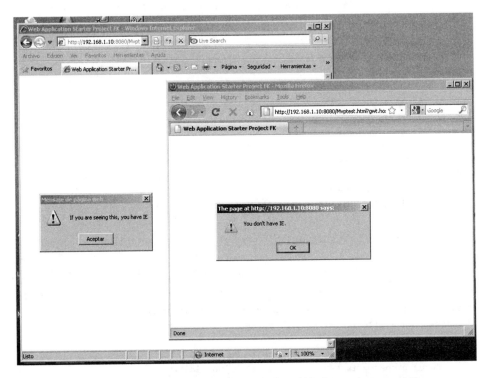

Figure 4.3 Browser detection, through deferred binding replacement. The generated code varies from a browser to another, enabling you to write specific browser-oriented code.

How could you take advantage of this? I previously mentioned a few situations: Depending on the browser type, you could create a `HTML` widget to allow viewing

---

8. Of course, this may change with future versions of GWT, as new versions of the browsers appear.

9. There's a third predicate, `<when-type-assignable class="some.class.name" />` that is true for any class that may be assigned to the given class.

videos (with the appropriate HTML 5 tags) or the correct tags (OBJECT or EMBED) for Flash, but please make sure you actually have to go this way.[10]

Code Generation

GWT also provides the capability of generating a class dynamically (and internationalization, which we'll see in Chapter 12, is the main example of that) so let's now see how code generators work and write up a sample generator of our own to help in a simple, but tedious, chore: creating a menu.

Whenever you include code to create an object by doing something like

```
MenuMaker newMenuBuilder = GWT.create(MenuMaker.class);
```

GWT invokes, at compile time, the corresponding generator, whose mission is to produce the code for the required class. Because creating a menu by hand can be tiresome, let's set up a MenuMaker class that can take care of doing that. We provide a simple configuration text file (sample.menu) such as the following one, for a fictitious video rental business.

```
menu Main
command RENT Rent a Movie
command BACK Return a Movie
command QUERY Search for Movies
command RESERVE Reserve a Movie
menu Reports
command LATE List late clients
command TOTALS Report total sales
endmenu
endmenu
menu Clients
command ADDCLIENT Add a new client
command SEARCHCLIENT Search for clients
command DELCLIENT Remove a client
endmenu
menu Movies
command ADDMOVIE Add a Movie
command SEARCHMOVIE Search for Movies
command DELMOVIE Remove a Movie
command LOSTMOVIE Enter a Movie as lost
endmenu
menu Other Functions
command LOGIN Log out
command BACKUP Make a backup
endmenu
```

10. For a discussion on the multiple ways to include Flash depending on each browser, check Bobby van der Sluis' article at www.alistapart.com/articles/flashembedcagematch.

The structure of the file is easy to understand. No blank or comment lines are allowed. A menu line creates a pop-up menu with the given text as a prompt. A command line invokes the history method providing the second parameter as a token and using the rest of the line as the menu prompt. Finally, an endmenu command just marks the finish of the corresponding menu. (Okay, this kind of menu definition isn't enough for all use cases, but it will do for an example. Also, we won't worry about syntax or content; we'll assume the file is perfectly correct, with no errors whatsoever, so the logic we write can be simpler.) The MenuMaker class we want, is simply defined as

```
package com.kereki.generator.client;

// ...imports...

public interface MenuMaker {

  public MenuBar createMenu();
}
```

Doing the following code produces a MenuBar object, with the structure provided in the sample.menu file.

```
final MenuMaker newMenuBuilder = GWT.create(MenuMaker.class);
final MenuBar mb = newMenuBuilder.createMenu();
RootPanel.get().add(mb);
```

The code for our generator class can be as follows. Most of the code is boilerplate (you'll always use it the same way) but you'll find it somewhat hard to learn the whys-and-wherefores; documentation for generators is somewhat scanty.

Your generator class must extend Generator, and implement the generate(...) method, which is responsible for producing all the code, or throwing UnableToCompleteException otherwise.

```
package com.kereki.generator.rebind;

// ...imports...

public class MenuGenerator
    extends Generator {

  @Override
  public String generate(
      final TreeLogger logger,
      final GeneratorContext context,
      final String typeName)
      throws UnableToCompleteException {

    try {
      final TypeOracle typeOracle = context.getTypeOracle();
```

```
final JClassType origType = typeOracle.getType(typeName);
final String packageName = origType.getPackage().getName();
final String origClassName = origType.getSimpleSourceName();
final String genClassName = origClassName + "Gen";

final ClassSourceFileComposerFactory classFactory =
  new ClassSourceFileComposerFactory(
    packageName, genClassName);
```

After this setup, we start producing code of our own. You must use `addImport(...)` to add all the packages and classes that your generated code will require and then `addImplementedInterface(...)` to generate the initial part of your class.

```
classFactory.addImport("com.google.gwt.user.client.ui.MenuBar");
classFactory
    .addImport("com.kereki.generator.client.HistoryCommand");
classFactory.addImplementedInterface(origType.getName());
```

Now we can create the required writer objects and start with our own logic, reading the menu file and producing output source code. For simplicity, I placed the `sample.menu` file at the output WAR directory; a better solution would have been using a source directory, but I wanted to write code as short as possible.

```
final PrintWriter printWriter = context.tryCreate(logger,
    packageName, genClassName);
final SourceWriter sourceWriter = classFactory
    .createSourceWriter(context, printWriter);

final File inFile = new File("sample.menu"); // at the WAR directory
final Scanner scanner = new Scanner(inFile);
String first, second, third;
int level = 0;

sourceWriter.println("public MenuBar createMenu() {");
sourceWriter.println("MenuBar stack[]= new MenuBar[20];");
sourceWriter.println("stack[0]= new MenuBar();");

while (scanner.hasNext()) {
  first = scanner.next();

  if (first.equals("menu")) {
    second = scanner.nextLine().trim();
    level++;
    sourceWriter.println("stack[" + level
        + "]= new MenuBar(true);");
    sourceWriter.println("stack[" + (level - 1) + "].addItem(\""
        + second + "\", stack[" + level + "]);");
```

```
    } else if (first.equals("command")) {
      second = scanner.next();
      third = scanner.nextLine().trim();
      sourceWriter.println("stack[" + level + "].addItem(\""
          + third + "\", new HistoryCommand(\"" + second + "\"));");

    } else /* first.equals("endmenu") assumed */{
      level--;
    }
  }
  scanner.close();
  sourceWriter.println("return stack[0];");
  sourceWriter.println("}");
```

After having emitted all the code, it's time to commit it, and return the name of the generated class, because that's required of generator classes.

```
  sourceWriter.commit(logger);

  final String genClassQualifiedName = origType
      .getParameterizedQualifiedSourceName()
      + "Gen";
  return genClassQualifiedName;

} catch (final Exception e) {
  throw new UnableToCompleteException();
  }
 }
}
```

So GWT can invoke this generator, we must add a few lines to the `gwt.xml` file.

```
<generate-with class="com.kereki.generator.rebind.MenuGenerator">
  <when-type-assignable class="com.kereki.generator.client.MenuMaker" />
</generate-with>
```

Running a sample application won't produce any visible code (the generated code is fed to the compiler but you won't get to see it) though the results will be obvious. See Figure 4.4 for the generated code in action.

If you want to take a look at the produced code, there's a simple trick: Modify the generator by adding an erroneous line guaranteed not to compile, such as `sourceWriter.println("Cave adventure = new xyzzy();")` so the produced code will generate "unknown type" errors. When you try to compile your code, GWT will produce a message and create a snapshot file with the problematic code.[11]

---

11. Note that you'll have to stop and restart your development session before trying a new version of a generator, because it's not client-side code, and rather part of your GWT development environment.

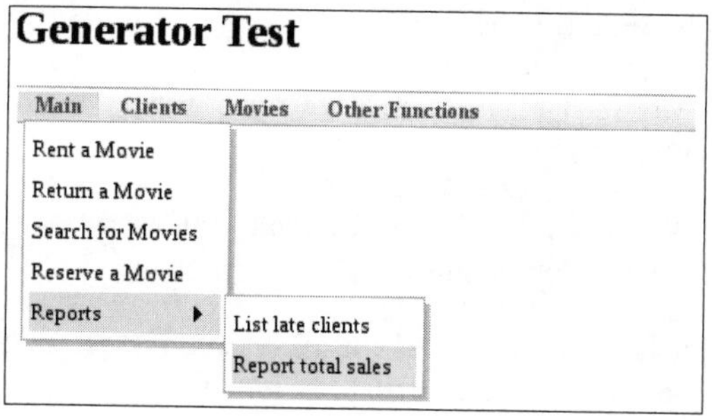

Figure 4.4 This menu was created automatically by a generator.

```
11:25:04.443 [ERROR][generator] Errors in
  'gen://CBF9B236.../com/kereki/generator/client/MenuMakerGen.java'
11:25:04.628 [ERROR][generator] Line 9: Cave cannot be resolved to a type
11:25:04.628 [ERROR][generator] Line 9: xyzzy cannot be resolved to a type
11:25:04.695 [INFO] [generator] See snapshot:
  /tmp/MenuMakerGen3442554202856735591.java
```

If you check out the contents of the snapshot file, you see what code you were generating—with the added error line also included, of course! For example, notice the name of the created class (MenuMakerGen, the name of the original interface, plus Gen tagged at the end), which is what the generator class returned.

```
package com.kereki.generator.client;

import com.google.gwt.user.client.ui.MenuBar;
import com.kereki.generator.client.HistoryCommand;

public class MenuMakerGen implements MenuMaker {
  public MenuBar createMenu() {
  Cave adventure = new xyzzy();
  MenuBar stack[]= new MenuBar[20];
  stack[0]= new MenuBar();
  stack[1]= new MenuBar(true);
  stack[0].addItem("Main", stack[1]);
  stack[1].addItem("Rent a Movie", new HistoryCommand("RENT"));
  stack[1].addItem("Return a Movie", new HistoryCommand("BACK"));
  stack[1].addItem("Search for Movies", new HistoryCommand("QUERY"));
  stack[1].addItem("Reserve a Movie", new HistoryCommand("RESERVE"));
  stack[2]= new MenuBar(true);
  stack[1].addItem("Reports", stack[2]);
  stack[2].addItem("List late clients", new HistoryCommand("LATE"));
  stack[2].addItem("Report total sales", new HistoryCommand("TOTALS"));
  stack[1]= new MenuBar(true);
  stack[0].addItem("Clients", stack[1]);
  stack[1].addItem("Add a new client", new HistoryCommand("ADDCLIENT"));
```

```
stack[1].addItem("Search for clients",
  new HistoryCommand("SEARCHCLIENT"));
stack[1].addItem("Remove a client", new HistoryCommand("DELCLIENT"));
stack[1]= new MenuBar(true);
stack[0].addItem("Movies", stack[1]);
stack[1].addItem("Add a Movie", new HistoryCommand("ADDMOVIE"));
stack[1].addItem("Search for Movies",
  new HistoryCommand("SEARCHMOVIE"));
stack[1].addItem("Remove a Movie", new HistoryCommand("DELMOVIE"));
stack[1].addItem("Enter a Movie as lost",
  new HistoryCommand("LOSTMOVIE"));
stack[1]= new MenuBar(true);
stack[0].addItem("Other Functions", stack[1]);
stack[1].addItem("Log out", new HistoryCommand("LOGIN"));
stack[1].addItem("Make a backup", new HistoryCommand("BACKUP"));
return stack[0];
  }
}
```

There's more to generators, from ways to indent or unindent the generated code (why worry, since nobody will get to see it but the GWT compiler?) to processing annotations to parameterize the code generation, or using reflection to learn about the classes to be produced, but describing all the possibilities would likely require a book of its own. This kind of usage I have shown is quite powerful, however, and can be applied to many different situations.

Recognizing Older Explorers

GWT is geared toward reasonably modern browsers, but unhappily there are still plenty of users with old versions of every browser that has ever been used, and Internet Explorer 5 and 6 (released in 1999 and 2001, respectively) are at the top of the list of "antique browsers."

You can't just kick out those users (well, if you insist, you can...) but at least your site should have an appropriate warning. You might use code such as we saw in the previous section, but for IE browsers, there is a more specific solution. The "IE6 No More" site has a simple script (available in different languages) that you should include at the beginning of your HTML source.[12] A simpler version could be as follows.

```
<!--[if lt IE 7]>
<b>This website won't work well with older Internet Explorer browsers. Please <a
href="www.microsoft.com/windows/Internet-explorer/default.aspx">update to IE8</a>,
or try out <a href="www.firefox.com">Mozilla Firefox</a>, <a
href="www.apple.com/safari">Safari</a>, or <a
href="http://www.google.com/chrome">Google Chrome</a>.</b>
<![endif]-->
```

12. Check the "IE6 no more" site at www.ie6nomore.com/ and MSDN's site at
http://msdn.microsoft.com/en-us/library/ms537509(VS.85).aspx for more on recognizing IE.

This code uses conditional comments, which work only in Internet Explorer. With other browsers, the code will be just considered a comment.[13]

No JavaScript?

Finally, to wrap up possible problems, the biggest showstopper for a GWT application is disabled JavaScript. The solution for this—unless you want to code everything twice: once with JavaScript, Ajax, the works, and once again with the most basic HTML!—is pretty classic, and the `projectCreator` script already takes care of that for you.

(And no, this isn't such a rare situation. Different estimations coincide in showing that about 10% of all users have disabled JavaScript as a safety measure, so you really need to consider and solve this problem.)

For a simple solution, just include in the main HTML of your page code such as the following, which was actually taken from a GWT project. Note that this code is created by `webAppGenerator` and will thus be included in every project you create.

```
<noscript>
<div style="width: 22em; position: absolute; left: 50%;
    margin-left: -11em; color: red; border: 1px solid red;
    padding: 4px; font-family: sans-serif">
Your web browser must have JavaScript enabled in order for this
application to display correctly.
</div>
</noscript>
```

Remember the old `<noscript>` tag? If the user disables JavaScript, he gets a red bordered warning instead of your GWT application. It won't let him run the application (which wouldn't have run anyway) but at least he'll get an explanation.

Summary

We have dealt with some browser-related themes. First, we studied how to work with History, allowing the user to use the Back and Forward commands at will, leading to a general launcher for any application. Second, we dealt with browser recognition code in two different ways (run-time and compile-time), which let us take a look at GWT's deferred binding replacement and code generation techniques. And, finally, we also studied automatic code generation, another deferred binding technique, that lets us produce code in a fully automatic way.

---

13. See more on conditional comments in the Quirksmode site at www.quirksmode.org/css/condcom.html.

5

Programming the User Interface

Designing the User Interface (UI) of your application has serious implications for your whole system. Applying a right design pattern such as Model-View-Presenter (MVP) makes for highly testable, well-layered implementations. The minimalistic view programming we apply is further reduced by using UiBinder (a GWT 2 novelty), which enables you to create the view layer by using XML, with practically no Java code at all. In this chapter we'll work at developing the UI, applying all the mentioned tools and methods.[1]

Thinking About UI Patterns

Earlier in the book we mentioned we'd be throwing some criticism at the standard GWT created "Hello World" type application. (You'll remember it just has a name textbox and a button; when you click the button, it uses RPC to call a servlet, and finally displays a panel with some information, and waits for you to click a button to close the panel.) The coding style is typical of common efforts for interactive forms, insofar as it mixes display logic (for showing values), application logic (what to do with the values), and business logic (what the servlet does); what problems does it cause?

Before answering this important question, let's get a bit ahead and think about testing. (We'll do a lot of testing in Chapter 13, "Testing Your GWT Application.") For example, going beyond our sample application

- How would you test a form that was supposed to produce an "alert" window? Sure, you can run the application and see if the alert shows up, but it would force you to run the tests by yourself without any automation help.

---

1. Note, however, that we won't be doing a tutorial on basic UI programming; if you need to refresh your knowledge about this, check http://code.google.com/webtoolkit/doc/latest/tutorial/gettingstarted.html or google for "GWT UI tutorial."

- How would you test a form that required clicking or value inputs by the user? Having to do the clicks or data entry on your own isn't very agreeable.
- How would you test a form that calls a servlet (such as the sample application does), if the servlet did actual work, such as updating a data base or posted a tweet? Every time you tested the applications, you would be causing serious side effects.

There are some ways around these problems (even without using such tools as we use later) but let's try to work out a solution that will be easily tested, and also offer several other advantages.

The servlet problem seems to be the harder one, but the solution is easy; it hinges on a pattern called Dependency Injection. If the form connects to the service on its own, and then uses that connection, there will be no way out. Thus, the idea is to separate the user of a service from the provider of the service: The form will use a service, and some other component of our system will provide it with the service it should call. It will be easy then, during testing, to arrange so that the form will be provided a fake service, with no negative side effects.

Dependency Injection also solves the "alert" problem; you should inject an object into the UI, so the latter, instead of directly doing `Window.alert(...)` on its own, would call a method of the injected object, which would do the alert. For production, the injected object would just do the alert, and for testing, we'd have a fake "alert-er" that would just register that an alert was called for, without interrupting the flow of testing.

This problem has been around long enough, and the corresponding solution has been given a name: the Humble Dialog or, more generally, Humble Object.[2] Basically, the idea is to split the UI into parts, so testing can be done more simply, and responsibilities are clearly assigned. The purely display-related logic will be in a simple object (the View), which will be injected into a supervisor object, which in turn shall be in charge of controlling and commanding the view. Let's first give a view to MVC, a long-standing solution to the problem, and then move over to MVP, a more streamlined pattern.

MVC: A Classic Pattern

Since Smalltalk in the 80s, the MVC (Model-View-Controller) pattern has been used, in many guises, for designing user interfaces.[3] Basically, the system is composed of

- The Model, which comprises all business logic. For web-based systems, this means servlets, web services, or any other kind of implementation residing server-side.
- The View includes all necessary widgets for user interaction. For web-based systems, the View usually resides client-side.

---

2. See www.objectmentor.com/resources/articles/TheHumbleDialogBox.pdf for the original paper by Michael Feathers, "The Humble Dialog Box."

3. See http://heim.ifi.uio.no/~trygver/themes/mvc/mvc-index.html for a history of the development of MVC by Trygve M. H. Reenskaug, its creator.

- The Controller, which stands between them and translates user actions into model updates. Depending on which framework you use, you may find the Controller either client- or server-side, but that's not relevant here.

How do these components relate to each other? (See Figure 5.1.) Basically, the Controller observes the View, and in response to user events, it can trigger model changes (by sending commands to the Model) or update the View to show the results of methods or events. The View can send queries to the Model (to get data) and also observe model change events, to eventually update itself. Finally, the Model receives update commands from the View, answers queries from the View, and communicates model changes to the View.

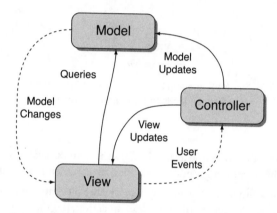

Figure 5.1 The MVC (Model-View-Controller) design pattern has been around since the 80s, but isn't optimal for GWT UI programming.

For GWT development, the View/Model interaction causes some difficulties. First, having the Model communicate changes to the View is complicated (though you may do with Comet, but that's not usually practical) because of the server/client separation. Reciprocally, having the View send queries to the Model makes testing harder (as we'll see in Chapter 13) because it requires using GWTTestCase, which is slower.[4]

MVP: A More Suitable Pattern

Recently, a variant of MVC in which the Controller role is taken over by a Presenter, with changed responsibilities, has proved to be more appropriate for GWT applications. (See Figure 5.2.)

---

4. If tests are harder to write and slower to run than need be, it's highly likely that they won't be written or run, despite what your development rules say, so it's in our interest to work toward easily tested design patterns.

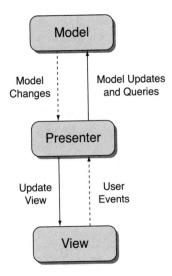

Figure 5.2 The MVP is adequate because it reduces the number and ways of connections between components.

In this pattern:

- The Model has the same role as in MVC, but it communicates only with the Presenter, which can send it both model update commands and queries.

- The View has a similar role as in MVC, but it doesn't communicate with the Model any more. Whenever the user does an action, the View informs the Presenter about the event, which may in turn ask the View to update itself.

- The Presenter is key in this pattern, for it is a bridge between the Model and the View. In response to the user events, it can communicate with the Model, and depending on its answers, send update commands to the View.

In this pattern, the (humble) View is quite simple and practically has no logic at all. Mostly, it will have code to create and displays widgets to get or set their values and to dispatch user events to the Presenter. If the user enters a value in a widget, the View won't do any validation; rather, it will notify the Presenter about the data change, and the Presenter will be responsible for the validation.[5]

In terms of testing, we hope to be available to skip testing the View (because of its simplicity) and work with a mocked instance of it, which we'll access only through its Display interface.

5. Because of this characteristic, this pattern is also called Passive View. Martin Fowler has "retired" the MVP pattern (see http://martinfowler.com/eaaDev/ModelViewPresenter.html) but in this case, his views haven't been universally adopted, and MVP is still commonly used.

Implementing MVP

We have seen the advantages of MVP; now let's study what we need to implement this pattern. Apart from a few auxiliary classes, implementation will be simple. Of course, you may think that for a simple login form—the example we'll use—it could be considered overkill, but that's usually the case with too-simple forms.

Callbacks Galore

Before implementing MVP, let's look at callbacks. The first "A" in Ajax stands for asynchronous, and you must get used to calling a function and not waiting for the answer. This will be true not only when you use RPC (as we'll do in Chapter 5, "Programming the User Interface," and Chapter 6, "Communicating with Your Server") but also when you are waiting for some input from the user.

Callbacks aren't that beloved, though. Because of the complexity they can add to a program, and the extra difficulties when debugging, they have been compared to the satirical "come from" statement.[6] In any case, because we'll be having rather a lot of them, let's consider an accessory `SimpleCallback` class that can help us writing shorter code.

```
import com.google.gwt.user.client.rpc.AsyncCallback;

public abstract class SimpleCallback<T> implements
    AsyncCallback<T> {

  @Override
  public final void onFailure(Throwable caught) {
    // Should never be used...
  }

  @Override
  public final void onSuccess(T result) {
    goBack(result);
  }

  public abstract void goBack(T result);
}
```

The standard GWT interface `AsyncCallback` always requires your coding both the `onSuccess` and the `onFailure` methods. However, in many cases you won't be dealing with the latter case; for example, you won't allow the user to leave the login form until he has entered a right user/password combination, so there can only be a "successful" return from it. Our `SimpleCallback` class makes `onSuccess` and `onFailure` final (so you cannot implement them) and defines an abstract `goBack` (as an alternative to

---

6. For the "come from" statement, see www.fortranlib.com/gotoless.htm—even if you are not up to par with FORTRAN coding, the examples will be clear enough (or obscure enough!) to make their point.

"return," which is a reserved word) method, which you need to implement. If your call-back won't pass any results to the caller, just use goBack(null).[7]

Implementation Details

Now, after the aside with callbacks, let's turn to implementing MVP in GWT and use the login screen as an example. Our application requires some client-side attributes and methods; we can easily imagine storing the username and password, or having menu creation and application launching methods (we did mention that in advance in Chapter 4, "Working with Browsers") so let's use an Environment singleton object for all that, and not forget to include a getModel() method. The Model object itself will have several methods for accessing all server-side services (we'll get to this in Chapter 6) but for now we'll make do with just a LoginService; it's easy to guess what it does![8]

Our login form requires a LoginFormPresenter and a LoginFormView, which extends appropriate abstract classes. We'll have LoginView implement the LoginDisplayInterface declared within the presenter's code, with all the needed getters and setters; working this way will simplify mocking the view for our automatic testing.

We'll inject the appropriate Environment and View into the Presenter through its constructor. The Presenter will inject its callbacks into the View through the methods defined in the Display interface; this is done so the View will know what method to call on each relevant user event. See Figure 5.3 for a UML explanation of the design.

In terms of code, the Presenter class would be

```
abstract public class Presenter {
    String params;
    Display display;
    Environment environment;
    KeyValueMap kvm;

    public Presenter() {
    }

    public Presenter(String someParams, Display aDisplay,
        Environment anEnvironment) {
        super();
        params = someParams;
        display = aDisplay;
        environment = anEnvironment;
```

7. You might also want to use a Runnable object and implement its Execute(...) method instead of a SimpleCallback with a goBack(...); moreover, when no results are passed back to the caller. I opted for going with callbacks only for generality. You could also object that hiding the onFailure(...) method isn't a good practice, even if it never gets called.

8. Note that Singleton objects are hard to test (and thus run against the grain of Chapter 13) but we aren't actually using it that way; rather, we are working with the object by dependency injection, so we can mock it as needed for our automatic tests.

```
  // ...get parameters from someParams...
}


public Environment getEnvironment() {
  return environment;
}


public Display getDisplay() {
  return display;
}


// ...we'll also have a getter for parameters...

}
```

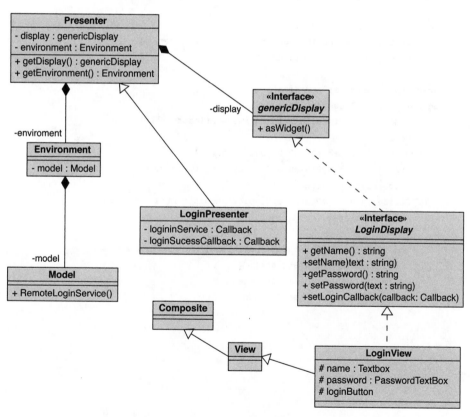

Figure 5.3 A UML class diagram for our MVP setup. Note that for client-side data and methods, we end up having an Environment class.

The `LoginFormPresenter` class will then be as follows. The **PLACE** string will be used for bookmarks and history management in the next chapter. Also note that the used login method isn't the safest; we look at alternatives in Chapter 10, "Working with Servers."

```
public class LoginFormPresenter extends Presenter {
  static String PLACE = "login";

  // define loginService and loginSuccessCallback as callbacks

  public LoginFormPresenter(final String params,
    final PresenterDisplay loginDisplay,
    final Environment environment,
    final SimpleCallback<String> callback) {

    super(params, loginDisplay, environment);

    loginSuccessCallback = callback;
    loginService = LoginFormPresenter.this.getEnvironment()
      .getModel().getRemoteLoginService();

    loginDisplay.setName("federico");
    loginDisplay.setPassword("");
    loginDisplay.setLoginCallback(new SimpleCallback<Object>() {
        @Override
        public void goBack(final Object result) {
          String name = ((PresenterDisplay) LoginFormPresenter.this
            .getDisplay()).getName();
          String pass = ((PresenterDisplay) LoginFormPresenter.this
            .getDisplay()).getPassword();

          loginService.getSomething(name, pass,
            new AsyncCallback<String>() {
              // on successful login, execute
              // the loginSuccessCallback
            });
        }
      });
  }
}
```

The `getSomething(...)` method is just a placeholder for the actual login method, which we'll get to implement in Chapter 10.[9]

We also require the `PresenterDisplay` interface that will be implemented by `LoginView`.

```
interface LoginFormDisplay extends Display {
  /**
   * Access the Name field
   *
   * @return Whatever the user entered in the Name field
   */
  String getName();


  /**
   * Initialize the Name field
   *
   * @param s
   *            Set the name field to s; most commonly just
   *            "" or possibly a saved name from an earlier
   *            session.
   */
  void setName(String s);


  /**
   * Access the Password field
   *
   * @return Whatever the user entered in the Password
   *            field
   */
  String getPassword();
```

---

9. Note: the following discussion can be considered a bit bizantine! It could be argued that a reference such as `getEnvironment().getModel().getRemoteLoginService()` violates the Law of Demeter, because the caller must know internal details of the `Model` to use it. As an argument for it, we use the `Environment` object as a sort of repository for all global objects, constants, and variables; the `Model` could certainly be a separate object, and we would just have to inject both of them when creating a form. Furthermore, the `Model` has nothing but these methods; it has no behavior *per se*. However, as an argument "against," when we get to optimization (in Chapter 14, "Optimizing for Application Speed") we will see that directly accessing a RPC service disallows some performance enhancing patterns, so we would probably opt for writing something such as `getEnvironment().doSomething(...)` and not violate Demeter's law.

```
/**
 * Initialize the Password field
 *
 * @param s
 *          Set the password field to s; usually just ""
 */
void setPassword(String s);

/**
 * Initialize the login callback, which shall be
 * executed when the user clicks the "Login" button
 *
 * @param acb
 *          Set the login callback to acb. The Presenter
 *          will have to get the Name and Password
 *          fields (by using the methods above) and
 *          perform the needed checks.
 */
  void setLoginCallback(SimpleCallback<Object> acb);
}
```

The LoginFormView class extends View, which itself extends Composite; it could directly extend the latter class, but it would be more obscure. (Using that class is logical because a form is composed by many widgets. This definition mandates including an initWidget(...) call; miss it, and you won't see any widgets.)

The view also needs to implement the LoginFormDisplay interface that was defined in LoginFormPresenter. Finally, the view constructor must define all necessary widgets, place them onscreen, and add a handler to the Login button that will call the (presenter-provided) callback.

```
public class LoginFormView extends View implements
    LoginFormPresenter.LoginFormDisplay {

  AsyncCallback<Object> loginCallback;
  final TextBox nameTextBox = new TextBox();
  final TextBox passwordTextBox = new PasswordTextBox();
  final Button loginButton = new Button("Log in");
  final FlexTable flex = new FlexTable();
  final DockPanel dock = new DockPanel();


  /**
   * Defines the view for the Login Form. Since this will be
   * shown in the main screen, we take care of centering the
   * fields (by using a DockPanel) so it will look nicer.
   */
```

```
public LoginFormView() {
  loginButton.addClickHandler(new ClickHandler() {
    public void onClick(final ClickEvent event) {
      loginCallback.onSuccess(null);
    }
  });

  flex.setWidget(0, 0, new Label("User name:"));
  flex.setWidget(0, 1, nameTextBox);
  flex.setWidget(1, 0, new Label("Password:"));
  flex.setWidget(1, 1, passwordTextBox);
  flex.setWidget(2, 1, loginButton);

  dock.setWidth("100%");
  dock.setHeight("100%");
  dock.setHorizontalAlignment(DockPanel.ALIGN_CENTER);
  dock.setVerticalAlignment(DockPanel.ALIGN_MIDDLE);
  dock.add(flex, DockPanel.CENTER);

  initWidget(dock);
}
```

The following are simple getters and setters for the Presenter to invoke.

```
@Override
public final String getName() {
  return nameTextBox.getValue();
}

@Override
public final String getPassword() {
  return passwordTextBox.getValue();
}

@Override
public final void setName(final String s) {
  nameTextBox.setValue(s);
}

@Override
public final void setPassword(final String s) {
  passwordTextBox.setValue(s);
}

@Override
public final void setLoginCallback(
  final SimpleCallback<Object> acb) {
```

```
    loginCallback = acb;
  }

  @Override
  public final Widget asWidget() {
    return LoginFormView.this;
  }
}
```

How does all this come together? We have already seen part of this in the menu code in Chapter 4, but let's complete that. The launching code for the login form will be in the `Environment` singleton, and will

- Create a `LoginFormView`.
- Create a callback for the `LoginFormPresenter`, with code to be executed after a successful user login; at the very least, the username will be stored, but let's not delve into that now.
- Create a `LoginFormPresenter`, and inject the view and the environment itself into the Presenter via its constructor. (The Presenter will use the environment to contact the Model to validate the user/password pair.)
- Show the `LoginFormPresenter` onscreen.

The Presenter must initialize the `LoginFormView` user and password fields, and set the view's callback to a method that will

- Get the user and password fields from the form.
- Through the Environment, call the Model's login validation method.
- If the attempt is successful, execute the callback that was provided by the Environment, passing whatever the Environment expects; at the very least, the username.
- If the attempt is unsuccessful, warn the user.

With this, we can now complement the launcher code from Chapter 4. Our menu code would do something as

```
if (token.equals(DummyOnePresenter.PLACE)) {
    panel.add(new DummyOnePresenter(args, new DummyOneView(), this)
        .getDisplay().asWidget());
} ...
```

There are two actions to be done. First, we construct an appropriate Presenter, by giving it a list of arguments, the View to use, and the current Environment (`this`). And second, we get the Display from the Presenter as a Widget, and we add it to the `panel` so it will get shown; you can only add widgets to a panel, and that's why we need to get the Display as one.

Some Extensions

On first meeting the MVP pattern, one usually has several questions about implementing specific behaviors; let's give a look to some usual problems and solutions. We create a second Login form, but just highlight the changes for the code we previously saw.

Many e-commerce sites have warnings Don't Click This Button Again because a payment would be processed twice or another similar fate would doom the double-clicking user. Solving this can be quite easy—just a matter of disabling the button after the first click—but how do you manage when the View and the Presenter are separate? We just need to add an `enableLoginButton(...)` method to the Display interface and implement it in the View.

(If you prefer, you could rather have two separate parameterless methods, `disableLogin()` and `enableLogin()`; do whatever suits you! I opted for having a single method, because that would allow me shorter code to enable or disable the login button in a blur handler; we'll get to that later.)

```
@Override
public void enableLoginButton(boolean b) {
  loginButton.setEnabled(b);
}
```

Then, the Presenter can easily disable the button after it's clicked and enable it again in case the login attempt was unsuccessful; we'd just have to add a pair of lines to our original code:

```
public void goBack(final Object result) {
  String name = (LoginFormPresenter.this.getDisplay()).getName();
  String pass = (LoginFormPresenter.this.getDisplay()).getPassword();
  LoginFormPresenter.this.getDisplay().enableLoginButton(false);

  loginService.getSomething(name, pass, new AsyncCallback<String>() {
    public void onFailure(final Throwable caught) {
      LoginFormPresenter.this.getEnvironment().showAlert("Failed login");
      LoginFormPresenter.this.getDisplay().enableLoginButton(true);
      loginSuccessCallback.onFailure(new Throwable());
    }

    public void onSuccess(final String result) {
      // ...as before...
    }
  });
```

In a similar vein, we can modify the login form so the Login button won't be enabled unless the user has entered both the name and password, and this will let us share a handler. We have to add a "blur" handler to the name and password fields, so the Presenter can learn when they have been changed; then, using the same `enableLoginButton(...)` method we just saw, it can enable or disable the button as needed.[10]

In the Display interface we'll add

```
/**
 * Initialize the name blur callback, which shall be
 * executed when the user changes the name textbox.
 *
 * @param acb
 *          Set the name blur callback to acb.
 */
void setNameBlurCallback(SimpleCallback<Object> acb);
```

Both setters are trivial; just a matter of storing the given callbacks in the `nameBlurCallback` and `passwordBlurCallback` private attributes. Then, in the View constructor we'll add

```
nameTextBox.addBlurHandler(new BlurHandler() {
  @Override
  public void onBlur(BlurEvent event) {
    nameBlurCallback.onSuccess(null);
  }
});

passwordTextBox.addBlurHandler(new BlurHandler() {
  @Override
  public void onBlur(BlurEvent event) {
    passwordBlurCallback.onSuccess(null);
  }
});
```

The Presenter must define the Callback and define how to do the enabling and disabling of the Login button. In its constructor, we create the handler and also use it after having initialized the name and password fields. (Why? A good point: Widgets aren't displayed when the View is created, and you should have initialized them before firing any events or doing any processing.)

```
SimpleCallback<Object> commonBlurHandler = new SimpleCallback<Object>() {
  @Override
  public void goBack(final Object result) {
    String name = LoginFormPresenter.this.getDisplay().getName();
    String pass = LoginFormPresenter.this.getDisplay().getPassword();
    boolean canLogin = !(name.isEmpty()) & !(pass.isEmpty());

    (LoginFormPresenter.this.getDisplay()).enableLoginButton(canLogin);
  }
};
```

10. Note that listeners are (since GWT 1.6) deprecated, and handlers is the way to go in GWT.

```
loginDisplay.setName("federico");
loginDisplay.setPassword("");
commonBlurHandler.goBack(null);
```

Working this way, no matter what event or condition you want to consider, the implementation always consists of

- Adding the required methods in the Display interface, so the Presenter can use them to inject the needed code
- Defining (in the Presenter) what code will be executed on each event, and use the Display setters to inject them into the view
- Modifying the View so it connects the UI events to the Presenter callbacks

This isn't exactly rocket science, and you may be feeling that this is actually quite a bother; after all, it's too much overhead for a simple form with three widgets! The first point that needs to be made is that splitting your UI code in this way doesn't lessen your coding possibilities; anything you could do in the old "all-together" style, you can still do now. And, as a second point, being able to unit test the code in a simpler way will pay off with the overall code quality; just remember not all screens will be this short, and the overhead won't mean as much![11]

Declarative UI

Isn't there a way to avoid all the object creation and object placement code? Building any kind of UI requires at least two or three lines per field, and that can quickly add up to large numbers. Furthermore, the Swing-like style of programming doesn't enable for quick changes in layout; you might end up having to rewrite large parts of your code because of a "little" change. And, finally, the produced code is too verbose (meaning, almost unreadable) making it hard to deduce or explain what kind of layout will be produced: Communication between UI designers (who "speak" HTML, CSS, and XML, rather than Java) and GWT coders will be more complex than needed.

Fortunately, GWT 2 introduces UiBinder, which alleviates the problem by letting you define the interface declaratively, using an XML markup scheme, which is transformed into Java code at compile time. You can even add handlers to fields, which helps make the view code even shorter; a good aid in making the View as simple as possible, without getting tempted into adding Presenter logic to it. CSS styling can be applied locally, and internationalization (i18n) is also supported, as we see in Chapter 12, "Internationalization and Localization."

Let's start with a simple example, by creating yet a third version of our Login form, and then delve more deeply into UiBinder's capabilities.

A Basic UiBinder Example

To use UiBinder, you need to add the `<inherits name="com.google.gwt.uibinder`
`.UiBinder"/>` declaration to the `gwt.xml` module description file for your application. For each object that uses UiBinder, you also need to create (at least) one `ui.xml`
file (with the layout for your view, including both HTML code and GWT widgets) and
include some annotations so the right code is generated. You can also rest assured that
UiBinder checks (at compile time) all cross references between your XML declaration
file and your Java code, to weed out mistakes; the Google Plugin for Eclipse is UiBinder-
aware, and errors appear with the classical red, wiggly underline.

Of course, before going any further, you should understand that UiBinder is not your
usual template interpreter. All code generation is done at compile time and not at runtime. There are no loops or conditional layout statements, as usual with template engines.
And, of course, there is no data binding and no value loading; getting data to and from
your widgets is still your View's responsibility.

Defining the Template

Let's do a login view, with name and password fields and a login button. (We work with
this form in Chapter 4.) Create a `LoginFormView.ui.xml` file in the same directory as
`LoginFormView.java`, with the following contents:

```
<?xml version="1.0" encoding="UTF-8"?>
<!DOCTYPE u:UiBinder SYSTEM "http://dl.google.com/gwt/DTD/xhtml.ent">
<u:UiBinder xmlns:u='urn:ui:com.google.gwt.uibinder'
            xmlns:g='urn:import:com.google.gwt.user.client.ui'>
  <g:HTMLPanel>
    <table>
      <tr>
        <td><g:Label text="User Name:"/></td>
        <td><g:TextBox u:field='nameTextBox'/></td>
      </tr>
      <tr>
        <td><g:Label text="Password:"/></td>
        <td><g:PasswordTextBox u:field='passwordTextBox'/></td>
      </tr>
      <tr>
        <td></td>
        <td><g:Button text='Login' u:field='loginButton'/></td>
      </tr>
    </table>
  </g:HTMLPanel>
</u:UiBinder>
```

(An aside: If you use Eclipse, you can create this file—and the corresponding Java
code—by selecting File, New, UiBinder. (See Figure 5.4.) Similarly, to edit an already
created template, right-click it and pick Open with, UI Template Editor.)

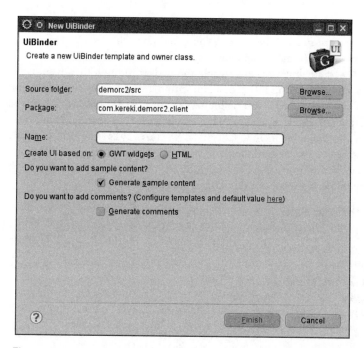

Figure 5.4 The newest GWT Plugin for Eclipse enables you to create
UiBinder templates easily.

Now, back to the template. Its first line (`<?xml...`) just declares the file type and encoding, in usual XML way. The second line (`<!DOCTYPE...`) includes a whole bunch of `<!ENTITY` definitions, for all HTML standard entities such as ` ` or `&aacute;`[12] XML doesn't know about HTML, so excluding this line will cause an `Error parsing XML (line 8): The entity "nbsp" was referenced, but not declared` message, and your code won't run.[13]

The third line (`<u:UiBinder...`) not only defines the root element for the XML document, but also defines a namespace prefix (g, as in `xmlsn:g`) that implies that all the classes in the `com.google.gwt.user.client.ui` package can be used as elements, by combining the defined prefix with the Java class name and writing something such as `g:TextBox` or `g:Button`.[14]

---

12. You can find a complete list of HTML entities at www.w3.org/TR/html5/named-character-references.html but check before at http://dl.google.com/gwt/DTD/xhtml.ent to make sure it's included.

13. The contents of this file are included in the compiler, so GWT won't have to connect to the Internet to compile your UI definition.

14. Note that the other namespace definition ("u") enables you to use the `UiBinder` class itself.

(In this example, we use `HTMLPanel` because it enables mixing HTML code and widgets; if you just needed the former, you could go with `HTML`. You can use HTML code only with panels that implement the `HasHTML` interface.)

The `u:field` attribute makes available the widget through the given name and relates it to a corresponding `@UiField` annotation; more on this, next. Note that this also applies to DOM elements; if you define `<span u:field='mySpan'/>` you can define `@UiField SpanElement mySpan` and use it as in `mySpan.setInnerText("some text")`.

You can also define or include CSS styles with `u:style`, but most probably you won't be using that, because it's unlikely you will want to define particular, specific styles for a view, instead of using a general CSS file for the complete application—the same reason why inline styles are not desired, and overall styles are preferred.[15]

Defining the Java Side

Let's now turn to the Java part. We need to declare to which template we'll be binding our code, which objects are to be used as widgets in it, and what handlers shall be attached to events.

```
public class LoginFormView {
  @UiTemplate("LoginFormView.ui.xml")
  interface Binder extends UiBinder<HTMLPanel, LoginFormView> {}
  private static final Binder binder= GWT.create(Binder.class);

  @UiField TextBox nameTextBox;
  @UiField PasswordTextBox passwordTextBox;
  @UiField Button loginButton;

  public LoginFormView() {
    HTMLPanel dlp= binder.createAndBindUi(this);
    initWidget(dlp);
  }

  // ...any other methods...
}
```

The `@UiTemplate` annotation lets you define the corresponding template file; by default, the same name of the class (so in this case the annotation isn't actually needed) but ending with `.ui.xml` instead of `.java`, is used. You must extend the `UiBinder<U,O>` generic interface: `U` represents the generated widget class (in this case, `HTMLPanel` as we saw in the template) and `O` stands for the owning class (the class we are defining right now). Finally, you must `GWT.create(...)` an instance of your interface (another case of deferred binding, which we saw in Chapter 4) which will be bound to the UiBinder created object when you call its `createAndBindUi(this)` method.

---

15. Okay, if you really insist on applying styles for each template, check http://code.google.com/ webtoolkit/doc/latest/DevGuideUiBinder.html#Hello_Stylish_World for a description of the `style` element.

The @UiField annotation relates your Java objects to the template widgets. Note that you just provide the object declaration here; actual object creation and binding will be done by UiBinder. (See the "Dealing with Constructors" section, for some exceptions.) A small detail: Tthe Java objects cannot be private, because in that case they couldn't be accessed and bound.

Finally, you can use the @UiHandler annotation to assign handlers to widgets.

```
@UiHandler("loginButton")
void uiOnLoginButton(ClickEvent event) {
  // ...your event handling code...
}
```

This takes care of creating the needed Handler and assigning it to the template widget. Note, however, that you can use this only with widget objects and not for DOM elements; you can assign an event to a <g:Button> (as in this example) but not to a mere HTML <button>.

More Complex Examples

Let's now examine a few other uses for UiBinder, such as setting widgets attributes, using constructors, adding your own packages, handling several views, and more.

Presetting Properties

You can preset most widget properties through the XML file. In our case, you could disable the login button by writing <g:Button text='Login' u:field='loginButton' enabled='false' /> or preload the username TextBox with <g:TextBox u:field= 'nameTextBox' value='default user' />. Any attribute that can be set with a widget.setAttribute(...) call can be initialized in this way.[16]

Using Your Own Widgets

You can also use any widgets you have created. For simplicity, let's say you created (in the com.fkereki.mvpproject.client package) a ReadOnlyTextBox that disables itself.

```
public class ReadOnlyTextBox extends TextBox {
  /**
   * A simple textbox that just disables itself
   */
  public ReadOnlyTextBox() {
    super();
    setEnabled(false);
  }
}
```

16. This style is basically the same as used with JavaBeans; see http://java.sun.com/javaee/5/docs/tutorial/backup/update3/doc/JSPIntro8.html for more on this.

If you want to use this kind of widget in a UiBinder template, you just have to add a new namespace:

```
<u:UiBinder xmlns:u='urn:ui:com.google.gwt.uibinder'
            xmlns:g='urn:import:com.google.gwt.user.client.ui'
            xmlns:h='urn:import:com.fkereki.mvpproject.client'>
```

which enables you to use your widget as in `<h:ReadOnlyTextBox ...../>`. In a sense, this works like a wildcard import in Java; you can use not only `ReadOnlyTextBox`, but any other widget defined in the same package as well.

Dealing with Constructors

All widgets declared in templates are created via `GWT.create(...)` meaning that they must provide a default zero argument constructor. If you need a special constructor, there are ways to work around UiBinder's restriction: You can either create the widget yourself or provide a factory method that will create it, or let UiBinder know about the required constructor so it will use it itself.

The first and simplest solution is creating the widget yourself. Suppose you want to use your own constructed `loginButton` in the preceding form. By changing the `@UiField` annotation, UiBinder won't create the widget, and its creation will be up to you.

```
@UiField(provided = true)
  Button loginButton;
```

Then, before binding the UI, you need to create the `provided=true` objects:

```
public LoginFormView3() {
  loginButton = new Button("My Own Login");
  HTMLPanel dlp = binder.createAndBindUi(this);
  initWidget(dlp);
```

A second way of achieving this is by providing a Factory method that creates and returns the appropriate object. Say we have a different `ReadOnlyTextBox2` class that requires its initial value as a constructor parameter.

```
public class ReadOnlyTextBox2 extends TextBox {
  public ReadOnlyTextBox2(String init) {
    super();
    setEnabled(false);
    setValue(init);
  }
}
```

We have to include a provider with:

```
@UiFactory ReadOnlyTextBox2 makeROTB2(String init) {
  return new ReadOnlyTextBox2(init);
}
```

UiBinder will use this Factory to construct all `ReadOnlyTextBox2` objects in the template.

Finally, you could tell UiBinder to directly use the new constructor. We annotate the `ReadOnlyTextBox2` constructor with `@UiConstructor` as follows:

```
public class ReadOnlyTextBox2 extends TextBox {
  public @UiConstructor ReadOnlyTextBox2(String init) {
    ...
  }
}
```

Now, we can use it within a template as `<h:ReadOnlyTextBox2 init='initial value'/>` and the provided constructor will be used.

Working with More Complex Layouts

What do you do if you require a more complex layout, which you cannot get with UiBinder templates? For example, say you want to have several templates in a `TabPanel` or a `Grid`? You can't directly create or position any such widgets with UiBinder (at most, you'll get zero tabs or a 0×0 grid) so you have to create the container yourself, then create the template objects, and finally assign them to your container.

Creating several template objects is simple, but you'll require a separate auxiliary class for each.

- Create all needed auxiliary classes, each with its own `@UiTemplate` annotation, interface, and binder objects. Each class should extend `Composite`.

- In your main form, create an instance of each auxiliary class. (The auxiliary classes may have nonempty constructors, which you would use to pass parameters for the widget creation and binding.) These instances will be populated with all the widgets you defined.

- Add each created object to your `TabPanel`, `Grid`, or whatever. Each panel or cell will now show whatever group of widgets you defined in the corresponding auxiliary classes.

Although the auxiliary classes would look much like the example we already worked out, your main class might include code such as

```
tp = new TabPanel();
tp.add(new Auxiliary1(...), "One");
tp.add(new Auxiliary2(...), "Two");
tp.add(new Auxiliary3(...), "Three");
```

It should be clear that this solution, although more Java-heavy than our previous examples, can easily be generalized to any kind of container and applied to any graphic design you might want.

Summary

We have studied ways to design the UI architecture, settling on the MVP pattern (with a "humble" View and a controlling Presenter) and we have applied UiBinder to more easily construct the View component. We have worked with testing in mind, and the resulting code will be simpler to test. Applying the techniques given here, you can design the UI in an easier way (because the XML templates can be used by nonprogrammers) and the View code will be minimized for faster development. In future chapters we build on the structure we created in Chapter 4 and this one, and code will follow the styles shown here.

6

Communicating with Your Server

Remote Procedure Calls (RPC) can bring client- and server-side code together and therefore are one of GWT's more potent tools. In this chapter we'll analyze how RPC works and show several patterns of its usage, including live suggestions, client-side data prevalidation, and connecting to Enterprise Java Beans (EJB). We shall even be providing a more complicated example of MVP, with an RPC-enabled composite widget.

Introduction to RPC

RPC enables GWT programmers to work almost as if the client- and server-side code resided at the same machine, making the connection practically invisible. There are some differences, however. For example, server-side code can use any class and package in the Java repertory, but client-side code is still limited. Also, some classes might not be transferred back and forth because of serialization problems; we'll touch on that next. Finally, of course connecting to a server and processing without waiting for an answer moves us out of the "synchronous world"; callbacks will be used everywhere for asynchronous coding.[1]

For implementation, RPC uses Ajax throughout, and GWT also provides the HTTP client classes (which we'll get to use in Chapter 7, "Communicating with Other Servers") if you need to connect to non-GWT server-side code. On the server side, servlets are used, by means of extending the `RemoteServiceServlet`. You aren't limited, however, to this architecture; you can use, say, Enterprise Java Beans (EJB) or Restful Services if you want, so your GWT application can connect to practically any kind of server side services architecture.

The most common usage of RPC is, obviously, accessing server-side servlets or EJBs, but it has a less obvious application, code splitting: a way to reduce the load time of your application, which we see in Chapter 15, "Deploying Your Application."

1. This is the big difference between RMI (well known to Java programmers) and RPC; the former is synchronous (blocking), whereas the latter is always asynchronous (nonblocking).

Implementation

Let's just give a once-over to the central concepts regarding RPC and then move to specific use cases and applications.

Though there have been some changes in how RPC was implemented as GWT evolved, the basic mechanism (involving a couple of client-side interfaces plus a RemoteService extended server-side class) is still the same.[2] In particular, "magic naming" is still applied (meaning GWT expects classes and interfaces names to follow certain rules) so for example, for a WorldService remote service you would have[3]

- `public interface WorldService extends RemoteService`, with the client-side specification of the provided services
- `public interface WorldServiceAsync`, which describes a "stub" that will mediate with the server and pass the results to the caller via an `AsyncCallback`, which will be used to pass the server-returned value to the caller
- `public class WorldServiceImpl extends RemoteServiceServlet implements WorldService`, which provides the actual server-side implementation code

(We shall see more of this `WorldService` remote servlet soon.)

Servlet mapping has also changed. In the current style, you need to annotate the client-side `WorldService` with `@RemoteServiceRelativePath(...)` providing the relative path for the remote service as a parameter. This annotation causes the client-side proxy to use `GWT.getModuleBaseURL()+"`*theAnnotatedValue*`"` as the service entry point for the servlet. You also need to provide more data on the remote servlet in the `war/WEB-INF/lib/web.xml` file, using both the `<servlet>` and `<servlet-mapping>` elements.[4]

```
<servlet>
  <servlet-name>
     worldServlet
  </servlet-name>
  <servlet-class>
     com.fkereki.mvpproject.server.WorldServiceImpl
  </servlet-class>
</servlet>
```

---

2. Check http://code.google.com/webtoolkit/doc/latest/DevGuideServerCommunication.html, and in particular the "Plumbing Diagram," if you want to refresh your RPC knowledge.

3. A small bother: The GWT Plugin for Eclipse doesn't help create these three files, but the GWT4NB plugin for Netbeans and the IntelliJ GWT plugin do. However, if you change one of the three files, the plugin can help you fix the other two.

4. In earlier versions of GWT, you would have had to add `<servlet path="..." class="..."/>` elements to your `gwt.xml` file. Currently, you need to do so only if you run `GWTTestCase` code.

```
<servlet-mapping>
  <servlet-name>
    worldServlet
  </servlet-name>
  <url-pattern>
    /mvpproject/world
  </url-pattern>
</servlet-mapping>
```

Note that the servlet-class element value is the fully qualified name of the service implementation class, and that the url-pattern element must match the relative path location of the servlet itself.

Calling a remote servlet still uses the same sequence: First create the client-side proxy to the remote servlet by writing `WorldServiceAsync worldService= GWT.create (WorldService.class)`, and then call any server-side method by using `worldService .anyMethod(...)` and including an `AsyncCallback<...>` matching whatever `anyMethod(...)` returns.[5]

A final point: When running in development mode, previous versions of GWT included a Tomcat server; GWT 2 uses Jetty instead. (Actually, in development you could use any other server, by providing the `-noserver` parameter for your development launcher configuration.) Of course, when you deploy your application (see Chapter 15) you can use either of them, or any other equivalent servers.

Serialization

Serialization is handled transparently through deferred binding, and appropriate serialization/deserialization methods are created at compile time for each class you want to send over the wire. (Note that GWT analyzes your code, and these methods will be provided only for the classes you actually send over the wire.) Java serialization isn't used (a GWT serialized object is different from a Java serialized object) because GWT makes a far simpler usage of serialization (for example, version IDs aren't needed) and only a few JRE classes are supported. However, since GWT 1.4, `java.io.Serializable` can be used instead of `IsSerializable`, but be aware that it is treated as a synonym; GWT's own serialization is still used.[6]

The rules that define what types are serializable, are simple:

- Primitive types (char, byte, short, and so on) and their wrappers (Character, Byte, Short, etc.) are serializable.

---

5. It should be noted that GWT hasn't ever provided, and still doesn't include, any synchronous RPC facilities. There are good reasons for this (such as JavaScript not being multithreaded) and you simply have no option to specify a non-Async call.

6. If your company uses Java heavily, `java.io.Serializable` is probably the way to go, but only for source code compatibility; keep in mind that GWT's methods are actually used. I personally prefer to use `IsSerializable`, because that won't let me forget I'm using GWT's serialization style.

- Enumerations, strings, and dates are serializable.[7]
- Throwables are serializable.
- Arrays of serializable types are serializable.
- Not all JRE emulation classes are serializable; however, ArrayList, HashMap, HashSet, Stack, and Vector (among others) are.
- `java.lang.Object` isn't serializable; avoid services that simply pass `Objects` along.[8]

A class will be serializable if all its attributes are of serializable types, with the exception that `transient` and `final` attributes are ignored and don't get serialized and transferred. You must implement the `IsSerializable` interface and also provide a default (no arguments) constructor.[9] Note that this interface actually has no methods and is only used to let the GWT compiler learn that you are planning to use the implementing class for RPC.

For efficiency considerations, try to be quite specific and go for concrete implementations rather than interfaces when declaring the types of your attributes. For example, in the `SuggestBox` implementation (which we'll develop later in this chapter) I declare final `ArrayList<SuggestionItem> suggestionsList=...` whereas the standard practice would have called for using `List<SuggestionItem>`; doing it this way helps the compiler optimize the produced code, for it can tell it needs just the `ArrayList` serialization code.

Note that it is even possible to define your own serialization/deserialization methods for any **xxxx** class, by defining (in the same package of the original class) a **xxxx_ CustomFieldSerializer** class (magic naming, again) that provides appropriate public static `serialize(...)`, `deserialize(...)` and `instantiate(...)` methods.[10] Some possible reasons would be efficiency (serializing "heavy" objects) or availability (legacy objects that do not implement `Serializable` or `IsSerializable` or that don't provide the default constructor).

As a test, I created a standard application with the GWT Plugin for Eclipse and then modified it a little. First, I created a `RpcResponse` class with a few—most, useless— fields; this class was meant to be returned by `GreetingService`:

```
package com.kereki.stdserialize.client;

import com.google.gwt.user.client.rpc.IsSerializable;
```

---

7. Note, however, that only the enumeration names will be sent over; if you have any member variables, they won't be included.

8. Furthermore, if you had Object as a return type, the GWT compiler would have to include code for all possible actual classes, thus generating lots and lots of unused code.

9. It's easy (ask me how I know!) to forget this no arguments constructor, because even if you don't require it for anything, GWT does.

10. Check http://code.google.com/p/wogwt/wiki/CustomFieldSerializer for more on this.

```
public class RpcResponse
    implements IsSerializable {
  public String aText;
  public String anotherText;
  public float aNumber;
  public boolean aBoolean;
}
```

Then I modified `GreetingService` so it would return a `RpcResponse` object instead of a `String`. (This also required substituting `RpcResponse` for `String` in the other RPC files.) The `GreetingServiceImpl` class would change as follows.

```
public RpcResponse greetServer(String input) {

    String serverInfo= getServletContext().getServerInfo();
    String userAgent= getThreadLocalRequest().getHeader(
        "User-Agent");

    RpcResponse answer= new RpcResponse();
    answer.aText= "Hello, " + input + "!<br><br>I am running "
        + serverInfo + ".";
    answer.anotherText= "It looks like you are using:<br>"
        + userAgent;
    answer.aNumber= 220960;
    answer.aBoolean= true;

    return answer;
  }
```

I ran the modified program, and used Firebug (which we installed in Chapter 2, "Getting Started with GWT 2") to check what was sent from the server to the client:

```
//OK[3,2,220960.0,1,1,["com.kereki.stdserialize.client.RpcResponse/3480033907",
"Hello, kereki!<br><br>I am running jetty-6.1.x.","It looks like you are
using:<br>Mozilla/5.0 (X11; U; Linux i686; en-US; rv:1.9.1.6) Gecko/20091201
SUSE/3.5.6-5.1 Firefox/3.5.6"],0,5]
```

Now I added a `RpcResponse_CustomFieldSerializer` class to the client-side code. Any serializer class must implement

- `public static void deserialize(...)` which takes a Stream reader and an object (an instance of the class you want to load) as parameters and must initialize the object with the data read from the reader.

- `public static void serialize(...)` which takes a Stream writer and an object as parameters and must serialize the latter (i.e., create an equivalent string from it) by writing to the former.

- an `initialize` method, that must return an instance of your class. This method is actually required only if your class doesn't have a empty constructor.

Reading and writing to the streams is helped by several convenience methods such as writeString(...), writeFloat(...), writeBoolean(...), and so on, plus the corresponding readString(...), readFloat(...), readBoolean(...) and more. Note that you can write anything you want to the stream; if you check the following serialize(...) method, you can see I included a my own serializer! string that is totally unneeded! Your only requirement is that, given the serialized contents, you must reconstruct the original object. Note, too, that while in serialize(...) you can write the values in any order; the deserialize(...) method must read them in the same order they were written.

```
package com.kereki.stdserialize.client;

import com.google.gwt.user.client.rpc.SerializationException;
import com.google.gwt.user.client.rpc.SerializationStreamReader;
import com.google.gwt.user.client.rpc.SerializationStreamWriter;

public class RpcResponse_CustomFieldSerializer {
  public static void deserialize(
      SerializationStreamReader reader,
      RpcResponse instance)
      throws SerializationException {

    if (instance == null) {
      throw new NullPointerException("Null RpcResponse!");
    } else {
      String dummy= reader.readString();
      instance.aText= reader.readString();
      instance.anotherText= reader.readString();
      instance.aNumber= reader.readFloat();
      instance.aBoolean= reader.readBoolean();
    }
  }

  public static RpcResponse instantiate(
      SerializationStreamReader reader)
      throws SerializationException {

    return new RpcResponse();
  }

  public static void serialize(
      SerializationStreamWriter writer,
      RpcResponse instance)
      throws SerializationException {

    if (instance == null) {
      throw new NullPointerException("Null RpcResponse!");
```

```
      } else {
        writer.writeString("my own serializer!");
        writer.writeString(instance.aText);
        writer.writeString(instance.anotherText);
        writer.writeFloat(instance.aNumber);
        writer.writeBoolean(instance.aBoolean);
      }
    }
  }
```

I ran the modified application (remember you have to restart Development mode, so the new server code will be recognized) and checked again with Firebug what was sent, and I could confirm that my serializer was used, because the data format changed; moreover, my useless string was there in plain sight!

```
//OK[1,220960.0,4,3,2,1,["com.kereki.stdserialize.client.RpcResponse/424577744",
"my own serializer!","Hello, kereki2!<br><br>I am running jetty-6.1.x.","It looks
like you are using:<br>Mozilla/5.0 (X11; U; Linux i686; en-US; rv:1.9.1.6)
Gecko/20091201 SUSE/3.5.6-5.1 Firefox/3.5.6"],0,5]
```

As a final note, keep in mind that if you extend a class with a custom serializer, you must also provide custom serializers for the subclasses; otherwise, they will fall back to the standard GWT serializer. In any case, writing your own serializer methods is probably something you won't be doing, but it's good to know that you can do so if you need to.

Direct Evaluation RPC

Finally, as an example of nonstandard serialization, a new RPC subsystem is being developed, though not still at production-quality level.[11] Direct Evaluation RPC (or deRPC, for short) creates a string somewhat akin to JSON for serialization (insofar it includes both attribute names and values, instead of just values as with GWT's standard serialization) that enables faster serialization and deserialization processes. Using deRPC instead of the standard RPC is simple and requires

- Inherit com.google.gwt.rpc.RPC in your application gwt.xml file

- Extend RpcService and RpcServlet, instead of RemoteService and RemoteServiceServlet

I further modified the standard greeting application from the previous section, and running it produced visibly different results; in particular, note that the attribute names are included in the response.

```
R1~Lcom.kereki.stdserialize.client.RpcResponse~I4~"42~com.kereki.stdserialize
.client.RpcResponse~"8~aBoolean~Z1~@1~"7~aNumber~F220960.0~@1~"5~aText~"48~Hello,
kereki3!<br><br>I am running jetty-6.1.x.~@1~"11~anotherText~"127~It looks like
you are using:<br>Mozilla/5.0 (X11; U; Linux i686; en-US; rv:1.9.1.6)
Gecko/20091201 SUSE/3.5.6-5.1 Firefox/3.5.6~
```

11. You can check http://code.google.com/webtoolkit/doc/latest/DevGuideServerCommunication
.html#DevGuideDeRPC for the status of deRPC.

Despite the declared advantages, it should be repeated that deRPC is still considered experimental code, "available as a technology preview for early adopters" as the GWT developers put it, so keep it in mind, but don't use it for production code yet.[12]

RPC Patterns of Usage

In this section, let's consider several RPC use cases, such as database bound widgets, live suggestions, on-the-fly validation, and more. Oh, and by the way, we shall also be showing a MVP interesting detail: how to include views within other views, and how everything gets wired together.

The World Cities Service

To have meaningful examples, we work with a regular-sized database, with information on countries, regions, and cities of the world. I used MaxMind's free cities table along with the International Organization for Standardization (ISO) 3166 table of country codes and both the ISO 3166-2 and Federal Information Processing Standards (FIPS) 10-4 tables of region codes.[13] (This was required because the United States cities' data used the common two-letter codes—such as NY for New York—instead of the numeric ISO codes.) The needed data was provided as comma-separated values (CSV) files, so loading it into MySQL tables was easy.

To follow the next examples, note that

- Countries are identified by a two-letter code (for example, US stands for the United States) and have a name.
- Countries are divided into states (or depending on the country, provinces, departments, regions, and more), which are identified by a numeric code (except for the US). The state code is unique only within the country. Each state also has a name.
- Cities are located in states and have a pure ASCII name, an accented name (possibly including foreign characters), a population (or zero, if unknown), a latitude, and a longitude. City names are unique only within a given state of a country; you can find several dozen "Springfield" cities just in the United States!

The world database can be created with

```
CREATE DATABASE world
  DEFAULT CHARACTER SET latin1
  COLLATE latin1_general_ci;

USE world;
```

12. Being a "preview" also implies there could be important changes in it, which could impact your code.

13. You can get these tables at www.maxmind.com/app/worldcities.

```
CREATE TABLE cities (
    countryCode char(2) COLLATE latin1_general_ci NOT NULL,
    cityName varchar(50) COLLATE latin1_general_ci NOT NULL,
    cityAccentedName varchar(50) COLLATE latin1_general_ci NOT NULL,
    regionCode char(2) COLLATE latin1_general_ci NOT NULL,
    population bigint(20) NOT NULL,
    latitude float(10,7) NOT NULL,
    longitude float(10,7) NOT NULL,
    KEY `INDEX` (countryCode,regionCode,cityName),
    KEY cityName (cityName),
    KEY cityAccentedName (cityAccentedName)
) ENGINE=MyISAM DEFAULT CHARSET=latin1 COLLATE=latin1_general_ci;

CREATE TABLE countries (
    countryCode char(2) COLLATE latin1_general_ci NOT NULL,
    countryName varchar(50) COLLATE latin1_general_ci NOT NULL,
    PRIMARY KEY (countryCode),
    KEY countryName (countryName)
) ENGINE=MyISAM DEFAULT CHARSET=latin1 COLLATE=latin1_general_ci;

CREATE TABLE regions (
    countryCode char(2) COLLATE latin1_general_ci NOT NULL,
    regionCode char(2) COLLATE latin1_general_ci NOT NULL,
    regionName varchar(50) COLLATE latin1_general_ci NOT NULL,
    PRIMARY KEY (countryCode,regionCode),
    KEY regionName (regionName)
) ENGINE=MyISAM DEFAULT CHARSET=latin1 COLLATE=latin1_general_ci;
```

I defined a WorldService remote service, with several functions that we use next, specifically

- addCity(...) can be used to add a new city to the database.
- cityExists(...) checks whether a given city already exists within a given state of a country.
- getCities(...) returns cities from a state of a country; you have to specify how many cities you want, and from which starting point in the list of all cities in the state.
- getCitiesStartingWith(...) returns all cities in a certain state, whose name starts with a given substring.
- getCountries(...) simply returns a list of all existing countries.
- getStates(...) returns a list of all states in a given country.

But, before we start with the actual code, let's give a thought to a little problem: How do we share code between the client and the server?

Code Sharing

The more checks you do client-side, before sending anything to the server, the more spry your application will feel. (And note that we show a related design pattern, "Prevalidation", next in this chapter.) With usual web development tools, that would imply having to code all checks twice (once in JavaScript for the client-side code, and once in any other language for the server-side code) but with GWT, within limits, you can use the same Java code on both sides. The only limitation, as we have already seen before, is that client-side code is restricted to a subset of the Java language; the source code for any shared objects will have to be located in a client-side package to insure it can be compiled and processed.

You require a server-side version of the object, with two special extra methods: a constructor that can initialize the server-side object with the client-side object, and a method that can produce a client-side object out of a server-side object. (Obviously, if you could use the same code client- and server-side, you wouldn't require two classes. Furthermore, according to the standard layout we save in Chapter 3, "Understanding Projects and Development," we'd place the common code in the shared directory.)

We have `ClientCityData` and `ServerCityData` classes to show this pattern. As previously described, the client-side code implements the `IsSerializable` interface so objects can be sent back and forth as described. Note that the validation method does only client-side valid operations.

```
package com.fkereki.mvpproject.client.rpc;

import com.google.gwt.user.client.rpc.IsSerializable;

public class ClientCityData
    implements IsSerializable {
  public String countryCode;
  public String regionCode;
  public String cityName;
  public String cityAccentedName;
  public int population;
  public float latitude;
  public float longitude;
```

We have two constructors: the required empty one, and another with all the city data.

```
  public ClientCityData() {
  }

  public ClientCityData(
      final String pCC, final String pRC, final String pCN,
      final String pCAN, final int pPop, final float pLat,
      final float pLong) {

    countryCode= pCC;
    regionCode= pRC;
    cityName= pCN;
```

```
      cityAccentedName= pCAN;
      population= pPop;
      latitude= pLat;
      longitude= pLong;
   }
```

You can't do so many validations client-side as you could server-side because of the Java restrictions imposed by GWT for your client code. (We have a more complete routine in our server-side code.) Let's have the validation function return an empty string if there are no problems with the data, or an explanation instead.

```
   public String validationProblems() {
     if (countryCode.isEmpty()) {
       return "No country specified";
     } else if (regionCode.isEmpty()) {
       return "No region specified";

     // ...more checks...

     } else {
       return "";
     }
   }
}
```

Our other version, **ServerCityData**, includes both special methods previously described and also implements more checks. Note how we import the client-side version of the class, which we extend.

```
package com.fkereki.mvpproject.server;

import com.fkereki.mvpproject.client.rpc.ClientCityData;

public class ServerCityData
    extends ClientCityData {
```

As described, we have a constructor that can take a client-side object and use it to construct a server-side one.

```
   public ServerCityData(
       final ClientCityData pObject) {

     countryCode= pObject.countryCode;
     regionCode= pObject.regionCode;
     cityName= pObject.cityName;
     cityAccentedName= pObject.cityAccentedName;
     population= pObject.population;
     latitude= pObject.latitude;
     longitude= pObject.longitude;
   }
```

Here's the other mandatory method: one that can produce a client-side version of a server-side object, so you can send it back from the server to the client.

```
public ClientCityData asCityData() {
  return new ClientCityData(countryCode, regionCode, cityName,
      cityAccentedName, population, latitude, longitude);
}
```

Our server-side validation code must be complete; we probably redefine and "amplify" the client-side checks here. Of course, there's no need to recode everything; we can still access the original validations by means of super.validationProblems(...).

```
@Override
public String validationProblems() {
  final String svp= super.validationProblems();
  if (!svp.isEmpty()) {
    return svp;
  } else {
    final WorldServiceImpl wsi= new WorldServiceImpl();
    if (wsi.cityExists(countryCode, regionCode, cityName)) {
      return "City exists.";
    } else {
      return "";
    }
  }
}
```

Now that we have seen how to pass city objects back and forth, let's get to the actual coding of the services we need.

Coding the Server Side Services

The WorldService.java interface is as follows:

```
package com.fkereki.mvpproject.client.rpc;

// ...several imports...

@RemoteServiceRelativePath("world")
public interface WorldService extends RemoteService {
  public String addCity(ClientCityData cd);

  public Boolean cityExists(String pCountry,
    String pRegion, String pCity);

  public LinkedHashMap<String, ClientCityData> getCities(String pCountry,
      String pRegion, int pFrom, int pQuantity);
```

```
public LinkedHashMap<String, ClientCityData> getCitiesStartingWith(
    String pCountry, String pRegion, String pStart);

public LinkedHashMap<String, String> getCountries();

public LinkedHashMap<String, String> getStates(String pCountry);
}
```

The corresponding Async interface is easily derived from it. (If you just code the preceding interface, the Google Plugin for Eclipse can detect the need for the Async interface and offer to create it automatically.) The code is a direct parallel of the preceding code; the added `AsyncCallback` parameters are the only difference.

```
package com.fkereki.mvpproject.client.rpc;

// ...imports...

public interface WorldServiceAsync {
  void addCity(ClientCityData cd, AsyncCallback<String> ac);

  void cityExists(String pCountry, String pRegion,
    String pCity, AsyncCallback<Boolean> ac);

  void getCities(String pCountry, String pRegion,
    int pFrom, int pQuantity, AsyncCallback<LinkedHashMap<String,
    ClientCityData>> ac);

  void getCitiesStartingWith(String pCountry, String pRegion,
    String pStart, AsyncCallback<LinkedHashMap<String,
    ClientCityData>> callback);

  void getCountries(AsyncCallback<LinkedHashMap<String, String>> ac);

  void getStates(java.lang.String country,
      AsyncCallback<LinkedHashMap<String, String>> ac);
}
```

We'll use all these methods in our examples, and since this is pure Java server-side code, let's study all the code at once. Note I defined a `gwtuser` user with a `gwtpass` password for the `world` database. The actual algorithms are straightforward. Because the services can be programmed using the full Java facilities, you might also use OpenJPA or Hibernate, but I didn't want to add an extra complication (which doesn't have to do with GWT in any case) so I just used a simple, clear definition and left optimization details for other books.

```
package com.fkereki.mvpproject.server;

// ...several imports...
```

```
public class WorldServiceImpl
    extends RemoteServiceServlet
    implements WorldService {
  private static final long serialVersionUID = 1L;

  /*
   * MySQL and JDBC related constants and variables
   */
  static String jdbc_url = "jdbc:mysql://127.0.0.1/world";
  static String mysql_user = "gwtuser";
  static String mysql_password = "gwtpass";
  private Connection conn = null;
```

Let's start with some simple utility methods for connecting and getting disconnected from the database. The methods are quite simple and require little explanation. (However, it should be commented that actual implementation of this service would probably access a JNDI pool of connections for efficiency considerations, but that doesn't have anything to do with GWT, so let's also skip that.)

```
private void connectToDatabase() throws Exception {
  DriverManager.registerDriver(new com.mysql.jdbc.Driver());
  Class.forName("com.mysql.jdbc.Driver").newInstance();
  conn = DriverManager.getConnection(jdbc_url,
    mysql_user, mysql_password);
}

private void disconnectFromDatabase() throws Exception {
  conn.close();
}
```

The addCity(...) method tries to add a new city to the database. For simplicity, we have it return an empty string if it succeeded or an error message otherwise. Note how we construct a ServerCityData object out of the ClientCityData object that we received as a parameter. After checking for possible validation problems, we use a pre-pared statement (never forget about possible SQL injection attacks!) to actually insert the new city in the database.

```
public String addCity(final ClientCityData cd) {
  final ServerCityData scd = new ServerCityData(cd);
  final String svp = scd.validationProblems();
  if (!svp.isEmpty()) {
    return svp;
  } else {
    try {
      connectToDatabase();
      final PreparedStatement ps = conn
          .prepareStatement("INSERT INTO cities "
              + "(countryCode, regionCode, "
              + "cityName, cityAccentedName, "
```

```
                    + "population, latitude, longitude) "
                    + "VALUES (?,?,?,?,?,?,?)");

        ps.setString(1, scd.countryCode);
        ps.setString(2, scd.regionCode);
        ps.setString(3, scd.cityName);
        ps.setString(4, scd.cityAccentedName);
        ps.setInt(5, scd.population);
        ps.setFloat(6, scd.latitude);
        ps.setFloat(7, scd.longitude);
        ps.executeUpdate();

        ps.close();
        disconnectFromDatabase();
      } catch (final Exception e) {
        return "Error adding city: " + e.getMessage();
      }
      return "";
    }
  }
```

Let's now write the `cityExists(...)` method, that checks whether a city with a given name already exists in a region of a country. Doing a simple count is enough to do that check. (And yes, I should have used a `PreparedStatement` here too!) Note that with RPC, objects must always be returned, and thus the `Boolean` type.

```
public Boolean cityExists(final String pCountryCode,
    final String pRegionCode, final String pCityName) {
  boolean result = false;
  try {
    connectToDatabase();
    final Statement stmt = conn.createStatement();
    final ResultSet rs = stmt
        .executeQuery("SELECT COUNT(*) FROM cities WHERE countryCode='"
            + pCountryCode + "' AND regionCode='" + pRegionCode
            + "' AND cityName='" + pCityName + "'");

    rs.first();
    result = rs.getInt(1) > 0;

    stmt.close();
    disconnectFromDatabase();
  } catch (final Exception e) {
    e.printStackTrace();
  }

  return new Boolean(result);
}
```

For a cities browsing example we'll develop, we'll require getting all the cities from a region of a country. As we'll page through the result set, we'll need to specify how many cities to return (pQuantity) and at which offset (pFrom) to start. The result will be a linked hash map ordered by city name. Note that we use ClientCityData objects in the map because we couldn't send it back to the client otherwise.

```java
public LinkedHashMap<String, ClientCityData> getCities(
    final String pCountryCode,
    final String pRegionCode,
    final int pFrom,
    final int pQuantity) {

  final LinkedHashMap<String, ClientCityData> citiesList =
    new LinkedHashMap<String, ClientCityData>();

  try {
    connectToDatabase();
    final Statement stmt = conn.createStatement();
    final ResultSet rs = stmt
        .executeQuery("SELECT * FROM cities WHERE countryCode='"
            + pCountryCode + "' AND regionCode='" + pRegionCode
            + "' ORDER BY cityName LIMIT " + pFrom + "," + pQuantity);

    while (rs.next()) {
      citiesList.put(rs.getString("cityName"), new ClientCityData(rs
          .getString("countryCode"), rs.getString("regionCode"), rs
          .getString("cityName"), rs.getString("cityAccentedName"), rs
          .getInt("population"), rs.getFloat("latitude"), rs
          .getFloat("longitude")));
    }

    stmt.close();
    disconnectFromDatabase();
  } catch (final Exception e) {
    e.printStackTrace();
  }

  return citiesList;
}
```

For the SuggestBox example we have already mentioned, we'll require getting a list of all cities, in a certain region of a country, whose names start with a given string.

```java
public LinkedHashMap<String, ClientCityData> getCitiesStartingWith(
    String pCountryCode, String pRegionCode, String pStart) {

  final LinkedHashMap<String, ClientCityData> citiesList =
    new LinkedHashMap<String, ClientCityData>();
```

```
  try {
    connectToDatabase();
    final Statement stmt = conn.createStatement();
    final ResultSet rs = stmt
        .executeQuery("SELECT * FROM cities WHERE countryCode='"
            + pCountryCode + "' AND regionCode='" + pRegionCode
            + "' AND cityName LIKE '" + pStart
            + "%' ORDER BY cityName");

    while (rs.next()) {
      citiesList.put(rs.getString("cityName"), new ClientCityData(rs
          .getString("countryCode"), rs.getString("regionCode"), rs
          .getString("cityName"), rs.getString("cityAccentedName"), rs
          .getInt("population"), rs.getFloat("latitude"), rs
          .getFloat("longitude")));
    }

    stmt.close();
    disconnectFromDatabase();
  } catch (final Exception e) {
    e.printStackTrace();
  }

  return citiesList;
}
```

The implementation of countries and regions `ListBox` widgets will require getting all countries and all regions from a country. This first method produces a `LinkedHashMap` with all countries in alphabetical order, so as to simplify the handling of the list.

```
public LinkedHashMap<String, String> getCountries() {
  final LinkedHashMap<String, String> countriesList =
    new LinkedHashMap<String, String>();

  try {
    connectToDatabase();
    final Statement stmt = conn.createStatement();
    final ResultSet rs = stmt.executeQuery(
        "SELECT countryCode,countryName "
        + "FROM countries ORDER BY 2");

    while (rs.next()) {
      countriesList.put(rs.getString(1), rs.getString(2));
    }

    stmt.close();
    disconnectFromDatabase();
  } catch (final Exception e) {
```

```
      e.printStackTrace();
   }

   return countriesList;
 }
```

This method returns all regions from a country. The region codes are used as keys and the region names as values. The `LinkedHashMap` is ordered by region name, alphabetically, to simplify loading the corresponding `ListBox`.

```
public LinkedHashMap<String, String> getStates(
   final String pCountryCode) {

   final LinkedHashMap<String, String> regionsList =
     new LinkedHashMap<String, String>();

   try {
     connectToDatabase();
     final Statement stmt = conn.createStatement();
     final ResultSet rs = stmt
        .executeQuery("SELECT regionCode,regionName FROM regions "
           + "WHERE countryCode='" + pCountryCode + "'  ORDER BY 2");

     while (rs.next()) {
       regionsList.put(rs.getString(1), rs.getString(2));
     }

     stmt.close();
     disconnectFromDatabase();
   } catch (final Exception e) {
     e.printStackTrace();
   }

   return regionsList;
 }
}
```

It was quite a stretch of code, but with it out of the way, let's get now to specific usages of RPC.

Database-Related Widgets and MVP

A common usage of RPC is to populate `ListBox` or similar widgets. For example, we might want to have a country/state pair of `ListBox` fields; the first `ListBox` should include all countries, and whenever the user picks a different country, the second `ListBox` should be filled with the appropriate states from the World database. With the given services, doing the first task is quite simple:

```
// ...show "Loading..." in the Countries ListBox
getEnvironment().getModel().getCountries(
    new SimpleCallback<LinkedHashMap<String, String>>() {
      @Override
      public void goBack(LinkedHashMap<String, String> result) {
        // ...use result to load the countries ListBox...
      }
    });
```

Similarly, loading the correct states after the selected country changes is a trivial variation that requires defining a `ValueChangeHandler` for the countries widget, and a few
lines such as

```
// ...empty the states ListBox...
if (!getDisplay().getCountry().isEmpty()) {
  getEnvironment().getModel().getStates(getDisplay().getCountry(),
    new SimpleCallback<LinkedHashMap<String, String>>() {
      @Override
      public void goBack(LinkedHashMap<String, String> result) {
        // ...use result to load the states ListBox...
      }
    });
}
```

Of course, managing this isn't hard, and a basic example at that, so let's spice it up a
little by creating a `Composite` widget that we can reuse in different forms. (And we'll do
that for the prevalidation example; see next.) How shall we split the code?

Each composite widget will be a View by itself, with a corresponding Presenter,
which shall take care of all required code for event processing. As a View (in our code)
actually extends `Composite`, we can include a View anywhere within another View and
even use UiBinder for that. Finally, whenever an included widget changes or causes any
similar event, it fires an appropriate event so the including View can respond to it. See
Figure 6.1.

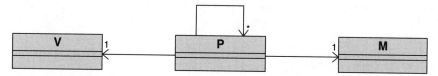

Figure 6.1 Composite widgets are split into a View (V) and a Presenter (P).
The main Presenter can include other Presenters, each bound to a
different View (themselves all included within the main View) and all
sharing the same Model (M).

Because the previous explanation might be hard to visualize, let's show how to build a
`CountryStateView` widget and how to use it. Let's start by looking at its design; we can

use UiBinder for this—though it's simple enough (just a couple of `ListBox` widgets side by side!) that we can manage by creating it directly through pure Java code!

```
<?xml version="1.0" encoding="UTF-8"?>
<!DOCTYPE u:UiBinder SYSTEM "http://dl.google.com/gwt/DTD/xhtml.ent">
<u:UiBinder xmlns:u='urn:ui:com.google.gwt.uibinder'
            xmlns:g='urn:import:com.google.gwt.user.client.ui'>
  <g:HTMLPanel>
    <g:ListBox u:field="countryCode"/>
    <g:ListBox u:field="stateCode"/>
  </g:HTMLPanel>
</u:UiBinder>
```

The corresponding View code is more interesting. We just define the required Display interface with two getters for the Country and State values, two setters for their corresponding `ListBox` widgets (more on this next), and a couple of callback related methods for their value changes.

```
package com.fkereki.mvpproject.client.countryState;
// ...imports...

public interface CountryStateDisplay
  extends Display, HasValueChangeHandlers<Object> {

  String getCountry();
  String getState();

  void setCountryList(LinkedHashMap<String, String> cl);
  void setStateList(LinkedHashMap<String, String> sl);

  void setOnCountryChangeCallback(SimpleCallback<Object> acb);
  void setOnStateChangeCallback(SimpleCallback<Object> acb);
}
```

The initial part is standard, though—just definitions, and the UiBinder related code.

```
package com.fkereki.mvpproject.client.countryState;

// ...imports...

public class CountryStateView
  extends View
  implements CountryStateDisplay {

  @UiTemplate("CountryStateView.ui.xml")
  interface Binder extends UiBinder<HTMLPanel, CountryStateView> {
  }
```

```
private static final Binder binder = GWT.create(Binder.class);

@UiField ListBox countryCode;
@UiField ListBox stateCode;

SimpleCallback<Object> onCountryChangeCallback;
SimpleCallback<Object> onStateChangeCallback;

public CountryStateView() {
  super();
  HTMLPanel dlp = binder.createAndBindUi(this);
  initWidget(dlp);
}
```

Because `CountryStateView` needs to fire a `ValueChangeEvent` whenever any of its components changes (otherwise, how would the including View otherwise learn about those changes?) we need to define an `addValueChangeHandler` method, so a handler can be added to our new widget:

```
@Override
public HandlerRegistration addValueChangeHandler(
    ValueChangeHandler<Object> handler) {
  return addHandler(handler, ValueChangeEvent.getType());
}
```

The rest of the code is simple. Note, in particular, that the Presenter doesn't directly work with the `ListBox` widgets; rather, it uses `setCountryList(...)` and `setStateList(...)` to provide the required lists of values, and a quite short code loads those values into the widgets.[14] (We use an empty string as the value for the "Select a country" text, so we can tell whether the user has actually selected a country; the same is done for the states `ListBox`.) The `getCountry(...)` and `getState(...)` methods are also simple enough that we dare use them with little testing.

```
@Override
public String getCountry() {
  int current = countryCode.getSelectedIndex();
  return current == -1 ? "" : countryCode.getValue(current);
}

@Override
public String getState() {
  int current = stateCode.getSelectedIndex();
  return current == -1 ? "" : stateCode.getValue(current);
}
```

14. This can be considered an application of the Adapter (or Wrapper) design pattern; see www.oodesign.com/adapter-pattern.html for more on this.

```
@Override
public void setCountryList(LinkedHashMap<String, String> cl) {
  countryCode.clear();
  if (cl != null) {
    countryCode.addItem("--Select a country--", "");
    for (final String it : cl.keySet()) {
      countryCode.addItem(cl.get(it), it);
    }
  }
}

@Override
public void setStateList(LinkedHashMap<String, String> sl) {
  stateCode.clear();
  if (sl != null) {
    stateCode.addItem("--Select a state--", "");
    for (final String it : sl.keySet()) {
      stateCode.addItem(sl.get(it), it);
    }
  }
}
```

To finish, we just need to store the Presenter callbacks and to call them when appropriate.

```
@Override
public void setOnCountryChangeCallback(SimpleCallback<Object> acb) {
  onCountryChangeCallback = acb;
}

@Override
public void setOnStateChangeCallback(SimpleCallback<Object> acb) {
  onStateChangeCallback = acb;
}

@UiHandler("countryCode")
void uiOnCountryChange(ChangeEvent event) {
  onCountryChangeCallback.onSuccess(null);
}

@UiHandler("stateCode")
void uiOnStateChange(ChangeEvent event) {
  onStateChangeCallback.onSuccess(null);
}
}
```

Let's finish with the Presenter, which is neither long nor complicated. Particularly note that it follows the same standards we used earlier in the book; this reinforces the notion that any particular View can be used within any other View.

```
package com.fkereki.mvpproject.client.countryState;

// ...imports...

public class CountryStatePresenter
    extends Presenter<CountryStateDisplay> {

  public CountryStatePresenter(
     final String params,
     final CountryStateDisplay countryStateDisplay,
     final Environment environment) {

    super(params, countryStateDisplay, environment);
```

Until we get the countries list via RPC, we can make do by just displaying Loading... in the Countries ListBox.

```
    LinkedHashMap<String, String> emptyCountriesList =
      new LinkedHashMap<String, String>();
    emptyCountriesList.put("", "Loading...");
    getDisplay().setCountryList(emptyCountriesList);
    getEnvironment().getModel().getCountries(
        new SimpleCallback<LinkedHashMap<String, String>>() {
          @Override
          public void goBack(LinkedHashMap<String, String> result) {
            getDisplay().setCountryList(result);
          }
        });
```

Whenever the country value changes, if an actual country were chosen (i.e., if the country value isn't empty) we use RPC to get the corresponding states list.

```
    getDisplay().setOnCountryChangeCallback(new SimpleCallback<Object>() {
      @Override
      public void goBack(Object result) {
        getDisplay().setStateList(null);
        if (!getDisplay().getCountry().isEmpty()) {
          getEnvironment().getModel().getStates(getDisplay().getCountry(),
              new SimpleCallback<LinkedHashMap<String, String>>() {
                @Override
                public void goBack(LinkedHashMap<String, String> result) {
                  getDisplay().setStateList(result);
                  ValueChangeEvent.fire(getDisplay(), null);
                }
              });
        }
      }
    });
```

Finally, so the encompassing View can learn whenever the user has picked a different country/state pair of values, we add firing event logic to the state change handler.

```
getDisplay().setOnStateChangeCallback(new SimpleCallback<Object>() {
  @Override
  public void goBack(Object result) {
    ValueChangeEvent.fire(getDisplay(), null);
  }
});
}
}
```

Now, how shall we use this new widget? Let's move to the next section and develop a simple paging application that can let us inspect all the cities in a given state of a country. We'll come back to this in Chapter 14, "Optimizing for Application Speed," when we consider using caching for enhancing performance.

A Look at MVP

With the work we have done up to now, we can now look to the Model, the last component of MVP, which we had left aside. (We mentioned the Environment object would be a singleton, and it would include a Model object to connect with the server, but that was as far as we had gotten in Chapter 5, "Programming the User Interface.") Anything that has to do with servlets (RPC) or services, shall be in the Model.

We have to provide the necessary services (built with GWT.create(...) as shown earlier in this chapter) but since they can be reused, it makes sense to create them only once, store them in local variables, and use them whenever needed. We can even go one better and not create them until actually needed ("lazy evaluation").

```
public class Model {
  private LoginServiceAsync loginService;
  private WorldServiceAsync worldService;
  private XhrProxyAsync xhrProxy;

  public LoginServiceAsync getRemoteLoginService() {
    if (loginService == null) {
      loginService = GWT.create(LoginService.class);
    }
    return loginService;
  }

  public WorldServiceAsync getRemoteWorldService() {
    if (worldService == null) {
      worldService = GWT.create(WorldService.class);
    }
    return worldService;
  }
```

```
public XhrProxyAsync getRemoteXhrProxy() {
  if (xhrProxy == null) {
    xhrProxy = GWT.create(XhrProxy.class);
  }
  return xhrProxy;
}
}
```

We haven't yet seen the **XhrProxy** service; we'll get to it in the next chapter. We'll add some methods later to this class, because having code all over our application using services directly is not a good design. (Also, it won't help with testing of the kind we'll do in Chapter 13, or some optimizations we'll see in Chapter 14.) We should rather concentrate all such communication tasks within the Model class, and no other part of the system should know about the actual implementation details, but we'll get to this later.

A Country/State Cities Browser

Given the Country/State composite widget we just developed, we can use it (even with UiBinder) to produce a simple city paging form. We could have developed it without using the new widget (see the provided source code for that) but it wouldn't give us any code reusing. The form (please, no snide comments about my graphic design abilities!) should look like Figure 6.2.

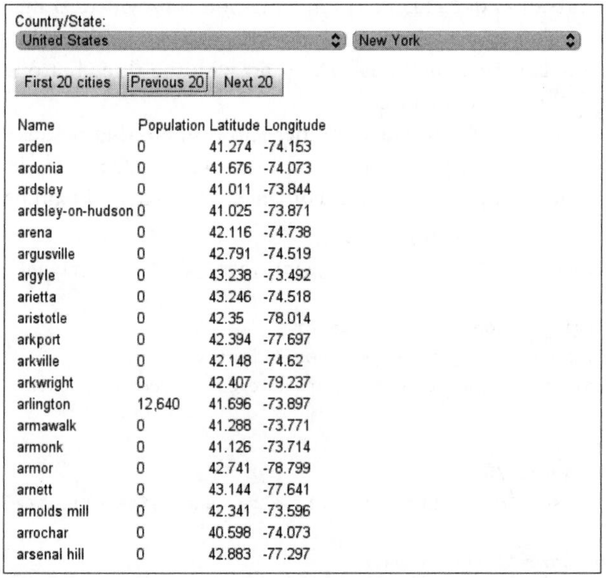

Figure 6.2 A simple city browser application enables us to page through the cities in any state of any country. The country/state pair is actually a separate widget, also developed with the MVP design pattern, and included within another MVP patterned form.

The Display interface for the View is short. Note how the `setCityData(...)` method receives the number of the line to set (`i`) as a parameter; thus, the Presenter can initialize a whole table row by row, a line at a time.

```
package com.fkereki.mvpproject.client.citiesBrowser2;

// ...imports...

public interface CitiesBrowserDisplay extends Display {

  CountryStateDisplay getCountryState();
  void setCityData(final int i, final String name, final String pop,
      final String lat, final String lon);

  void setOnCountryStateChangeCallback(SimpleCallback<Object> acb);

  void setOnFirstClickCallback(SimpleCallback<Object> acb);
  void setOnNextClickCallback(SimpleCallback<Object> acb);
  void setOnPreviousClickCallback(SimpleCallback<Object> acb);
}
```

The `getCountryState(...)` method provides access to the included View (but defined in terms of its interface) so it can be injected into its own presenter, as shown next. The `setCityData(...)` method loads a grid row with city data. The `setOnCountryStateChangeCallback(...)` method is provided so that the Presenter can learn whenever there was a change, to erase the grid data and set things up for a new city. Finally, the last three methods have to do with the three buttons used for paging back and forth through the cities.

The main view is defined through UiBinder and is interesting because it includes our composite Country/State widget by means of the `cs` namespace. This file should be called `CitiesBrowserView.ui.xml` in accordance with standard naming rules.

```
<?xml version="1.0" encoding="UTF-8"?>
<!DOCTYPE u:UiBinder SYSTEM "http://dl.google.com/gwt/DTD/xhtml.ent">
<u:UiBinder
    xmlns:u='urn:ui:com.google.gwt.uibinder'
    xmlns:g='urn:import:com.google.gwt.user.client.ui'
    xmlns:cs='urn:import:com.fkereki.mvpproject.client.countryState'  >

  <g:HTMLPanel>
    <h1>CitiesBrowser2</h1>
    Country/State:<cs:CountryStateView u:field="countryStateView"/>
    <br />
    <g:Button u:field="firstButton"/>
    <g:Button u:field="previousButton"/>
    <g:Button u:field="nextButton"/>
    <br />
    <br />
```

```
   <g:FlexTable u:field="cg"/>
  </g:HTMLPanel>
</u:UiBinder>
```

As to the View code, the most interesting parts are the UiBinder related matters, and the use of the composite Country/State widget. Note that the grid headings must be initialized through Java code because you cannot do that with UiBinder. The `CITIES_PAGE_SIZE` constant will be used for paging.

```
package com.fkereki.mvpproject.client.citiesBrowser2;

// ...imports...

public class CitiesBrowserView
  extends View
  implements CitiesBrowserDisplay {

  @UiTemplate("CitiesBrowserView.ui.xml")
  interface Binder extends UiBinder<HTMLPanel, CitiesBrowserView> {
  }

  public static final int CITIES_PAGE_SIZE = 20;
```

Let's bind the form to the UiBinder design. Note that we are constructing some of the buttons on our own, but we could have let UiBinder create them, and then set their properties in our code.

```
  private static final Binder binder = GWT.create(Binder.class);

  @UiField
  CountryStateView countryStateView;

  @UiField
  FlexTable cg;

  @UiField(provided = true)
  Button firstButton = new
    Button("First " + CITIES_PAGE_SIZE + " cities");

  @UiField(provided = true)
  Button previousButton = new
    Button("Previous " + CITIES_PAGE_SIZE);

  @UiField(provided = true)
  Button nextButton = new
    Button("Next " + CITIES_PAGE_SIZE);

  SimpleCallback<Object> onFirstClickCallback;
  SimpleCallback<Object> onPreviousClickCallback;
```

```
SimpleCallback<Object> onNextClickCallback;
SimpleCallback<Object> onCountryStateChangeCallback;
```

Creating the View is simple; the only remarkable point is that we have to finish the cities grid (cg) formatting ourselves because there isn't any way (at least yet) to do so with UiBinder.

```
public CitiesBrowserView() {
  super();
  HTMLPanel dlp = binder.createAndBindUi(this);
  initWidget(dlp);

  cg.setText(0, 0, "Name");
  cg.setText(0, 1, "Population");
  cg.setText(0, 2, "Latitude");
  cg.setText(0, 3, "Longitude");
}
```

There are just two methods related to the CountryStateView widget.

```
@Override
public CountryStateDisplay getCountryState() {
  return countryStateView;
}

@UiHandler("countryStateView")
void uiOnChange(ValueChangeEvent<Object> event) {
  onCountryStateChangeCallback.onSuccess(null);
}
```

The rest of the methods are trivial.

```
@Override
public void setCityData(int i, String name, String pop, String lat, String lon)
{
  cg.setText(i, 0, name);
  cg.setText(i, 1, pop);
  cg.setText(i, 2, lat);
  cg.setText(i, 3, lon);
}

@Override
public void setOnCountryStateChangeCallback(SimpleCallback<Object> acb) {
  onCountryStateChangeCallback = acb;
}

@Override
public void setOnFirstClickCallback(SimpleCallback<Object> acb) {
  onFirstClickCallback = acb;
}
```

```
// ...setOnNextClickCallback and setOnPreviousClickCallback are similar

@UiHandler("firstButton")
void uiOnFirstClick(ClickEvent event) {
  onFirstClickCallback.onSuccess(null);
}


// ...the handlers for the two other buttons are similar
}
```

Finally, let's look to the Presenter, which must deal not only with the grid and buttons, but also with the Country/State widget changes.

```
package com.fkereki.mvpproject.client.citiesBrowser2;

// ...imports...

public class CitiesBrowserPresenter
  extends Presenter<CitiesBrowserDisplay> {
  public static String PLACE = "citybrowse";

  int currentStart = 0;

  CountryStatePresenter csp;

  public CitiesBrowserPresenter(final String params,
      final CitiesBrowserDisplay citiesBrowserDisplay,
      final Environment environment) {

    super(params, citiesBrowserDisplay, environment);

    csp = new CountryStatePresenter("", getDisplay().getCountryState(),
        environment);

    clearCities();
```

Note how the following methods implement paging. The `displayCities(...)` method can be used for displaying actual cities, whereas `displayEmptyCities(...)` just displays empty placeholders; see the `clearCities(...)` method, for example.

```
    getDisplay().setOnFirstClickCallback(new SimpleCallback<Object>() {
      @Override
      public void goBack(Object result) {
        if (checkCountryAndState()) {
          currentStart = 0;
          getAndDisplayCities();
        }
      }
    });
```

```
// ...setOnPreviousClickCallback is similar, but does
// currentStart -= CitiesBrowserView.CITIES_PAGE_SIZE
// while setOnNextClickCallback does
// currentStart += CitiesBrowserView.CITIES_PAGE_SIZE;

getDisplay().setOnCountryStateChangeCallback(new
  SimpleCallback<Object>() {
  @Override
  public void goBack(Object result) {
    clearCities();
  }
});
}
```

Because we associated empty values to the `Select...` messages in both listboxes, checking if the user has picked something in both fields is easy.

```
boolean checkCountryAndState() {
  return !getDisplay().getCountryState().getCountry().isEmpty()
      && !getDisplay().getCountryState().getState().isEmpty();
}

void clearCities() {
  currentStart = 0;
  displayEmptyCities(0, "");
}

/**
 * Display all cities in citiesList in the grid.
 * If there aren't enough cities
 * to fill out the grid, empty the extra rows.
 *
 * @param pCitiesList
 *          Hash map ordered alphabetically by city name, with up to
 *          CITIES_PAGE_SIZE cities.
 */
void displayCities(final LinkedHashMap<String,
  ClientCityData> pCitiesList) {
  final NumberFormat nf = NumberFormat.getDecimalFormat();

  int i = 0;
  for (final String it : pCitiesList.keySet()) {
    i++;
    final ClientCityData cd = pCitiesList.get(it);
    getDisplay().setCityData(i, cd.cityName, nf.format(cd.population),
        nf.format(cd.latitude), nf.format(cd.longitude));
  }
```

```
      displayEmptyCities(i, "");
  }


  /**
   * Blank out all lines in the cities grid,
   * from the line pSince up to the end.
   *
   * @param pSince
   *            First line to blank
   *
   * @param pDisplayText
   *            Text to display in the first column;
   *            may be "Loading..." or ""
   */
  void displayEmptyCities(int pSince, final String pDisplayText) {
    while (pSince < CitiesBrowserView.CITIES_PAGE_SIZE) {
      pSince++;
      getDisplay().setCityData(pSince, pDisplayText, "", "", "");
    }
  }
```

Now we get to the actual display code. We use the `displayEmptyCities(...)` method to display a `Loading...` text, which will be replaced by the actual cities names when their data arrives. Should there not be enough cities to fill the table, blank lines would be displayed instead.

```
  void getAndDisplayCities() {
    if (currentStart < 0) {
      currentStart = 0;
    }

    displayEmptyCities(0, "Loading...");
    getEnvironment().getModel().getCities(
        getDisplay().getCountryState().getCountry(),
        getDisplay().getCountryState().getState(), currentStart,
        CitiesBrowserView.CITIES_PAGE_SIZE,
        new SimpleCallback<LinkedHashMap<String, ClientCityData>>() {
          @Override
          public void goBack(LinkedHashMap<String, ClientCityData> result) {
            displayCities(result);
          }
        });

  }
}
```

Note that the main `CitiesBrowserView` includes the smaller `CountryStateView`, but doesn't "know" about its inner changes unless the latter's presenter fires a

ValueChangeEvent; the behavior and attributes of the CountryStateView are totally encapsulated and only accessible to its presenter. With regard to the main CitiesBrowserView, the CountryStateView behaves just as any run-of-the-mill widget.

We'll return to this form in Chapter 13, when we'll study a performance-enhancing design pattern: prefetching.

Live Suggestions

Want to do live suggestions, as Google does whenever you type in a search? GWT provides an useful SuggestBox, but to actually make it work, you need to get the possible options dynamically. The standard, simple way of using these widgets depends on a predetermined list of options, as GWT's own documentation shows:

```
MultiWordSuggestOracle oracle = new MultiWordSuggestOracle();
oracle.add("Cat");
oracle.add("Dog");
oracle.add("Horse");
oracle.add("Canary");
SuggestBox box = new SuggestBox(oracle);
```

This widget never shows other options than the four given animals. To get a more useful widget, you need to program your own MultiWordSuggestOracle. I coded a (really simple!) form including just a single SuggestBox that connects to the server to provide New York state cities' suggestions (see Figure 6.3).

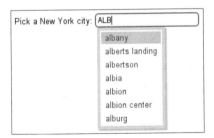

Figure 6.3 Our SuggestBox uses RPC to get all NY state cities whose name start with whatever the user has typed.

The oracle code (including RPC) will be in the Presenter, but the View will have the actual widget creation code. The form Display interface is simplicity itself, including just a method to get the city name and another to set the SuggestBox oracle:

```
package com.fkereki.mvpproject.client.suggest;

import com.fkereki.mvpproject.client.Display;
import com.google.gwt.user.client.ui.MultiWordSuggestOracle;
```

```
public interface SuggestDisplay
    extends Display {

  String getCityName();

  void setCitiesOracle(MultiWordSuggestOracle oracle);
}
```

Given that the View is simple, using UiBinder would have been overkill. The methods that interest us are the two final ones, `getCityName(...)` and `setCitiesOracle(...)`. Note that (at least at present) there's no way to inject an oracle into a `SuggestBox`, so you actually have to create a new widget.[15]

```
package com.fkereki.mvpproject.client.suggest;

// ...imports...

public class SuggestView
    extends View
    implements SuggestDisplay {

  FlexTable ft = new FlexTable();
  SuggestBox sb;

  public SuggestView() {
    ft.setWidget(0, 0, new Label("Pick a New York city:"));
    ft.setWidget(0, 1, new SuggestBox());
    initWidget(ft);
  }

  @Override
  public String getCityName() {
    return sb.getValue();
  }

  @Override
  public void setCitiesOracle(MultiWordSuggestOracle oracle) {
    sb = new SuggestBox(oracle);
    ft.setWidget(0, 1, sb);
  }
}
```

15. There is a way to get the oracle, `getSuggestOracle(...)`, but there's no corresponding `setSuggestOracle(...)`. You might work around this by using the `wrap(...)` method, but it feels sort of patchy. Another possibility would be using `@UiBinder(provided=true)` and writing a Factory to construct the widget with the needed oracle.

Each time the user modifies the input text box, the oracle's `requestSuggestions(...)` method (see next) is called, with a request parameter (from which you can get the letters the user typed) and a callback (which you call after you get the suggestions). We query the server, get a list of cities matching whatever the user typed, and provide an `ArrayList` with the found `SuggestionItem` data. The `SuggestionItem` class isn't provided by GWT; I defined it to ease producing the required list. Note the empty constructor (mandatory for serialization), the alternative constructor (which constructs a suggestion out of a given string) and the trivial `getDisplayString(...)` and `getSuggestString(...)` methods.[16]

```
package com.fkereki.mvpproject.client.suggest;

// ...imports...

public class SuggestionItem
    implements SuggestOracle.Suggestion, IsSerializable {
  private String suggestionText;

  public SuggestionItem() {
    super();
  }

  public SuggestionItem(String text) {
    super();
    suggestionText = text;
  }

  @Override
  public String getDisplayString() {
    return suggestionText;
  }

  @Override
  public String getReplacementString() {
    return suggestionText;
  }
}
```

With this, our Presenter code is reasonably straightforward.

```
package com.fkereki.mvpproject.client.suggest;

// ...imports...
```

16. You can have a different text appear in the suggestion list than in the input text box, but I didn't find that useful.

```
public class SuggestPresenter extends Presenter<SuggestDisplay> {
  public static String PLACE = "baz";

  public SuggestPresenter(String params, SuggestDisplay suggestDisplay,
      Environment environment) {

    super(params, suggestDisplay, environment);

    getDisplay().setCitiesOracle(new MultiWordSuggestOracle() {
      @Override
      public void requestSuggestions(Request request, Callback callback) {
        final Request savedRequest = request;
        final Callback savedCallback = callback;
        final Response response = new Response();
        final ArrayList<SuggestionItem> suggestionsList =
          new ArrayList<SuggestionItem>();

        /*
         * If the query is more than two characters long, search;
         * otherwise, just return no suggestions. Also return no
         * suggestions if the search happens to fail for some reason.
         */
        String beginning = request.getQuery();
        if (beginning.length() > 2) {
          getEnvironment().getModel().getRemoteWorldService()
              .getCitiesStartingWith("US", "NY", request.getQuery(),
                new AsyncCallback<LinkedHashMap<String,
                  ClientCityData>>() {
                  @Override
                  public void onFailure(Throwable caught) {
                    response.setSuggestions(suggestionsList);
                    savedCallback.onSuggestionsReady(
                      savedRequest,
                      response);
                  }

                  @Override
                  public void onSuccess(
                      LinkedHashMap<String, ClientCityData> result) {

                    for (final String it : result.keySet()) {
                      suggestionsList.add(new SuggestionItem(
                          result.get(it).cityName));
                    }
                    response.setSuggestions(suggestionsList);
                    savedCallback.onSuggestionsReady(
```

```
                        savedRequest,
                        response);
                }
            });
        } else {
          response.setSuggestions(suggestionsList);
          callback.onSuggestionsReady(request, response);
        }
      }
    });
  }
}
```

Note that we don't care to search until the user has typed at least three letters; you would have to receive too much data. Some other optimizations you might care to consider include

- Use a `Timer` to delay the actual search, so it won't be attempted unless the user has paused typing. (As is, it would try making many calls to the server and be limited by the maximum number of allowed connections—and, furthermore, most of those calls would be redundant or useless.) If `requestSuggestions` is called again, `cancel(...)` the timer and `schedule(...)` a new call.

- Check, before providing the list of suggestions, if the `SuggestBox` still has the same contents as when you did the RPC, and if not, ignore the received results. Note that the user might have edited the `SuggestBox` while your search was running, and you could be providing a totally useless list of suggestions.

- Modify the service so if it finds more than, say, 50 cities, it returns an empty list. (We cannot hog the connection!) In MySQL you can manage this by adding the `LIMIT` clause to the `SELECT` statement and by using `SELECT FOUND_ROWS()` afterward to see if your limit was attained.

Data Prevalidation

A rule of Internet programming states that all checks must always be done server-side, because you cannot safely assume that data has not been tampered with client-side. This said, it doesn't make much sense to wait until the user finished with data entry before advising him of a trivial error. For example, let's consider a city entry form, which lets the user enter a city's data (country, state, name, population, and so on) and then add it to the database. (See Figure 6.4.)

After the user enters a city name, you can use RPC to check whether there already exists a such named city, and if so, show a warning, highlight the field, and so on. See Figure 6.5.

Figure 6.4   A simple city input form. If the user enters the name of an already existing city, he should get a warning so that he can fix it before trying to commit the entered data.

Figure 6.5   If the city already exists, we can use CSS to highlight the field, provide a warning, and more.

Let's hit the main points of the application. The UiBinder form is simple.

```
<?xml version="1.0" encoding="UTF-8"?>
<!DOCTYPE u:UiBinder SYSTEM "http://dl.google.com/gwt/DTD/xhtml.ent">
<u:UiBinder xmlns:u='urn:ui:com.google.gwt.uibinder'
  xmlns:g='urn:import:com.google.gwt.user.client.ui'
  xmlns:h='urn:import:com.fkereki.mvpproject.client.countryState'>
  <g:HTMLPanel>
    <table>
      <tr>
        <td>Country/State:</td>
        <td><h:CountryStateView u:field="countryState" /></td>
      </tr>
      <tr>
        <td>Name:</td>
        <td><g:TextBox u:field="cityName" /></td>
      </tr>
```

```
    <tr>
      <td>Accented Name:</td>
      <td><g:TextBox u:field="cityAccentedName" /></td>
    </tr>
    <tr>
      <td>Population:</td>
      <td><g:TextBox u:field="cityPopulation" /></td>
    </tr>
    <tr>
      <td>Latitude:</td>
      <td><g:TextBox u:field="cityLatitude" /></td>
    </tr>
    <tr>
      <td>Longitude:</td>
      <td><g:TextBox u:field="cityLongitude" /></td>
    </tr>
  </table>
  <br />
  <g:Button u:field="addCityButton" text="Add City" />
 </g:HTMLPanel>
</u:UiBinder>
```

In the View, we need to assign a value change handler, which calls a (presenter provided) method. Note that we must assign the handler both to the country/state widget and to the city name textbox, because all those fields are involved in the validation we want to do.

```
@UiHandler("cityName")
void uiOnCityChange(ChangeEvent event) {
  onCityNameChangeCallback.onSuccess(null);
}

@UiHandler("countryState")
void uiOnChange(ValueChangeEvent<Object> event) {
  onCountryStateChangeCallback.onSuccess(null);
}
```

In the presenter, we have to set up a method that will (1) get the current country, state, and city name values, (2) if none is missing, use RPC to check whether that city is already in the database, and (3) depending on the check result, set the CSS style for the city name either as normal or as an error.

```
SimpleCallback<Object> ch= new SimpleCallback<Object>() {
  @Override
  public void goBack(Object result) {
    final String country=
      getDisplay().getCountryState().getCountry();
```

```
    final String state=
      getDisplay().getCountryState().getState();
    final String city= getDisplay().getCityName();

    if (!country.isEmpty() && !state.isEmpty()
        && !city.isEmpty()) {

      getEnvironment().getModel().getRemoteWorldService()
          .cityExists(country, state, city,
              new AsyncCallback<Boolean>() {

                public void onFailure(
                    final Throwable caught) {
                  // ...warn about the problem...
                }

                public void onSuccess(
                    final Boolean result) {
                  if (result.booleanValue()) {
                    /*
                      * That city already exists!
                      */
                    getEnvironment()
                        .showAlert(
                            "That city is already in the database");
                    getDisplay().setCityNameCssStyle(
                        "gwt-Textbox-Error");
                  } else {
                    getDisplay().setCityNameCssStyle(
                        "gwt-TextBox");
                  }
                }
              }
          });
    }
};

getDisplay().setOnCityNameChangeCallback(ch);
getDisplay().setOnCountryStateChangeCallback(ch);
```

This code is simple but has a subtle, easy-to-miss error. What would happen if the user entered a duplicate city name, realized his error, and quickly fixed it before the RPC check was done? The result would come showing the duplicate value, and the presenter would highlight the new value of the field as duplicate, whereas the old one was the actual wrong value. A better way of coding the main part of the check requires storing the original country, state, and city name values and reporting the duplication if and only if those three values still match.

```
getEnvironment().getModel().getRemoteWorldService().cityExists(
    country, state, city, new AsyncCallback<Boolean>() {
        /*
         * In order to prevent spurious or redundant messages or
         * actions, let's store the original parameters for the service
         * call...
         */
        String originalCountry = country;
        String originalState = state;
        String originalCityName = city;

        public void onFailure(final Throwable caught) {
          // ...as before...
        }

        public void onSuccess(final Boolean result) {
          /*
           * ...and avoid doing anything unless the parameters still
           * match.
           */
          if (originalCountry.equals(getDisplay().getCountryState()
              .getCountry())
                && originalState.equals(getDisplay().getCountryState()
                  .getState())
                && originalCityName.equals(getDisplay().getCityName()))) {

            if (result.booleanValue()) {
              //...as before...
```

This pattern appears in different guises in other examples in the book. You must always assume a RPC call might take several minutes (!) and the user could use that time to change everything from the way it was before the call.

Enterprise Java Beans

Using GWT for the client-side of your application doesn't mean you cannot use Enterprise Java for the server-side code. (And using the existing Java infrastructure might become a necessity and a requirement for your new GWT application, so it can coexist happily with the already in-use code.) You cannot directly call an EJB from your client, but you can call a RemoteServlet via RPC, and this servlet can in turn connect to the EJB.

As a test, I coded and deployed (using GlassFish) a truly simple EJB that received a first name and a last name and returned it in a normalized "LAST, FIRST" format. I then coded an EjbAccess remote servlet that received two strings (first and last name) connected to the EJB and returned the produced normalized string to the client-side caller. A bare-bones code sample using a EJB could be as follows.

```java
package com.kereki.ejbcall.server;

//...imports...

@SuppressWarnings("serial")
public class EjbAccessImpl
    extends RemoteServiceServlet
    implements EjbAccessService {

  public String normalizeName(String firstName, String lastName) {

    String xxx= "";

    Context ctx;
    try {
      /*
       * We are connecting to GlassFish v.3, where our EJB is posted
       */
      Properties props= new Properties();

      props.put(Context.INITIAL_CONTEXT_FACTORY,
          "com.sun.jndi.cosnaming.CNCtxFactory");

      props.put("java.naming.factory.url.pkgs",
          "com.sun.enterprise.naming");

      props.put(Context.PROVIDER_URL,
        "iiop://localhost:3700/");

      ctx= new InitialContext(props);

      BookServiceEJBRemote ejb= (BookServiceEJBRemote) ctx
       .lookup("java:global/EJBModule/BookServiceEJBBean!"+
       "gwt.book.integration.BookServiceEJBRemote");

      xxx= ejb.getNormalizedName(firstName, lastName);

    } catch (NamingException ex) {
      ex.printStackTrace();

    }

    return xxx;
  }
}
```

This kind of proxying is easy to implement and can also help connect to other services, including non-Java based ones; we'll see more on this in Chapter 7. Of course, there are more ways of solving this: For example, you could use the EJB container to host the GWT components, and you could look up the local interfaces in JNDI. This is, however, a server-side consideration, and goes beyond GWT, so we won't be studying it any further.

Summary

We have studied several usage patterns that involve RPC, showing how its application can enhance performance, a recurring theme in this book. We also took advantage of an application of RPC to build a database bound widget, and saw how to do and use it with MVP in mind, going further than we had in previous chapters. We also saw how to share code (even incompatible classes) between client- and server-side code.

In the next chapter we'll keep to server connection-related themes but consider using Ajax more directly, instead of indirectly through RPC.

7

Communicating with Other Servers

If you cannot or won't use GWT servlets on the server (possibly because your company has already set up a different environment, with a services-oriented architecture, probably based in scripting languages such as PHP) you can still do direct Ajax calls and process other kind of responses, such as XML (or JSON, which we'll see later on). In this chapter we will study the usage of XmlHttpRequests and connect to services both to get and to send XML data.

RPC calls are very useful in GWT, but in today's computing environments, it's highly likely that your GWT application will have to coexist with other, previously developed, separate applications. Your company might already have in place a service-oriented architecture, and it wouldn't pay to redevelop and revalidate all that code, just to use RPC.

Fortunately, the GWT developers didn't forget about Ajax, and also provide direct access to `XMLHttpRequest` calls, which means you can connect to other kinds of services; you can even deploy a complete system using GWT exclusively for client-side code and never develop a single line of server-side Java code!

Of course, a web service can return any kind of data, and a most likely option is the usage of XML, so in this chapter we will develop a simple form that will both get and send XML data, and do so in several different ways. (And we will be seeing more ways of getting such data, through JSONP or external APIs, in the next chapters.)

But, before getting to work with all these examples, we need to analyze and solve a possibly show-stopping problem: the Same Origin Policy, a security measure that could stop all our connections cold and leave us without any way to test our application!

The Same Origin Policy (SOP) Restriction

The Same Origin Policy (SOP) is a security restriction that won't let a page, which was loaded from a certain origin (taken as the trio formed by protocol, host, and port) to access any data from any URL that changes a part of that trio. (Internet Explorer is rather cavalier about the SOP, and only forbids accesses when you change protocol or host, but allows port changes. However, for Ajax calls, it does pay attention to the port.) For example, if your GWT client-side application was loaded from `http://www.somesite.com:80/a/page/at/your/site`, SOP won't enable your application to attempt to get data from other URLs (this is called cross scripting) by blocking any calls to `https://www.somesite.com` (changed protocol), `http://www.othersiteofyours.com` (changed host), or even `www.somesite.com:8080` (changed port).[1]

SOP is, of course, a good browser security idea, because it makes it impossible for rogue JavaScript code from any origin to access and handle data taken from another, different, origin. Actually, managing to disable SOP would be a phisher's ultimate wish: You could be looking at a valid, legit page, while a third party could be monitoring your interactions with the page and learning your secrets along the way. With SOP in place, you can rest assured that any content you view will have been sent by the expected origin and that no code from any other (suspect) origin could be interfering.

On the other hand, for GWT development, SOP proves to be rather a bother. When you try your application in Development mode, it connects to port 8888, but you may be trying to connect to a PHP web service residing at the standard port 80, which means the call won't be allowed by SOP!

If your application doesn't use RPC and you deploy it with Apache (we will touch on Deployment in Chapter 15, "Deploying Your Application") the compiled version of your code won't have any problems calling the web service (because both will run at port 80) but having to compile and deploy your code after every little change would quickly become quite tiresome.

Is there a way out? It depends on how you plan to deploy your application, and what web services you want to connect to. A first solution implies adding the `-noserver` parameter to your development launch configuration and setting the port number to 80. If your code connects only to that port (i.e., not trying to access both servlets and other services, which reside at different ports) you won't have any problems. However, there are other situations you must consider.

- If the desired web services require a different protocol, or reside at another host, you are plumb out of luck; you will have to deploy a proxy on your server (we'll see how to do it next), access it through RPC, and let it connect to the other web service, post your parameters, get the answer, and then send it back to you for your own processing. JSONP (which we'll also study) can provide another solution.

- If you want to connect to a web service running on the same server, but at a different port, the simplest solution could be using Internet Explorer (an old version, at that) for Development mode, and in this case, the browser wouldn't complain about the different port: Internet Explorer's noncompliance with standards would come out to be an advantage! However, I couldn't seriously recommend this way

---

1. You can find a treatment of this at http://code.google.com/p/browsersec/wiki/Part2.

of working; your development work would hinge on a program not going along with standards and would limit you to a single browser, so even if this provides a quick workaround, it cannot be considered a definitive solution.

- In the same preceding situation, if you work with Linux and Firefox, the port change would be recognized and rejected, but Firefox 3.5 and later implements the W3C "Access Control Specification",[2] which enables the server to accept or rejects calls, by using new HTTP headers that describe what origins are allowed to use the service. For GET calls, if the caller is enabled to use the service, an accepted answer includes a header such as `Access-Control-Allow-Origin: http://an.accepted.site`, which Firefox will see. For POST methods (that could cause side effects on the server side) browsers are supposed to "preflight" the petition by sending an HTTP OPTIONS query, and only after receiving approval, sending the actual POST request. We won't get deeply into this; after all, it's a browser-and-server-code-related matter, which doesn't actually have much (or anything) to do with GWT. This is better than the Internet Explorer solution (at least it would work both under Linux and Windows) but it would also cause some pain and limit your development. This evaluation would change if Internet Explorer and other browsers aligned themselves with the W3C specification, but that's not the situation for the time being.

- Finally, if you want to connect to a different server, or use a different port, you are definitely out of luck. Even if you could get the service deployers to modify their code and send out the proper headers, it wouldn't help users who didn't run Firefox; you will have no way but to recur to a proxy, because SOP restrictions do not apply to code not running on a browser.[3]

So, let's work out a simple example and run it either with a proxy or by using Firefox's solution.

Our City Update Application

Let's plan a simple program, which will let us update the missing Population fields in most of our cities database. The user can enter the beginning of a city name, search for all cities matching that beginning, edit (in a grid) the populations of all those cities, and finally send the modified data back to the server so the database will be updated. See Figure 7.1 for a bare-bones form design.

---

2. See http://dev.w3.org/2006/waf/access-control/ for the specification, and https://developer.mozilla.org/En/Server-Side_Access_Control for a complete description of Firefox's implementation.

3. Okay, this isn't fully true; you could do, under certain circumstances, by using JSONP, as we will see in next chapter.

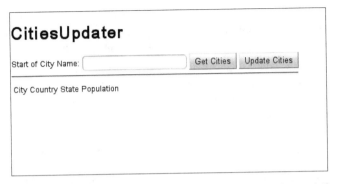

Figure 7.1   A simple design suffices for our cities population updating application. The user will get all cities whose names start with a given string, enter the populations for the matching cities, and send the data back to the server.

After the user keys in the city name start and gets the cities, he may see something such as Figure 7.2.

CitiesUpdater

Start of City Name: darwin   Get Cities   Update Cities

City	Country	State	Population
darwin	Argentina	Rio Negro	0
darwin	Australia	Northern Territory	93081
darwina	Iraq	As Sulaymaniyah	0
darwin downs	United States	Alabama	0
darwin	United States	California	0
darwin subdivision	United States	Georgia	0
darwin	United States	Illinois	0
darwin	United States	Minnesota	0
darwin	United States	Nevada	0
darwin	United States	Ohio	0
darwin	United States	Oklahoma	0
darwin	United States	Tennessee	0
darwin	United States	Virginia	0
darwin	Uruguay	Soriano	0
darwin	Zimbabwe	Mashonaland Central	0

Figure 7.2   Getting all cities whose names start with Darwin.

The design of the view is easy, so we won't show that code here. The Display interface for the view is more interesting, because it shows how to deal with grids and arrays of values in MVP fashion.

```
public interface CitiesUpdaterDisplay extends Display {

    void clearAllCities();

    String getCityNameStart();

    int getCityPopulation(final int i);

    void setCityData(
        final int i,
        final String cityName,
        final String countryName,
        final String stateName,
        final int population);

    void setOnCityNameStartChangeCallback(SimpleCallback<Object> acb);
    void setOnGetCitiesClickCallback(SimpleCallback<Object> acb);
    void setOnUpdateCitiesClickCallback(SimpleCallback<Object> acb);
}
```

The `clearAllCities( )` method enables the Presenter to empty the grid, whereas `setCityData(...)` enables filling the grid city by city, line by line. The `getCityPopulation(...)` method is used to get data back from the grid, and `getCityNameStart( )` accesses the city name field to provide its value. Finally, the three `set...Callback(...)` methods are used to handle city name change events plus click events on both buttons.

When the user clicks on Get Cities, the Presenter receives an XML file like the one shown (in a slightly abridged form) next. The root element is `<cities>`, which includes a `<city>` element for each returned city. The country and state values are returned in separate elements, using attributes for the code and name. (These values could have been returned as attributes of the `<city>` element, but here we want to show several XML processing features; this XML isn't actually optimal for our usage.) Finally, latitude and longitude are returned (once again, uselessly unless as an example) in the `<coords>` element. Finally, note that the `<pop>` element is included only for those cities (in our case, just the Australian "Darwin" city) whose population is known.

```
<?xml version="1.0" encoding="UTF-8"?>
<cities>
 <city name="darwin">
  <country code="AR" name="Argentina"/>
  <state code="16" name="Rio Negro"/>
  <coords>
    <lat>-39.2000008</lat>
```

```
    <lon>-65.7666702</lon>
  </coords>
</city>
<city name="darwin">
 <country code="AU" name="Australia"/>
 <state code="03" name="Northern Territory"/>
 <coords>
   <lat>-12.4666672</lat>
   <lon>130.8333282</lon>
 </coords>
 <pop>93081</pop>
</city>
...
... several <city> elements removed
...
<city name="darwin">
 <country code="UY" name="Uruguay"/>
 <state code="17" name="Soriano"/>
 <coords>
   <lat>-33.0999985</lat>
   <lon>-57.6333351</lon>
 </coords>
</city>
<city name="darwin">
 <country code="ZW" name="Zimbabwe"/>
 <state code="03" name="Mashonaland Central"/>
 <coords>
   <lat>-16.7833328</lat>
   <lon>31.5833340</lon>
 </coords>
 </city>
</cities>
```

The PHP code that runs on the server and produces this output is quite simple. Note that the method used for producing XML code is quite similar to the strings-based method we will develop for GWT. Also, note that the generated code uses both attributes and elements, just for variety; in actual life, you would go for the most compact possible representation.[4]

```
<?php
header("Content-type: text/xml");

$desiredCity= addslashes($_REQUEST["city"]);
```

4. Also, this is the simplest way to produce XML output, but there are alternatives, such as the XMLWriter class, or SimpleXML, or any of PEAR's XML-related functions and classes.

```php
$conn= mysql_connect("127.0.0.1", "mysqluser", "mysqlpass");
mysql_select_db("world");

$result= mysql_query("SELECT ci.cityName, ci.countryCode,".
        "co.countryName, ci.regionCode, re.regionName, ".
        "ci.population, ci.latitude, ci.longitude ".
        "FROM cities ci JOIN regions re ON ".
        "ci.countryCode=re.CountryCode AND ci.regionCode=re.regionCode ".
        "JOIN countries co ON ci.countryCode=co.countryCode ".
        "WHERE ci.cityName LIKE '%{$desiredCity}%' ".
        "ORDER BY ci.cityName, co.countryName, re.regionName ");

echo '<?xml version="1.0" encoding="UTF-8"?>'."\n";
echo '<cities>'."\n";

while ($row= mysql_fetch_assoc($result)) {
  echo ' <city name="'.htmlspecialchars($row['cityName']).'">'."\n";
  echo '  <country code="'.$row['countryCode'].'" ';
  echo 'name="'.htmlentities($row['countryName']).'"/>'."\n";
  echo '  <region code="'.$row['regionCode'].'" ';
  echo 'name="'.htmlentities($row['regionName']).'"/>'."\n";
  echo '  <coords>'."\n";
  echo '    <lat>'.$row['latitude'].'</lat>'."\n";
  echo '    <lon>'.$row['longitude'].'</lon>'."\n";
  echo '  </coords>'."\n";

  if ($row['population']>0) {
    echo '  <pop>'.$row['population'].'</pop>'."\n";
  }

  echo ' </city>'."\n";
}
echo '</cities>'."\n";
?>
```

Leaving aside (for the moment) the matter of actually getting the XML string, let's study how to process it in GWT.

Receiving and Processing XML

To use the XML library, you have to add `<inherits name="com.google.gwt.xml .XML"/>` to the `.gwt.xml` file of your application. You convert the string to a XML document by using `XMLParser.parse(...)` and access its root (`<cities>`, in this case) with the `getDocumentElement( )` method; after this, you are ready to walk through the XML.

GWT's XML parser is based on the browser's own JavaScript DOM routines. (This will affect our tests in Chapter 13, "Testing Your GWT Application"; we won't be able to test with just JUnit any XML using form.) Browser parsers often create empty text nodes for each tab or line break, and unless you remove them, your code will encounter unexpected elements, which might even cause your algorithm to fail; always use `removeWhitespace(...)` to clean up the generated document before attempting to process it. Another quirk: if you expect to process CDATA sections, you'll need to verify whether your browser `supportsCDATASection(...)`; if not, those sections will become text nodes, and your XML processing logic will have to vary.[5] Finally, note that your XML processing code will usually be full of casts; it's up to you to decide what kind of nodes you will process!

The Presenter code for our form is as follows. The logic also uses `HashMap<Integer, ClientCityData> cityList` to store the cities data, for later usage when updating the server.

```
void displayCities(String xmlCities) {
  clearCities();

  if (!xmlCities.isEmpty()) {
    final Document xmlDoc = XMLParser.parse(xmlCities);
    final Element root = xmlDoc.getDocumentElement();
    XMLParser.removeWhitespace(xmlDoc);
```

As we said, you must remember to `removeWhitespace(...)` from the produced Document; otherwise, you'll have to deal with plenty of empty nodes.

```
    final NodeList cities = root.getElementsByTagName("city");
    for (int i = 0; i < cities.getLength(); i++) {

      final Element city = (Element) cities.item(i);
      String cityName = city.getAttributeNode("name").getValue();

      final Element country = (Element)
          city.getElementsByTagName("country")
          .item(0);
      String countryCode = country.getAttributeNode("code").getValue();
      String countryName = country.getAttributeNode("name").getValue();

      final Element state = (Element)
          city.getElementsByTagName("state")
          .item(0);
      String stateCode = state.getAttributeNode("code").getValue();
      String stateName = state.getAttributeNode("name").getValue();
```

---

5. Keep in mind that GWT's XML parser depends on the underlying browser's parser, so you should be extra careful not to write any code that could depend on functionality not common to all browsers!

```
    int population = 0;
    Element popElem = (Element)
      city.getElementsByTagName("pop").item(0);
    if (popElem != null) {
      population =
        Integer.parseInt(popElem.getFirstChild().getNodeValue());
    }

    Element coords = (Element)
      city.getElementsByTagName("coords").item(0);
    Element lat = (Element) coords.getElementsByTagName("lat").item(0);
    Element lon = (Element) coords.getElementsByTagName("lon").item(0);
    float latitude =
      Float.parseFloat(lat.getFirstChild().getNodeValue());
    float longitude =
      Float.parseFloat(lon.getFirstChild().getNodeValue());
```

After having collected the complete city data, we just have to show it onscreen, by using the `setCityData(...)` method and add it to `cityList`.

```
    getDisplay().setCityData(i + 1,
        cityName, countryName,
        stateName, population);

    /*
     * Given the usage of cityList, we could have set latitude
     * and longitude to 0.0, and it would have worked all the same...
     */
    cityList.put(i + 1, new ClientCityData(countryCode, stateCode,
        cityName, "", population, latitude, longitude));
  }
 }
}
```

Notice the use of `getElementsByTagName(...)` to get an array of elements, `getAttributeNode(...)` to get at attributes, and `getNodeValue(...)` to get the value associated with a node. We still have to see how to produce XML (for our city updating service consumes XML too) but let's first finish the matter of getting the data from the server, with two variants.

Using Ajax Directly

If you solved the SOP problems, using Ajax directly is a no-brainer. GWT used to limit you to using GET and POST calls only (because Safari wasn't able to do otherwise) but for this application that's enough. In any case, it was always possible to emulate other requests by doing a POST and including an extra parameter specifying what method you actually wanted to use. And by the way, you might even have to use this emulation to do GET requests, but with too long an URL; if you must send over too many parameters, and the 256-character limit will be exceeded, you'll just have to recur to using a POST, and faking a GET.[6]

Because we assume the service is in the same server, we can use `GWT.getHostPage-BaseURL(...)` and massage it a bit (see the following `baseUrl` variable and the second parameter to `RequestBuilder`) to produce the actual URL to call. This way of working also helps during development; calls will be sent to your development machine instead of to the actual server, where they could be quite harmful!

```
void getCitiesViaRequestBuilder() {
    String baseUrl = "http:" + GWT.getHostPageBaseURL().split(":")[1];
    final RequestBuilder rb = new RequestBuilder(RequestBuilder.GET,
        URL.encode(baseUrl + ":80/bookphp/getcities1.php?city="
            + getDisplay().getCityNameStart()));

    try {
      rb.sendRequest(null, new RequestCallback() {
        @Override
        public void onError(Request request, Throwable exception) {
          //...inform about the error...
        }

        @Override
        public void onResponseReceived(Request request,
          Response response) {
          displayCities(response.getText());
        }
      });
    } catch (Exception e) {
      // ...inform about the error...
    }
}
```

Directly specifying a port in the desired URL isn't quite nice, even leaving aside the usage of hard-coded constants; if you set up your development environment properly and run your code on port 80, you won't have to do this fiddling. On the other hand, including the desired port number forces you to set things up properly, so it could be positive after all![7]

On receiving the answer, we just execute the `displayCities(...)` method we previously saw. Of course, error handling should be enhanced; just informing the user wouldn't probably do, but adding extra behavior isn't hard to do.

---

6. Emulating PUT and DELETE calls with POST and GET is common; for example, the prototype.js JavaScript library lets you change a GET into a DELETE by adding _method=DELETE to the parameters list; Ruby on Rails uses a similar solution, and there are many more examples.

7. I won't be repeating this comment, but note that all examples in this chapter force port 80 in this way.

Going Through a Proxy

If you cannot get past the SOP problems, you'll have to implement a `RemoteServlet` that acts as a proxy. You'll have to implement, at the very least, the GET and POST methods, but it's possible (depending on your requirements) that you will also have to add PUT, DELETE, and so on, but their implementations are quite similar (DELETE is similar to GET, and PUT to POST) so that won't be a problem.[8] We'll call our servlet `XhrProxy`, standing for `XMLHttpRequestProxy`.

(Of course, this solution has its own costs; mainly, you will be adding to the server load, because it will have to intermediate in all requests. However, if the server environment isn't Java-based, there's no way out other than using the proxy.)

We shall implement two methods: `getFromUrl(...)` and `postToUrl(...)`. Both methods will receive three parameters: the URL of the server providing the service, the path to the service (relative to the URL), and the parameter string in the usual `parameter=value&parameter2=value2&...` style; it's your responsibility to adequately escape all values. Implementing this method is more of a Java problem than a GWT one, and the use of a `BufferedReader` simplifies it.

```
package com.fkereki.mvpproject.server;

//...imports...

public class XhrProxyImpl
    extends RemoteServiceServlet
    implements XhrProxy {

  @Override
  public String getFromUrl(
      final String originalUrl,
      final String originalPath,
      final String parameters) {
    String result = "";

    try {
      final String urlToGet = originalUrl + "/" + originalPath
          + (parameters.isEmpty() ? "" : "?" + parameters);

      final URL url = new URL(urlToGet);

      final BufferedReader in = new BufferedReader(
          new InputStreamReader(url.openStream()));

      String inputLine;
      while ((inputLine = in.readLine()) != null) {
```

---

8. For the whole list of possible calls, check www.w3.org/Protocols/rfc2616/rfc2616-sec9.html.

```
        result += inputLine;
    }

    in.close();
    return result;

  } catch (final Exception e) {
    return "";
  }
}
```

Keep in mind this code is intended as an example, and not as production-ready code; in an actual implementation you would care more about error processing than mainly returning an empty string, for example.

Implementing POST is similar, but in this case we'll have to both read and write to the connection; first write to send the request and then read to get the results.[9]

```
@Override
public String postToUrl(
    final String originalUrl,
    final String originalPath,
    final String parameters) {

  String result = "";

  try {
    final String EOL = "\r\n";

    final URL url = new URL(originalUrl);
    final URLConnection connection = url.openConnection();
    connection.setDoOutput(true);

    final BufferedReader in = new BufferedReader(new InputStreamReader(
        connection.getInputStream()));
    final OutputStreamWriter out = new OutputStreamWriter(connection
        .getOutputStream());

    out.write("POST " + originalPath + EOL);
    out.write("Host: " + originalUrl + ":80" + EOL);
    out.write("Accept-Encoding: identity" + EOL);
    out.write("Connection: close" + EOL);
    out.write("Content-Type: application/x-www-form-urlencoded" + EOL);
    out.write("Content-Length: " + parameters.length() + EOL);
    out.write(EOL);
```

---

9. For sample Java code, see http://developers.sun.com/mobility/midp/ttips/HTTPPost/ and for all the possible headers, go to www.w3.org/Protocols/rfc2616/rfc2616-sec14.html.

```
      out.write(parameters);
      out.write(EOL);

      String inputLine;
      while ((inputLine = in.readLine()) != null) {
        result += inputLine;
      }

      in.close();
      out.close();

      return result;
    } catch (Exception e) {
      return "";
    }
  }
}
```

Again, there are shorter and more robust ways of writing this code, such as using the Apache HttpComponents HttpClient library (see `http://hc.apache.org/ httpcomponents-client/`) but for our example, the provided implementation is enough.

Producing and Sending XML

Now that we have seen how to send requests and process XML results, let's turn to producing XML output and sending it to the server. If the user updates any city population, we'll send an XML file with all the updated cities; we'll use the same format that we got, just so we can experiment a bit more. There are two ways of producing this output: Because XML is just text, we can work with strings and build up the XML output bit by bit, or we can internally generate an XML document and then convert it to a string with its `toString( )` method; let's go over both ways, but first let's look at the code that will decide which cities to update.

```
getDisplay().setOnUpdateCitiesClickCallback(
    new SimpleCallback<Object>() {
      @Override
      public void goBack(Object dummy) {
        HashMap<Integer, ClientCityData> newCityList =
          new HashMap<Integer, ClientCityData>();

        for (Integer i : cityList.keySet()) {
          int gridPop = getDisplay().getCityPopulation(i);
          ClientCityData thisCity = cityList.get(i);
          if (thisCity.population != gridPop) {
            thisCity.population = gridPop;
            newCityList.put(i, thisCity);
```

```
            }
        }
        String xmlToSend;
        /*
         * Create the XMl to send via any of the
         * two following calls (but not both!)
         */
        xmlToSend= citiesToXmlViaDom(newCityList);
        xmlToSend= citiesToXmlViaString(newCityList);

        /*
         * ...and then pick one of the two following
         * sentences to send the data to the server
         */
        sendCitiesToServerViaRequestBuilder(xmlToSend);
        sendCitiesToServerViaProxy(xmlToSend);
    }
});
```

In the `DisplayCities(...)` method we previously saw, we had created `CityList` with all the data on the received cities. Now, we loop over all the cities, get the (possibly updated) population from the grid by using `getDisplay().getCityPopulation(i);` if there were a change, we add the city data to `newCityList`, with which we shall construct the XML output code.

Creating XML with Strings

As XML is plain text, we can just loop through newCityList and build up the result string bit by bit. Note that we do not actually need to include line feeds or indent elements with spaces; this was done just for clarity.[10]

```
String citiesToXmlViaString(HashMap<Integer, ClientCityData> aList) {
  String result = "<?xml version=\"1.0\" encoding=\"UTF-8\"?>\n";

  result += "<cities>\n";
  for (int i : aList.keySet()) {
    ClientCityData thisCity = aList.get(i);

    result += "<city>\n";
    result += " <city name=\"" + thisCity.cityName + "\">\n";
    result += "  <country code=\"" + thisCity.countryCode + "\"/>\n";
    result += "  <state code=\"" + thisCity.stateCode + "\"/>\n";
    result += "   <pop>" + thisCity.population + "</pop>\n";
```

---

10. Though it may seem like bit-counting, for extra speed you should always be as concise as possible in every data you send back and forth; although I agree that in many cases, the difference may be unnoticeable.

```
    /*
     * In truth, putting latitude and longitude in the XML string isn't
     * needed; let's do it just for showing how it's done.
     */
    result += "   <coords>\n";
    result += "     <lat>" + thisCity.latitude + "</lat>\n";
    result += "     <lon>" + thisCity.longitude + "</lon>\n";
    result += "   </coords>\n";
    result += "</city>\n";
  }
  result += "</cities>\n";

  return result;
}
```

In this particular case, because we know that city names, country and state codes, and geographical coordinates are just letters and numbers, we need not worry about nonvalid characters, but if the text to be output might include < or apostrophes or other XML-used characters, we would have to pass every string through a function such as[11]

```
public static String htmlSpecialChars(final String inp) {
  String aux = inp;
  aux = aux.replace("&", "&amp;");
  aux = aux.replace("\"", "&quot;");
  aux = aux.replace("'", "&apos;");
  aux = aux.replace("<", "&lt;");
  aux = aux.replace(">", "&gt;");
  return aux;
}
```

This function changes the five characters that XML uses for itself, replacing them by their HTML equivalents; all other characters are left as-is. Be careful to first replace & with &, and only then do the other substitutions; otherwise, you would get &lt; for <.[12]

Creating XML Through the DOM

The second way to produce an XML string is by building up a XML document and then converting it to a string with its toString( ) method.

---

11. There are many other possibilities, such as Apache Commons own StringEscapeUtils.escapeXML( ) function.

12. The function is based on PHP's own htmlSpecialChars(...) function; see www.php.net/manual/en/function.htmlspecialchars.php for more on it.

```
String citiesToXmlViaDom(HashMap<Integer, ClientCityData> aList) {

  Document xml = XMLParser.createDocument();
  Element cities = xml.createElement("cities");
  xml.appendChild(cities);

  for (int i : aList.keySet()) {
    ClientCityData aCity = aList.get(i);

    Element city = xml.createElement("city");
    city.setAttribute("name", aCity.cityName);

    Element country = xml.createElement("country");
    country.setAttribute("code", aCity.countryCode);
    city.appendChild(country);

    Element region = xml.createElement("state");
    region.setAttribute("code", aCity.stateCode);
    city.appendChild(region);

    String pop = "" + aCity.population;
    Element popEl = xml.createElement("pop");
    Text popText = xml.createTextNode(pop);
    popEl.appendChild(popText);
    city.appendChild(popEl);

    /*
     * We actually don't use the <coords> element,
     * but let's build it up for the sake of it.
     */
    Element coords = xml.createElement("coords");
    Element lat = xml.createElement("lat");
    Text latText = xml.createTextNode("" + aCity.latitude);
    lat.appendChild(latText);
    coords.appendChild(lat);

    /*
     * If you want to write a little less, you can chain "create"
     * commands; check out the differences with the "lat" code above.
     *
     * Of course, with such brevity, legibility may suffer...
     */
    coords.appendChild(xml.createElement("lon").appendChild(
        xml.createTextNode("" + aCity.longitude)));

    city.appendChild(coords);
```

```
        cities.appendChild(city);
    }

    return "<?xml version=\"1.0\" encoding=\"UTF-8\"?>"
        + xml.toString();
}
```

We use `createElement(...)` and `createTextNode(...)` to build up the necessary nodes, `setAttribute(...)` to assign attribute values, and `appendChild(...)` to link objects together and form the DOM structure. Note how the `<longitude>` element is created with a single rather complex call; this way of achieving brevity at the cost of clarity appeals to some programmers, and that's why I included it—though I frown on it myself!

Sending the XML Data

Now that we have seen how to produce the XML data for updating the cities, let's see how to send the data. The PHP service that will receive the XML string and use it to update the database is simple; pay particular attention to the processing of the OPTIONS request to allow Firefox cross scripting.

```php
<?php

if($_SERVER['REQUEST_METHOD'] == "OPTIONS") {

  header('Access-Control-Allow-Origin: http://arunranga.com');

} elseif($_SERVER['REQUEST_METHOD'] == "POST") {

  $xml_str= $_POST["xmldata"];
  $xml_obj= simplexml_load_string($xml_str);

  $conn= mysql_connect("127.0.0.1", "mysqluser", "mysqlpass");
  mysql_select_db("world");

  foreach($xml_obj->children() as $city) {
    $name= addslashes($city['name']);
    $country= addslashes($city->country['code']);
    $region= addslashes($city->region['code']);
    $pop= addslashes($city->pop);
    $lat= addslashes($city->coords->lat);
    $lon= addslashes($city->coords->lon);

    mysql_query("REPLACE INTO cities ".
      "cityName, countryCode, regionCode, ".
      "population, latitude, longitude) VALUES (".
```

```
      "'{$name}', '{$country}', '{$region}', ".
      "'{$pop}', '{$lat}', '{$lon}')");
} else
  die("Not allowed operation");
}


?>
```

Now let's turn to actually sending the data from our GWT client application.

Sending XML Through Ajax

Using XMLHttpRequest to send the XML data to the server via Ajax is quite similar to getting the XML. We use the same kind of processing as earlier to get the baseUrl and from hence the final URL to call.

```
void sendCitiesToServerViaRequestBuilder(String xmlToSend) {
  String baseUrl = "http:" + GWT.getHostPageBaseURL().split(":")[1];
  final RequestBuilder rb = new RequestBuilder(RequestBuilder.POST,
      URL.encode(baseUrl + ":80/bookphp/setcities.php?" + "xmldata="
        + xmlToSend));

  try {
    rb.sendRequest(null, new RequestCallback() {
      @Override
      public void onError(Request request, Throwable exception) {
        // ...warn about the error...
      }

      @Override
      public void onResponseReceived(Request request, Response response) {
        // ...let the user know the data were processed...
      }
    });
  } catch (Exception e) {
    // ...warn about the error...
  }
}
```

After the routine learns that the XML data was successfully processed, it could inform the user, reenable the Send Data button (if it were disabled, applying the "double click" preventing logic that we saw in Chapter 5, "Programming the User Interface"), and so on.

Sending XML Through a Proxy

Using a proxy is practically the same. Do not forget to URL.encode(...) the data to be passed to the proxy.

```
void sendCitiesToServerViaProxy(String xmlToSend) {

    final String baseUrl = "http:"
        + GWT.getHostPageBaseURL().split(":")[1];
    final String realUrl = URL.encode(baseUrl);
    final String realPath = URL.encode("bookphp/setcities.php");
    final String params = URL.encode("xmldata=" + xmlToSend);

    XhrProxyAsync xhrProxy = getEnvironment().getModel()
        .getRemoteXhrProxy();

    xhrProxy.postToUrl(realUrl, realPath, params,
        new AsyncCallback<String>() {

        @Override
        public void onFailure(Throwable caught) {
          //...warn about the problem...
        }

        @Override
        public void onSuccess(String result) {
          //...let the user know the data were processed...
        }
      });
}
```

After the XML is processed, further steps would be the same as with the `RequestBuilder` previous call.

Summary

We have seen how to process and generate XML code, and also studied how to get it from a server either by using XMLHttpRequest calls or by having an intermediate proxy, called by RPC.

We return to XML processing in the next chapters, when we will build an RSS/Atom feed reader; we'll be getting the feeds either via JSONP (Chapter 8, "Mixing in JavaScript") or through external APIs (Chapter 9, "Adding APIs"), but the XML processing will be along the same lines we saw in this chapter.

## 8

Mixing in JavaScript

JavaScript is to GWT what assembly language is to classic compilers, and although you should be careful, mixing JavaScript in with your Java code can help. For example, you can attain better performance, or achieve otherwise hard-to-get results, including getting data from remote servers bypassing the Same Origin Policy we covered in previous chapters.

There are some circumstances when you will need to add some JavaScript to your application, and GWT provides a solution for this kind of situation. The GWT developers frequently use this to get low-level access to browser aspects, but there are other possible usages, such as taking advantage of prewritten JavaScript routines and libraries, using JSON (an alternative to XML) for connection with servers, or using JSONP as a way to avoid cross scripting SOP restrictions; we'll analyze examples of all these situations in this chapter.

JSNI

JavaScript Native Interface (JSNI) enables you to include JavaScript written routines within your GWT Java program. Your JavaScript code will fully interact (i.e., calling, or being called by) with the Java code, passing data back and forth, and even processing exceptions thrown by each other. In fact, you could think of JavaScript as the "assembly language" for GWT applications and use it the same way you would use Intel assembly code with C++, for example. (As an example of this, several History methods that we used in Chapter 4, "Working with Browsers," are actually programmed directly in JavaScript.)

Before going any further, some warnings need be given in advance. First, it should be obvious that by programming directly with JavaScript, you are foregoing GWT's advantages as to browser independence; for example, if your code deals with DOM aspects, you will have to take care of compatibility by yourself. (Deferred binding—which we saw in Chapter 4—is often used along with JSNI to produce browser-specific versions of classes; GWT does this all the time.) Memory leaks and hard to trace errors are also a possibility, and, of course, as we commented in Chapter 1, "Developing Your Application," JavaScript isn't so good from the software engineering point of view as Java itself; wasn't that a reason for using GWT? But, if you still decide to go ahead, JSNI will enable you to access low-level operations or reuse third-party libraries, and possibly even squeeze a drop more of speed and performance for your application.[1]

Other observation that needs be done is that JavaScript code will be harder to write (neither the Java compiler nor GWT will detect syntactic or semantic problems in your JavaScript code), debug (your Eclipse debugger won't be much help when debugging non-Java code) and test (you won't be able so easily mock classes that mix JavaScript and Java) so before going this way, you should certainly question yourself to see if pure GWT Java code isn't capable or good enough for your purposes.

In any case, we shall see more JSNI; for example, in Chapter 9, "Adding APIs," we use it to access third-party services (think Google Maps for a simple case) through specific JavaScript APIs.

Basic JSNI Usage

Because JSNI isn't so well known and used, let's give a quick once over to the basic rules. Calling a Java method from JavaScript requires a complex notation because your code must provide all necessary disambiguation information to distinguish among possibly overloaded methods. Calls are always in the form `instance.@classname::method(signature)(arguments)` in which

- *Instance* is the object whose method you'll be calling; you must omit it for `static` calls. Don't forget the dot before the @ symbol!
- *Classname* is the fully qualified class name, such as `com.kereki.nixietest.client.NixieDisplay` as we'll see in an upcoming example.
- *Method* is the name of the method you are calling.
- *Signature* is the internal Java Virtual Machine parameters signature for the method parameters, built from the following table below.[2] For example, if you were calling a method with `(int n, String s, int[] a)` parameters, the corresponding signature would be `ILjava/lang/String;[I`.
- *Arguments* is the actual list of arguments that you want to pass to the called method. Note that calls to *vararg* methods require passing an array of values.[3]

---

1. Of course, you may have to work really hard at beating the speed of GWT generated code.

2. See http://java.sun.com/j2se/1.5.0/docs/guide/jni/spec/types.html#wp276 for the specification of Java signatures.

3. See http://java.sun.com/j2se/1.5.0/docs/guide/language/varargs.html for more on this; the required JSNI creation of an array actually fits the old Java style for dealing with varargs.

Type	Signature
Boolean	Z
Byte	B
Char	C
Double	D
Float	F
Integer	I
Long	J
Short	S
all classes	L *fullyQualifiedClassName;* with dots replaced by forward slashes, as in `Ljava/lang/String;`
array of type	[*type*

Invoking a Java constructor follows the same rule, except that the method name is always new. Accessing Java fields from JavaScript also uses a similar syntax: `instance.@classname::field`. You should take into account the following rules regarding what types can be passed back and forth between Java and JavaScript:

- Java String types become JavaScript string values.
- Java Boolean types become JavaScript Boolean values.
- Java numeric types become JavaScript number values, with the exception that long types are not supported.[4]

JSNI methods can return void, a Java primitive, a Java Object (created by Java code, but possibly modified by JavaScript code), or a JavaScript created JavaScriptObject; the latter, as far as GWT is concerned, will behave like a black box, and only JSNI code will be able to access it.

Finally, you can handle Java exceptions within JavaScript code and vice versa (JavaScript exceptions become JavaScriptException objects for Java processing) but it's recommended that you handle Java exceptions in Java code and JavaScript exceptions in JavaScript code. (The reason for this is that JavaScriptException objects are untyped, which goes against the vein of usual programming. You can even then get at the original exception name and description by using the getName(...) and getDescription(...) methods if you still want to process the exception yourself.)

---

4. JavaScript doesn't provide an adequate substitution for long variables, so they are emulated by the compiler, but this prevents using such values with JSNI. See http://code.google.com/webtoolkit/doc/latest/DevGuideCodingBasicsJSNI.html for further explanation.

Hashing with JavaScript

Now, let's start out with several simple, short JSNI examples. As we'll see in Chapter 10, "Working with Servers," we can add a bit more security to logins and data exchanges by using *hashes*. (A hash function takes a string as input and produces another string. The important details are that there is no practical way to determine the input string from the output string, and that any change in the input string, small as it might be, will produce several changes in the output string.) Hashes are usually involved in authentication protocols, and that's the way we'll use them.

There are many possible such functions, such as MD5 or SHA-1, and because there are quite good, free JavaScript implementations available, we can just take advantage of them.[5]

Let's pick Paul Johnston's minified implementation of MD5 (at http://pajhome.org.uk/crypt/md5/) and produce a JSNI wrapper. You will have to add the appropriate `<script>` declaration to your HTML file:

```
<script type="text/javascript"
  language="javascript" src="md5-min.js">
</script>
```

An (even better from the point of view of packaging everything together) alternative would be adding `<script src="/md5-min.js"/>` to your `gwt.xml` module declaration file, as we saw in Chapter 3, "Understanding Projects and Development"; in both cases, you can be assured that your code won't be called until the script is loaded. The script itself should be placed in the `war` directory of your project.[6]

Given this, calculating the MD5 hash for any string can be done by just writing `md5("your string")` if you declare[7]

```
private static native String md5(String pText) /*-{
  return $wnd.hex_md5(pText);
}-*/;
```

Note particularly the usage of `$wnd` (which points to the current page's browser window) to access the `hex_md5(...)` method; because your GWT compiled code executes in a frame, you wouldn't get access to the window methods and variables. (Forgetting to use `$wnd` is a quite common error; remind me to tell you how I know!) Similarly, you would use `$doc` (which points to the current page's document object) to get at the current `document` properties.

---

5. For example, you can find MD5 implementations at http://www.webtoolkit.info/javascript-md5.html and http://pajhome.org.uk/crypt/md5/ and by searching a bit, you can find several more.

6. Previous versions of GWT used a `public` directory for this.

7. Note that the `/*-{...}-*/` notation is actually a comment; in Java (not GWT) `native` methods are pure object code, and you aren't allowed to specify a code block for them. With JSNI, you include your JavaScript within a comment that will be ignored by Java but recognized and processed by the GWT compiler.

Analogously, you could use other cryptographic methods for encoding or decoding, for example; just make sure your JavaScript implementation is well tested, even taking into account possible changes such as the previous usage of `$wnd`.[8]

Animations Beyond GWT

Although GWT does provide some help as to animations (see the `com.google.gwt` `.animation.client.Animation` for more on this) there are many well-tested and efficient libraries, such as jQuery (at http://jquery.com/) or script.aculo.us (at http://script.aculo.us/) that provide all kinds of animations, transitions, and effects.

Let's go with jQuery, and use it for a simple embellishment to highlight hyperlinks as you hover over them. First, you'll have to add the appropriate jQuery library to your HTML file, with `<script type="text/javascript" language="javascript" src="jquery-1.3.2.min.js"></script>`.

Then, we can write a JSNI `animateAllLinks(...)` function that will get all links on the current window (`$('a')` is a *selector*, the jQuery way of referring to all `<a>` links, and we already saw the need for `$wnd`) and make them grow to 150% size when the mouse goes over them, and reduce them back to normal size when the mouse moves out. (Yes, I know that the effect isn't that pretty, but on the other hand, it's simple to code!) The `stop(...)` method cancels any previous animation enabling a new one to proceed. The code is then

```
private static native void animateAllLinks() /*-{
  $wnd.$('a').hover(
    function() { // mouse in animation code
      $wnd.$(this).stop().animate({fontSize:'150%'}, 250);
    },
    function() { // mouse out animation code
      $wnd.$(this).stop().animate({fontSize:'100%'}, 250);
    });
}-*/;
```

If you call the `animateAllLinks(...)` function, jQuery will add the two animations to every `<a>` link it can find. Of course, you can do much better, by both doing animations and CSS styling, but that would be beyond this book; we just want to see how to use an external JavaScript library, and JSNI enabled us to do it quite simply.

A Steampunk Display Widget

Do you remember Nixie tubes? The earliest calculators (in the 70s before LED times) used them for displays. Basically, those tubes included several numeral-shaped cathodes,

---

8. If you want to test any implementation, there are many "test suites" such as the one at http://home.claranet.de/xyzzy/src/md5.cmd that you can use.

which glowed orange when power was applied to them.[9] Hobbyists are nowadays using these tubes to build Steampunk-styled appliances like clocks; let's build a widget enabling us to display numbers, as in Figure 8.1.[10]

James Bond is:

Darwin/Lincoln Birthdate:

All digits:

Figure 8.1 A Nixie display widget, showing vital information such as James Bond's secret agent number, Charles Darwin and Abraham Lincoln's shared birthday, and all the available digits.

Čestmír Hýbl provides, in his web site, both a useful routine and the needed images (see http://cestmir.freeside.sk/projects/dhtml-nixie-display/) with which we can build a Java `NixieDisplay` class.

```
package com.kereki.nixietest.client;

import com.google.gwt.core.client.JavaScriptObject;
import com.google.gwt.user.client.ui.HTMLPanel;

public class NixieDisplay
    extends HTMLPanel {

  JavaScriptObject display;

  public NixieDisplay(
    String pName,
    int pDigits,
    String pAlign) {

    super("<div id='" + pName + "'></div>");
    display = initNixieDisplay(pName, pDigits, pAlign);
  }
```

9. See www.tube-tester.com/sites/nixie/different/nixie-tube-links.htm for many links to Nixie tubes information.

10. I remember my father bringing home a desk calculator—Monroe or Sweda brand, I think—which used such tubes for its display... does this memory date me?

```
private native JavaScriptObject initNixieDisplay(
  String pName,
  int pDigits,
  String pAlign) /*-{
  var nd = new $wnd.NixieDisplay();
  nd.id = pName;
  nd.charCount = pDigits;
  nd.charWidth = 30;
  nd.charHeight = 50;
  nd.charGapWidth = 0;
  nd.urlCharsetImage= "nixielib/zm1080_d1_09bdm_30x50_8b.png";
  nd.align = pAlign;
  return (nd);
}-*/;

public native void setText(String pText) /*-{
 this.@com.kereki.nixietest.client.NixieDisplay::display.init();
 this.@com.kereki.nixietest.client.NixieDisplay::display.setText(pText);
}-*/;
}
```

Before getting into details, let's see how this class would be used. The following code produces the display that was shown earlier.

```
NixieDisplay display1 = new NixieDisplay("nd1", 5, "right");
NixieDisplay display2 = new NixieDisplay("nd2", 10, "left");
NixieDisplay display3 = new NixieDisplay("nd3", 12, "right");

FlexTable ft = new FlexTable();

ft.setWidget(0, 0, new Label("James Bond is:"));
ft.setWidget(0, 1, display1);
ft.setWidget(1, 0, new Label("Darwin/Lincoln Birthdate:"));
ft.setWidget(1, 1, display2);
ft.setWidget(2, 0, new Label("All digits:"));
ft.setWidget(2, 1, display3);

RootPanel.get().add(ft);

display1.setText("007 ");
display2.setText("02-12-1809");
display3.setText("-123456.7890");
```

The JavaScript routine needs a <div> (with an id) to display the characters, so extending HTMLPanel was a sensible choice. The constructor requires a name (for the <div id>), a length (in digits) and a default alignment ("left" or "right") for the text. To set a value, the setText(...) method is provided. The logic for constructing and updating a display were taken from the web site; in particular note the way of getting at an attribute of a Java object from JavaScript (which in this case happens to be a function) in the `setText(...)` method, with `this.@com.kereki.nixietest.client` `.NixieDisplay::display.init()`.

Okay, maybe this kind of widget isn't your "cup of tea," but if you like this retro look, check out Hýbl's site and code, and you'll learn how to use other tubes, or create a dynamic old-style clock or calculator for your web application. Using other JavaScript widget libraries is similar to the job we did here, in any case, and you can enhance your GWT applications this way.

JSON

JSON (JavaScript Object Notation) is an alternative to XML, with the extra advantage that it is quite easily processed by JavaScript.[11] GWT has always provided support for this protocol, and in particular GWT 2 includes several classes and methods that make JSON processing even easier.

Let's create a simple news reader, using a JSON data source, to examine how to get and process such data. We use Yahoo's search services[12] that searches for news and provides them in JSON format. (You can also get the feed in JSONP format, which makes for even easier processing; we'll touch on this next.)

A sample call to http://search.yahooapis.com/NewsSearchService/V1/newsSearch?appid= YahooDemo&query=computer&results=5&language=en&output=json provides a JSON string, with up to five news in English language that include the word "computer." With some added blanks for readability, and abridging some texts, the output might be as follows:

```
{"ResultSet": {
  "totalResultsAvailable":"19978",
  "totalResultsReturned":5,
  "firstResultPosition":"1",
  "Result":[
  {
    "Title":"Micro computer club meets Jan 12 in Hanover Twp.",
    "Summary":"HANOVER TWP. - The Micro Computer Club will meet ...",
    "Url":"http:\/\/recordernewspapers.com\/articles\/2010\/01\/09...",
    "ClickUrl":"http:\/\/recordernewspapers.com\/...",
    "NewsSource":"Hanover Eagle",
    "NewsSourceUrl":"http:\/\/www.recordernewspapers.com...",
```

11. See www.json.org/ for more information on JSON, including parsers and generators for several dozen languages and environments.

12. See http://developer.yahoo.com/search/web/V1/webSearch.html for a full specification of query strings.

```
    "Language":"en",
    "PublishDate":"1263082654",
    "ModificationDate":"1263082655"},
  {
    "Title":"The Hindu Business Line...",
    "Summary":"Over one lakh government schools...",
    ...},
  {...},
  {...}
  ]}
}
```

The JSON notation (a subset of JavaScript) is easy to read: Braces surround objects, brackets surround arrays, and attributes are followed by a colon and their values. This news server provides a `ResultSet` object, with three attributes (`totalResultsAvailable`, `totalResultsReturned`, and `firstResultPosition`) having to do with how many and which items were returned, and another attribute (`Result`) that is an array of objects itself, each one representing a news item. These objects have several attributes, including `Title`, `Summary`, `URL`, `NewsSource`, `Language`, among others.

(An aside, just for completeness: If you need to *produce* JSON code with client-side code—not a likely situation, because JSON is usually produced at the server and consumed at the client—you can use the `JsonUtils.escapeValue(...)` method to produce escaped, valid JSON strings, and a simple logic to build the output string piece by piece, in a similar way to what we did in Chapter 7, "Communicating with Other Servers," to produce XML output.)

The view for our reader will be simple: a `TextBox` for specifying what terms you want to search, a `Button` to do the call, and an `HTMLPanel` to display an appropriately built up string, with the news titles, summaries, and clickable links to the original web page. See Figure 8.2 for our simple form design.

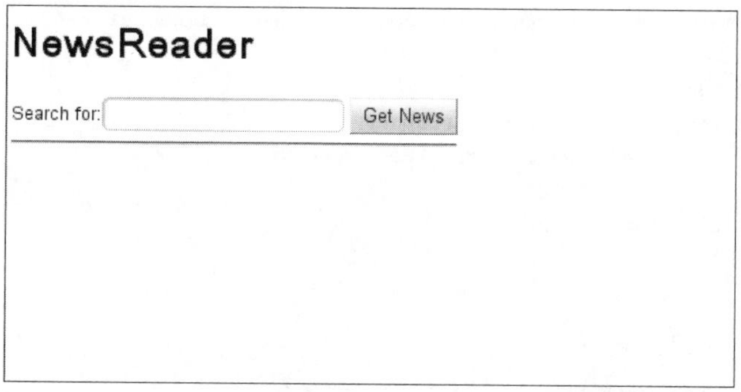

Figure 8.2 A simple news reader that will let us search for news on any search terms we want.

After a search for ABRAHAM LINCOLN you could get something such as Figure 8.3, showing a maximum of five news items. (This parameter can be changed.) Clicking on a title would open a new page with the original news web site.

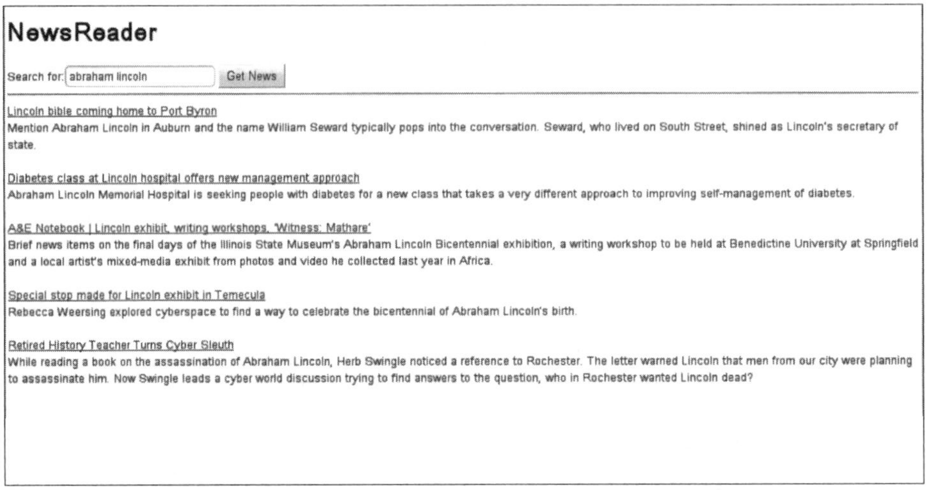

Figure 8.3 The results of searching for news regarding ABRAHAM LINCOLN, with a preset maximum of five news items.

The `NewsReaderView.ui.xml` and `NewsReaderView` files are quite simple, involving just a few fields and a single callback (when the button gets clicked). The `ui.xml` file is simply:

```
<?xml version="1.0" encoding="UTF-8"?>
<!DOCTYPE u:UiBinder SYSTEM "http://dl.google.com/gwt/DTD/xhtml.ent">
<u:UiBinder xmlns:u='urn:ui:com.google.gwt.uibinder'
            xmlns:g='urn:import:com.google.gwt.user.client.ui'>
  <g:HTMLPanel>
    <h1>NewsReader</h1>
    Search for:<g:TextBox u:field="searchFor"/>
    <g:Button u:field="getNews" text="Get News"/>
    <hr/>
    <g:HTML u:field="newsResult"/>
  </g:HTMLPanel>
</u:UiBinder>
```

The corresponding view is

```
package com.fkereki.mvpproject.client.newsReader;

// ...several imports...
```

```java
public class NewsReaderView
    extends View
    implements NewsReaderDisplay {
  @UiTemplate("NewsReaderView.ui.xml")
  interface Binder
      extends UiBinder<HTMLPanel, NewsReaderView> {
  }

  private static final Binder binder = GWT.create(Binder.class);

  @UiField TextBox searchFor;
  @UiField Button getNews;
  @UiField HTML newsResult;

  SimpleCallback<Object> onGetNewsCallback;

  public NewsReaderView() {
    super();
    HTMLPanel dlp = binder.createAndBindUi(this);
    initWidget(dlp);
  }

  @Override
  public String getTextToSearchFor() {
    return searchFor.getValue();
  }

  @Override
  public void setNews(String htmlNews) {
    newsResult.setHTML(htmlNews);
  }

  @Override
  public void setOnGetNewsCallback(SimpleCallback<Object> acb) {
    onGetNewsCallback = acb;
  }

  @UiHandler("getNews")
  void uiOnGetNewsClick(ClickEvent event) {
    onGetNewsCallback.onSuccess(null);
  }
}
```

The required NewsReaderDisplay interface is also quite simple, with methods for getting the textbox contents, setting the HTML list of news, and setting the button callback; let's examine it just for completeness:

```
public interface NewsReaderDisplay
    extends Display {

  String getTextToSearchFor();

  void setNews(String htmlNews);

  void setOnGetNewsCallback(SimpleCallback<Object> acb);
}
```

Now we can get to the more interesting part, and consider the `NewsReaderPresenter`
`.java` logic. The main part hinges on creating the "Get News" button callback, that will
construct the correct URL and connect to the news search service to get the latest news
items.

```
package com.fkereki.mvpproject.client.newsReader;

// ...imports...

public class NewsReaderPresenter
    extends Presenter<NewsReaderDisplay> {
  public static String PLACE = "newsReader";

  public NewsReaderPresenter(
      final String params,
      final NewsReaderDisplay newsReaderDisplay,
      final Environment environment) {

    super(params, newsReaderDisplay, environment);

    getDisplay().setOnGetNewsCallback(new SimpleCallback<Object>() {
      @Override
      public void goBack(final Object result) {
        getNewsViaXhr();
      }
    });
  }

  void displayNews(final NewsFeed data) {
    // format and show the news...
  }

  void getNewsViaXhr() {
    final String newsUrl = "http://search.yahooapis.com";
    final String newsPath = "NewsSearchService/V1/newsSearch";
    final String newsParams = "appid=YahooDemo&query="
        + URL.encode(getDisplay().getTextToSearchFor())
        + "&results=5&language=en&output=json";
```

```
    final XhrProxyAsync xhrProxy = getEnvironment().getModel()
        .getRemoteXhrProxy();

    xhrProxy.getFromUrl(newsUrl, newsPath, newsParams,
        new AsyncCallback<String>() {

            @Override
            public void onFailure(final Throwable caught) {
              // warn about the error...
            }

            @Override
            public void onSuccess(final String result) {
              final NewsFeed data = JsonUtils.unsafeEval(result);
              displayNews(data);
            }
        });
    }
}
```

If the Ajax call succeeds, we'll use the `JsonUtils.unsafeEval(...)` method—basically just a plain call to JavaScript's own `eval(...)` function, with no further safety measures; thus, the "unsafe" part of the name—to produce a `NewsFeed` object, an overlay for the underlying JavaScript object; let's study this a bit.

How do you work with a JavaScript object with Java code? You could go for the older `JSONParser` methods and build an object item per item, but it wouldn't be so efficient as using an overlay object that will encapsulate all accesses, hiding the underlying JavaScript object.

First, you should remember that you cannot create such an object by using Java's `new(...)` syntax; the whole idea of overlays is to graft an access to an already existing JavaScript object. Because we use `unsafeEval(...)` to get the JavaScript version of the news feed object, we are well on our way.[13]

Our `NewsFeed` overlay class will just provide four methods, because we are only interested in a few fields of the complete JSON result: We want to know how many news items there were, and their titles, summaries, and URLs. Note the protected constructor, that won't enable you to even try to construct a `NewsFeed` object with Java.

```
package com.fkereki.mvpproject.client.newsReader;

import com.google.gwt.core.client.JavaScriptObject;
```

---

13. This function is quite new in GWT; in fact, most online documentation shows how to accomplish the evaluation by means of a JavaScript method that directly calls `eval(...)`. By using this function you get the same result but keep to Java code.

```
public class NewsFeed
    extends JavaScriptObject {

  protected NewsFeed() {
  }

  public final native String getClickUrl(final int i) /*-{
    return this.ResultSet.Result[i].ClickUrl;
  }-*/;

  public final native String getSummary(final int i) /*-{
    return this.ResultSet.Result[i].Summary;
  }-*/;

  public final native String getTitle(final int i) /*-{
    return this.ResultSet.Result[i].Title;
  }-*/;

  public final native int getTotalResultsReturned() /*-{
    return this.ResultSet.totalResultsReturned;
  }-*/;
}
```

All methods must be `final` or `private`, so the compiler will resolve the call at compile time and generate optimized, possibly inlined, code. (We'll see the results of this optimization next.) Through overlays, your Java code can interact with the JavaScript object with no fuss. You could even add extra "Java-only" methods to NewsFeed; for example, we could write something like—and feel free to fill in the details—the `getAge(...)` method, which would tell how old is a piece of news.

```
public final long getAge(final int i) {
  // use a JSNI method to get the PublishDate attribute
  // of the i-th news item, and store it to newsTimeStamp

  // get the current timestamp by using new Date().getTime()
  // and store it to currentTimeStamp

  return currentTimeStamp - newsTimeStamp;
}
```

Note that this enables having a richer view of the underlying JavaScript object than the original object would have enabled.

Given the preceding class, the `displayNews(...)` method iterates through all news items (their quantity is obtained through the `getTotalResultsReturned(...)` method) and constructs a link (by using `getClickUrl(...)` and `getTitle(...)`) with the following `getSummary(...)` results. A couple of empty lines separate different news items.

```
void displayNews(NewsFeed data) {
  String show = "";
  final int news = data.getTotalResultsReturned();
  for (int i = 0; i < news; i++) {
    show += "<a href='" + data.getClickUrl(i) + "' target='_blank'>"
        + data.getTitle(i) + "</a><br/>" + data.getSummary(i)
        + "<br/><br/";
  }
  getDisplay().setNews(show);
}
```

Used in this way, JSON is easier to work with than XML. If you compile the project producing *Pretty* code (as we mentioned in Chapter 2, "Getting Started with GWT 2") you'll see the produced JavaScript code is as compact as it could be, and practically a one-by-one translation of your Java code:

```
function $displayNews(this$static, data){
  var i, news, show;
  show = '';
  news = data.ResultSet.totalResultsReturned;
  for (i = 0; i < news; ++i) {
    show += "<a href='" + data.ResultSet.Result[i].ClickUrl
      + "' target='_blank'>" + data.ResultSet.Result[i].Title
      + '<\/a><br/>' + data.ResultSet.Result[i].Summary
      + '<br/><br/';
  }
  dynamicCast(this$static.display_0,9).newsResult.element.innerHTML =
    show || '';
}
```

The produced code is exactly what you'd directly write in JavaScript (in passing, note that the calls to `data` methods were inlined, so there's no overhead there; this validates what we said about the need for `private`, `final` methods) so it will run faster than if it had received XML.

JSONP

Because you can load JavaScript code from other domains, and JSON objects are JavaScript code, it stands to reason that you can get JSON objects without regard to SOP restrictions… but how do you know when the object is ready? JSONP (JSON with Padding) provides a solution.

When you connect to a JSONP server, you add an argument that becomes a callback to a function, with the JSON data as a parameter. For example, the same call to the Yahoo! News search function, with an added `callback=yourownfunction` parameter, returns something like the following, minus extra spaces added for readability:

```
yourownfunction({"ResultSet": {
  "totalResultsAvailable":"19919",
  "totalResultsReturned":5,
  "firstResultPosition":"1",
  "Result": [{
    "Title":"Here are ...",
    "Summary":"Maybe you've resolved ...",
    "Url":"http:\/\/www.usatoday.com...",
    "ClickUrl":"...",
    "NewsSource":"USA Today",
    "NewsSourceUrl":"http:\/\/www.usatoday.com\/",
    "Language":"en",
    "PublishDate":"1262970718",
    "ModificationDate":"1262972040"},
    {"Title":"Final Glance: Computer companies",...},
    {...}...]}})
```

When the script is loaded, it will execute, and thus call `yourownfunction(...)`, which will process the received JSON string—a nice way to skip around cross origin restrictions!

(Of course, a serious warning must be given: If you connect to an untrusted site, receive a JSONP result, and blindly use it, anything may happen. You are purposefully avoiding SOP tests, so you must fully trust the downloaded code.)

Up to GWT 1.7, you had to code JSONP calls "by hand" (you had to do some DOM maneuvering to add a `<script>` node to your current page and then set its URL appropriately) but GWT 2 added the `JsonpRequestBuilder` class, which enables you to do JSONP calls in a fashion similar to Ajax calls. You must, however, add

```
<inherits name="com.google.gwt.jsonp.Jsonp"/>
```

to your `gwt.xml` module file, to use JSONP.

We can modify our news reader by providing a different method, that will replace `getNewsViaXhr(...)`.

```
void getNewsViaJsonp() {
  final String newsUrl = "http://search.yahooapis.com/"
      + "NewsSearchService/V1/newsSearch?appid=YahooDemo&query="
      + URL.encode(getDisplay().getTextToSearchFor())
      + "&results=5&language=en&output=json";

  final JsonpRequestBuilder jsonp = new JsonpRequestBuilder();
  jsonp.requestObject(newsUrl, new AsyncCallback<NewsFeed>() {

    @Override
    public void onFailure(final Throwable caught) {
      // ...warn about the problem...
    }
```

```
    @Override
    public void onSuccess(final NewsFeed result) {
      displayNews(result);
    }
  });
```

The code is quite similar, but note that the `AsyncCallback` for the JSONP call is defined to return a `NewsFeed` object and that you don't need to parse the result of the call, which is already converted into the appropriate format. Also observe that the URL we need to provide is exactly the same as in the Ajax version; the `&callback=...` attribute will be added by `JsonpRequestBuilder`. (And, should you require a different name for it—say, `_call`—you would have to set it via `jsonp.setCallbackParam(` `"_call")`. The default name for the JSONP callback routine is, as you might expect, `callback`.)

Because many important, well-known Internet companies (including Yahoo!, Google, Twitter, Flicker, and more) provide JSONP feeds, this method will enable us to produce Web 2.0-like mashup services, without recurring to proxies or anything else, for an extra bit of speed.

Summary

Directly coding in JavaScript by means of JSNI enables you to go beyond any possible limitations that you might find in GWT. Though obviously requiring a more careful approach (and somewhat complicated rules for Java/JavaScript interaction) JSNI is widely used by the GWT developers and is a worthy tool for you to learn and use—and we will keep working with it in the following chapter, using JSNI to interact with several important APIs.

9

Adding APIs

There are many JavaScript libraries and web services, and you can include their features in your application by adding JSNI (as we saw in Chapter 8, "Mixing in JavaScript,") and some GWT coding. In this chapter we see some examples and get to process data feeds to get weather information, use charts to provide a visual dashboard, and interact with geographic data working with maps.

Creating highly interactive, modern web applications doesn't mean reinventing the wheel for each specific purpose. Rather, we like to utilize the many available APIs for just about anything you might want.

(Of course, you should remember that you won't be getting the usual GWT benefits as to code optimization, dead code removal, and more, if you just produce a wrapper around a JavaScript library. If there's a GWT-only solution, you'll probably be better off using it.)

In this chapter we see how a mixture of Java and JavaScript coding can let you easily mix in several APIs into your application, with no particular complications. We won't restrict ourselves to Google-only routines, so you can get experience on handling APIs that might have not even been prepared for GWT.

A Weather Vane

Let's start by using some libraries to get weather information, which we could include in any site.[1] For my example, I wanted to get Montevideo, Uruguay (my birth place, and where I live) weather information—without merely looking out of my window!

Getting Weather Data

First, I needed a web service that would provide weather information. Out of the many available possibilities, I opted (no particular reason) for *Yahoo! Weather RSS Feed* (see

---

1. And yes, Weather Vane may not be a precise or correct name but is flashier sounding than Weather Widget!

http://developer.yahoo.com/weather/). To use it, I had to go to Yahoo's Weather site (at http://weather.yahoo.com/) and using the search function, let me learn that the WOEID[2] code for Montevideo was 468052. I got that directly from examining the URL for Montevideo's weather, which was http://weather.yahoo.com/uruguay/montevideo/montevideo-468052/. (Another example would be 2442047, which means Los Angeles, California, USA.) Given that code, accessing the feed at http://weather.yahooapis.com/forecastrss?w=468052&u=c would get Montevideo's (w=468052) weather information in Celsius (u=c) degrees.

If you want to consider other possibilities for getting weather information, you could check GeoNames' site (at www.geonames.org/) and in particular its web services (at www.geonames.org/export/JSON-webservices.html) that can provide JSON weather information. For example, knowing that Montevideo is at latitude −34.858 and longitude −56.171 (I googled for that information; mind having it in decimal format rather than in the more classic 34°51'29"S, 56°10'14"W style) I could then access http://ws.geonames.org/findNearByWeatherJSON?lat=-34.858&lng=-56.171 and get the (slightly edited and abridged) JSON result listed here.3

```
{"weatherObservation":{
  "clouds":"scattered clouds",
  "weatherCondition":"in vicinity:  rain",
  "observation":"SUAA 162100Z 15003KT 9999 VCRA SCT023 BKN040 23/18 Q1010",
  "windDirection":150,
  "ICAO":"SUAA",
  "elevation":54,
  "countryCode":"UY",
  "lng":-56.25,
  "temperature":"23",
  "dewPoint":"18",
  "windSpeed":"03",
  "humidity":73,
  "stationName":"Melilla",
  "datetime":"2010-01-16 21:00:00",
  "lat":-34.7666666666667,
  "hectoPascAltimeter":1010
  }
}
```

Just so you can see GWT's flexibility, you could also use several other RSS weather feeds, such as Accuweather's (see http://rss.accuweather.com/rss/liveweather_rss.asp?metric=1&locCode=SAM|UY|UY010|MONTEVIDEO) or The Weather Channel's (see

---

2. WOEID stands for Where On Earth ID and is a 32-bit number used by Yahoo! for its geographic GeoPlanet services and data; see http://developer.yahoo.com/geo/ for more on this.

3. If you are curious, ICAO stands for International Civil Aviation Organization, and SUAA is the code for the Ángel S. Adami Civil Airport in Melilla, near Montevideo.

http://rss.weather.com/weather/rss/local/UYXX0006?cm_ven=LWO&cm_cat=
rss&par=LWO_rss) among many.[4] Yet another possibility would be using Yahoo Pipes
(http://pipes.yahoo.com/pipes/) and build yourself an appropriate JSON service. Yahoo
Pipes lets you mash different feeds (such as the RSS feeds I mentioned) and produce
results in JSON, XML, and more formats.

Getting the Feed

Now, how do we get this feed? Of course we could do a proxy (as we saw in Chapter 7,
"Communicating with Other Servers,") and extract the weather information from the
RSS XML result, but the Google Ajax Feed API (see http://code.google.com/apis/
ajaxfeeds/) will help us. (Remember you cannot directly get the feed because of the
SOP restrictions we studied in Chapter 6, "Communicating with Your Server.") You can
use this API to download any public data RSS/Atom feed by using just JavaScript;
Google provides the necessary server-side proxy, and integrating a feed becomes easier.
Also, this library can return the feed data in either JSON (by default) or XML; because
we are working with client-side code, the first option is a natural for us. The (slightly
edited and abridged) string we'd be getting is

```
{"feed":{
  "title":"Yahoo! Weather - Montevideo, UY",
  "link":"http://us.rd.yahoo.com/...",
  "author":"",
  "description":"Yahoo! Weather for Montevideo, UY",
  "type":"rss20",
  "entries":[{
    "title":"Conditions for Montevideo, UY at 12:00 pm UYT",
    "link":"http://us.rd.yahoo.com/...",
    "author":"",
    "publishedDate":"Thu, 14 Jan 2010 12:00:00 -0800",
    "contentSnippet":"\nCurrent Conditions:\nFair, 26 C\nForecast:\nThu - Sunny.
High: 26 Low: 17\nFri - Mostly Sunny. High: 28 Low: 21\n\nFull Forecast at ...",
    "content":"\u003cimg src\u003d\"http://l.yimg.com/a/i/us/we/52/34.gif\
"\u003e\u003cbr\u003e\n\u003cb\u003eCurrent
Conditions:\u003c/b\u003e\u003cbr\u003e\nFair, 26
C\u003cbr\u003e\n\u003cbr\u003e\u003cb\u003e
Forecast:\u003c/b\u003e\u003cbr\u003e\nThu - Sunny. High: 26 Low:
17\u003cbr\u003e\nFri - Mostly Sunny. High: 28 Low: 21...",
    "categories":[]
  }]
  }
}
```

Finally, how do we get to use this API? We have to load it into memory and then
interact with it to get the data. The standard way is by using JavaScript but we can go
one better.

4. Be careful, however; different codes stand for the same cities, and of course, data formats vary.

```
<html>
  <head>
    <script type="text/javascript" src=http://www.google.com/jsapi  />
    <script type="text/javascript">

    google.load("feeds", "1");

    function initialize() {
      var url= "http://weather.yahooapis.com/forecastrss?w=468052&u=c";
      var feed= new google.feeds.Feed(url);
      feed.load(function(result) {
        // do something with result
      });
    }
    google.setOnLoadCallback(initialize);
    </script>
  </head>
  <body>
    ...rest of your site...
  </body>
</html>
```

We can use the GWT AjaxLoader API (see http://code.google.com/docreader/#p=
gwt-google-apis&s=gwt-google-apis&t=AjaxLoaderGettingStarted) to load the Feed
API, and then this API to get the RSS weather information, transformed into JSON...
sounds harder than it is, in fact!

By the way, loading the JavaScript library on demand helps providing a faster startup
time, along the lines of `RunAsync(...)`, which we'll use in Chapter 15, "Deploying
Your Application." Also note that after the library has been loaded, future load requests
won't reload it, so performance will be very good.

Getting Everything Together

Let's go at this step by step. To use the GWT AjaxLoader API, you have to add
`<inherits name="com.google.gwt.ajaxloader.AjaxLoader"/>` to your `gwt.xml`
file. You also have to get the `gwt-ajaxloader-1.0.0.tar.gz` file from Google's download site (at http://code.google.com/p/gwt-google-apis/downloads/list), extract the
`gwt-ajaxloader.jar` file from it, and add it to your project's client-side code build path.

(Note that Google provides several APIs that simplify using services, without having
to write JavaScript by yourself. In any case, in this chapter we use both such APIs and
JSNI-based methods to consider all possible solutions.)

First, you need to initialize `AjaxLoader` and then use it to load the Feeds library into
memory; you'll provide the library's name (`"feeds"`) and the version you want to use
(`"1"` at the time, but there can be new ones in the making). You also have to provide a
`Runnable` object, whose `run(...)` method will be used as a callback, after the API is

loaded. Code like the following should be used to initially load the JavaScript library and then to actually get the feed.

```
AjaxLoader.init();
final AjaxLoaderOptions options = AjaxLoaderOptions.newInstance();
AjaxLoader.loadApi("feeds", "1", new Runnable() {
  public void run() {
    getFeed();
  }
}, options);
```

Getting at the Feed Data with an Overlay

We'll get to the `getFeed(...)` routine soon, but let's first see how we'll process the feed. The easiest way to get the JSON data is through an overlay, as we saw in Chapter 8.

```
public class WeatherFeed
    extends JavaScriptObject {

  protected WeatherFeed() {
  }

  public final native String getFeedDescription() /*-{
    return this.feed.description;
  }-*/;

  public final native String getItemContent() /*-{
    return this.feed.entries[0].content;
  }-*/;

  public final native String getItemLink() /*-{
    return this.feed.entries[0].link;
  }-*/;

  public final native String getItemTitle() /*-{
    return this.feed.entries[0].title;
  }-*/;
}
```

The GWT method that uses the `WeatherFeed` data could be as simple as the following:

```
void processWeather(final WeatherFeed ww) {
  final VerticalPanel vp = new VerticalPanel();
  vp.add(new Anchor(ww.getFeedDescription(), ww.getItemLink()));
  vp.add(new HTMLPanel(ww.getItemContent()));
  RootPanel.get().add(vp);
  Window.alert("Check it out!");
}
```

Getting the Feed with JSNI

Now, let's get back to actually getting the data. A suitable `getFeed(...)` routine requires JSNI; a possible solution is

```
private native void getFeed() /*-{
  var myself= this;
  var url= "http://weather.yahooapis.com/forecastrss?w=468052&u=c";
  var feed= new $wnd.google.feeds.Feed(url);
  feed.load(function(result) {
    if (!result.error) {
      myself.@com.kereki.apisdemo.client.Apisdemo::processWeather
        (Lcom/kereki/apisdemo/client/WeatherFeed;)(result);
  }});
}-*/;
```

Notice the usage of `$wnd` to get at the `google.feeds` variable, and also the call to the Java `processWeather(...)` method, with the usual JSNI style we saw in Chapter 8. An important detail: you might think of writing that call as `this.@com...` instead of declaring and using the `myself` variable as given, but that would be an error because `this` would point to the recently created `function` object and not to yours.[5]

Dashboard Visualizations

For Management Information Systems (MIS) applications, adding a *dashboard* showing the most important business indicators is a good way to provide a bird's eye glance to the current situation of your company. Instead of showing plain numbers, graphics and charts are usually chosen, and we'll now turn to several ways of providing such visualizations.

The easiest way would probably be using the *Google Visualization API* (at http://code.google.com/docreader/#p=gwt-google-apis&s=gwt-google-apis&t=Visualization), which provides access to all kinds of graphs, both static (just an image) and animated (meaning you can click on chart items and fire events, for example).[6]

An example of the usage of this API (we'll get to details later) is shown in Figure 9.1.[7]

---

5. Bone up on JavaScript *closures* if you are not sure about this. A possible reference is https://developer.mozilla.org/en/Core_JavaScript_1.5_Guide/Working_with_Closures.

6. This API also provides a Table object (why, yes, a table is also a visualization tool, isn't it?) whose data can be sorted, paged, and formatted; check it out at http://code.google.com/apis/visualization/documentation/gallery/table.html.

7. By the way, the data I used for the examples were taken from *GeoHive* (at www.xist.org/); other possibilities (among many available) would be *The CIA World Factbook* (https://www.cia.gov/library/publications/the-world-factbook/) or *NationMaster* (www.nationmaster.com/).

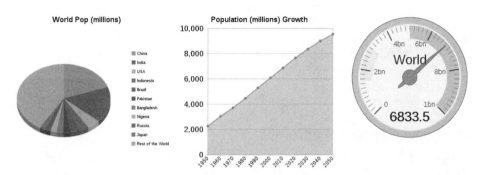

Figure 9.1 Some sample visualizations of basic world demographic data,
provided by the Google Visualizations API.

You can pick several other packages. Google provides the *Google Chart API* (at
http://code.google.com/apis/chart/), which can be used with JSNI, or directly by providing an appropriate URL; for example, by linking to http://chart.apis.google.com/
chart?chs=480x360&cht=bhs&chtt=World%20Population&chd=s:dZHFEEDDDD9&ch
xl=0:|Rest|Japan|Russia|Nigeria|Bangladesh|Pakistan|Brazil|Indonesia|USA|India|
China|1:|Population|2:|Countries|&chxt=y,x,t you can provide an image as shown in
Figure 9.2, but note that you'll have to do some coding to convert numbers (the populations, in this case) to letters (see the `chd` parameter in the URL above); not hard, anyway.

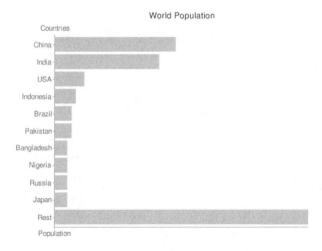

Figure 9.2 The Google API Chart has a rather complex interface but
enables you to produce charts by just linking to a specific URL.

Several more JavaScript or Flash-based libraries can help producing visualizations such as the ones in this chapter. Personally, I'd rather go for JavaScript than for Flash (after having said, in Chapter 1, "Developing Your Application," that using GWT was advantageous because you didn't require any plugins, it wouldn't do to actually recommend a Flash-based visualization library, would it?) but via JSNI you can interact with both of them.

With all libraries you might find that given chart styles might not run or be shown on all browsers; a nice solution to this is to apply the deferred binding techniques we used in Chapter 4, "Working with Browsers," and either provide an alternative chart style or at least give an adequate warning.

Using the Google Visualization API

Using this API requires adding `<inherits name='com.google.gwt.visualization .Visualization'/>` to your gwt.xml file. You won't have to use the GWT AjaxLoader API (as in the weather feed example) because the `VisualizationUtils` package already provides the necessary function; for example, you could load the API and set it up for displaying `PieChart` and `AreaChart` objects with the following line of code:[8]

```
VisualizationUtils.loadVisualizationApi(onVisualizationsLoadCallback,
    PieChart.PACKAGE, AreaChart.PACKAGE, Gauge.PACKAGE);
```

The `onVisualizationsLoadCallback` method will be called as soon as the API is loaded in memory and ready to be used; you can use it, for example, to initialize the visualizations for your page. (In Chapter 15 we'll see how we could split the code away, so it would actually be loaded only if needed.)

```
final Runnable onVisualizationsLoadCallback = new Runnable() {
  public void run() {

    final HorizontalPanel hp = new HorizontalPanel();

    final PieChart worldPopPie = new PieChart(create2010PopTable(),
        create2010PopOptions());
    hp.add(worldPopPie);

    final AreaChart popGrowthChart = new AreaChart(
        createPopGrowthTable(), createPopGrowthOptions());
    hp.add(popGrowthChart);

    final Gauge popGauge = new Gauge(createPopGaugeTable(),
        createPopGaugeOptions());
    hp.add(popGauge);

    RootPanel.get().add(hp);
  }
};
```

8. All Google provided visualizations include a PACKAGE String that identifies them.

Each visualization requires a data table and visualization options. Data tables can have many columns; you'll have to check what's appropriate for the type of visualization you are creating. For example, the world population pie chart uses a two-column data table, with the country names in the first column and populations in the second.

```
private void addIdentValueRow(
    final DataTable data,
    final String ident,
    final double value) {

  data.addRow();
  data.setValue(data.getNumberOfRows() - 1, 0, ident);
  data.setValue(data.getNumberOfRows() - 1, 1, value);
}


private AbstractDataTable create2010PopTable() {
  /*
   * 2010 Population Data taken from
   * http://www.xist.org/earth/population1.aspx
   */
  final DataTable data = DataTable.create();
  data.addColumn(ColumnType.STRING, "Country");
  data.addColumn(ColumnType.NUMBER, "Population (millions)");

  addIdentValueRow(data, "China", 1338.6);
  addIdentValueRow(data, "India", 1166.1);
  addIdentValueRow(data, "USA", 307.2);
  addIdentValueRow(data, "Indonesia", 240.2);
  addIdentValueRow(data, "Brazil", 198.7);
  addIdentValueRow(data, "Pakistan", 176.2);
  addIdentValueRow(data, "Bangladesh", 156.1);
  addIdentValueRow(data, "Nigeria", 149.2);
  addIdentValueRow(data, "Russia", 140.0);
  addIdentValueRow(data, "Japan", 127.1);
  addIdentValueRow(data, "Rest of the World", 2834.1);
  return data;
}
```

The required options for each visualization vary a bit. Also, if you have more than one type of visualization on your application, you have to qualify which `Options` class you want because all are named the same way. The world population pie had the following code; note the `PieChart.Options` specification.[9]

9. If you cannot find a wrapper function to set a desired parameter, you can use the generic `setOption(...)` call: `options.setOption("is3D", true)` is the same as `options.set3D(true)`, for example. Check online for the names of the necessary parameters.

```
private PieChart.Options create2010PopOptions() {
  final PieChart.Options options = PieChart.Options.create();
  options.setWidth(400);
  options.setHeight(360);
  options.set3D(true);
  options.setTitle("World Pop (millions)");
  return options;
}
```

Just for completeness, we can have the code required for the other two visualizations: an area chart showing the growth and estimated sizes of the world's population (a line chart would have done as well) and a gauge showing the current population.[10]

```
private Gauge.Options createPopGaugeOptions() {
  final Gauge.Options options = Gauge.Options.create();
  options.setWidth(300);
  options.setHeight(300);

  options.setGaugeRange(0, 10000);
  options.setGreenRange(1500, 3000);
  options.setYellowRange(3000, 5000);
  options.setRedRange(5000, 10000);

  options.setMajorTicks(new String[] {"0", "2bn",
    "4bn", "6bn", "8bn", "10bn" });
  options.setMinorTicks(10);

  return options;
}


private AbstractDataTable createPopGaugeTable() {
  /*
   * 2010 Population Data taken from
   * http://www.xist.org/earth/population1.aspx
   */
  final DataTable data = DataTable.create();
  data.addColumn(ColumnType.STRING, "Population");
  data.addColumn(ColumnType.NUMBER, "Millions");
  addIdentValueRow(data, "World", 6833.5);
  return data;
}
```

10. There is no surefire standard for the optimum world population, but several papers seem to agree that between 1.5 and 2 billion would be best, up to 5 could be acceptable, and that the current numbers are already too big. Anyway, do not read any intended political statements in this; I just needed some data that could logically be shown in a gauge!

```
private AreaChart.Options createPopGrowthOptions() {
  final AreaChart.Options options = AreaChart.Options.create();
  options.setWidth(400);
  options.setHeight(360);
  options.setTitle("Population (millions) Growth");
  options.setLegend(LegendPosition.NONE);
  options.setMin(0);
  options.setEnableTooltip(true);
  return options;
}

private AbstractDataTable createPopGrowthTable() {
  /*
   * World (actual and projected) Population Data from
   * http://www.xist.org/earth/his_proj.aspx
   */
  final DataTable data = DataTable.create();
  data.addColumn(ColumnType.STRING, "Decade");
  data.addColumn(ColumnType.NUMBER, "Pop (millions)");

  addIdentValueRow(data, "1950", 2255.9);
  addIdentValueRow(data, "1960", 3041.6);
  addIdentValueRow(data, "1970", 3711.8);
  addIdentValueRow(data, "1980", 4452.8);
  addIdentValueRow(data, "1990", 5282.4);
  addIdentValueRow(data, "2000", 6084.9);
  addIdentValueRow(data, "2010", 6866.9);
  addIdentValueRow(data, "2020", 7659.3);
  addIdentValueRow(data, "2030", 8373.1);
  addIdentValueRow(data, "2040", 9003.2);
  addIdentValueRow(data, "2050", 9539.0);
  return data;
}
```

Handling Events

You can also process events related to visualizations, such as `mouseOver`, `select`, and more. For example, say we want to let the user click on a pie wedge and then do something related to the picked country. Just after creating the object, we should add an appropriate handler to the pie chart by writing code such as

```
worldPopPie.addSelectHandler(new SelectHandler() {
  @Override
  public void onSelect(final SelectEvent event) {
    final JsArray<Selection> selections = worldPopPie
        .getSelections();
    final int chosenRow = selections.get(0).getRow();
```

```
        Window.alert("you clicked on country #" + (chosenRow + 1));
    }
});
```

The `getSelections(...)` method returns all clicked selections, and because on pie charts you can only click on a single wedge, by writing `selections.get(0).getRow()` we learn which row of the data table corresponds to the selected wedge. Of course, you would probably do something more meaningful than just letting the user know on which country he did click on!

Working with Maps

As a final example, let's work on building a widget that will allow us to enter or modify the geographic coordinates of a given point.

Currently, there are at least three major map APIs: Google Maps (at http://code.google.com/apis/maps/), Microsoft Bing Maps (at www.microsoft.com/maps/) and Yahoo! Maps (at http://developer.yahoo.com/maps/). Just for variety, let's go with the latter, which will require us a bit of XML processing and JSNI (unlike Google Maps, because we could use the GWT API at http://code.google.com/docreader/#p=gwt-google-apis&s=gwt-google-apis&t=MapsGettingStarted), and will enable us to both get interactive (clickable, draggable, and so on) maps and fixed maps (plain images) for less demanding applications.

Interactive Maps

The most interesting maps are interactive, meaning you can drag them around, zoom in or out, and pinpoint specific points of interest. We'll write a simple application that will show a map with a marker on it (arbitrarily set at the American Museum of Natural History, or AMNH; my favorite place to see in New York City!) and allow you to click on other position. The map will start centered at the AMNH, and each time you click on a different spot, the marker will move there and the map will be recentered. You'll have a continuously updated display of the latitude and longitude of the marker. See Figure 9.3 for a view of our application.

We shall work in the MVP style we have been using. The Display interface for this form will be quite simple—and for an actual application, you'd probably add more methods—and will just include a couple of getters (to gain access to the current coordinates of the marker) and a setter (to put the marker at a given position).

```
package com.fkereki.mvpproject.client.map1;

// ...imports...

public interface MapDisplay
    extends Display {

  double getLatitude();
```

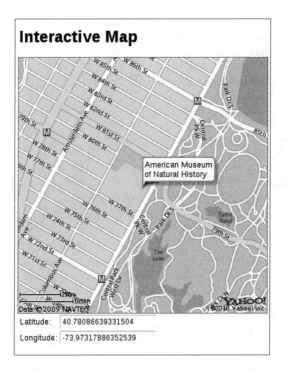

Figure 9.3 Our interactive map, showing the American Museum of National History in New York City. You can reposition the marker by clicking on any spot. The map can be dragged and zoomed, too. © 2010 NAVTEQ. All rights reserved. ©2010 Yahoo! Inc. YAHOO! and the YAHOO! logo are registered trademarks of Yahoo! Inc.

```
double getLongitude();

void setCoordinates(double latitude, double longitude);
}
```

The corresponding Presenter is trivial. We use **PLACE** as before to set up the menu and program the corresponding actions.

```
package com.fkereki.mvpproject.client.map1;

// ...imports...

public class MapPresenter
    extends Presenter<MapDisplay> {

  public static String PLACE = "map";
```

```
    public MapPresenter(
        final String params, final MapDisplay mapDisplay,
        final Environment environment) {

      super(params, mapDisplay, environment);
    }
}
```

The interesting logic lies at the View. Because it is responsible for creating the widgets, all the interaction with the Yahoo! Maps API will go here. You have to add the line
`<script type="text/javascript" language="javascript" src="http://`
`api.maps.yahoo.com/ajaxymap?v=3.8&appid=...yourKeyGoesHere...">`
`</script>` to your main HTML file, so the required API will be included. To use it,
you'll also have to get a key of your own; check the "How do I get started?" section at
http://developer.yahoo.com/maps/rest/V1/ for more details on that.

The Yahoo! Maps API specifies you must provide a `<div>` where the map will be
shown; we'll use a `HTML` object for this, with appropriate contents. We'll also define several widgets for the Latitude and Longitude fields, plus a `VerticalPanel` and a
`FlexTable` to organize everything. Finally, `yahooMap` will point to the actual map and
be a `JavaScriptObject`, defined and used only in JavaScript coding.

```
package com.fkereki.mvpproject.client.map1;

// ...imports...

public class MapView
    extends View
    implements MapDisplay {

  final VerticalPanel vp = new VerticalPanel();
  final HTML div = new HTML(
      "<div id='myveryownmap' style='height:50%;width:75%;'></div>");
  final FlexTable ft = new FlexTable();
  final TextBox lat = new TextBox();
  final TextBox lon = new TextBox();
  JavaScriptObject yahooMap = null;

  /*
   * AMNH= American Museum of Natural History, NYC
   */
  final double AMNHlat = 40.780411;
  final double AMNHlon = -73.974037;
  final String AMNHDescription = "American Museum<br/>of Natural History";
  public MapView() {
    super();

    vp.add(new InlineHTML("<h1>Interactive Map</h1>"));
```

```
ft.setWidget(0, 0, new Label("Latitude:"));
ft.setWidget(0, 1, lat);
ft.setWidget(1, 0, new Label("Longitude:"));
ft.setWidget(1, 1, lon);

vp.add(div);
vp.add(ft);

initWidget(vp);
}
```

The `getLatitude(...)`, `getLongitude(...)` and `setCoordinates(...)` methods are quite simple, and mainly access the corresponding `TextBox` fields.

```
@Override
public final double getLatitude() {
  return Double.parseDouble(lat.getValue());
}

@Override
public final double getLongitude() {
  return Double.parseDouble(lon.getValue());
}

@Override
public final void setCoordinates(
    final double latitude,
    final double longitude) {

  lat.setValue("" + latitude);
  lon.setValue("" + longitude);
}
```

Now, how and when should we initialize the map? We are just defining a `Composite` widget here, and it won't get displayed until later, so we cannot do any Maps API calls right now. Because we need the map to be initialized as soon as the form is shown, an easy way to achieve this is by redefining the `onAttach(...)` method, and our initialization code will be called the moment the widget is shown.[11]

```
@Override
public final void onAttach() {
  super.onAttach();
  yahooMapInit();
  setCoordinates(AMNHlat, AMNHlon);
  yahooMapDisplay(AMNHlat, AMNHlon, AMNHDescription);
}
```

11. The `onLoad(...)` method could also be used.

The most interesting parts come now. Initialization requires calling the **YMap** function to produce a map, setting its type to whatever we want (we are going for a regular map; other options include satellite and hybrid versions), and saving it to the **yahooMap** attribute we defined earlier. Note the usage of the usual JSNI **$wnd** prefix, and the rather long way for accessing **yahooMap**. You could get fancier and add several types of controls if you want; check the API documentation for that.

```
private final native void yahooMapInit()
/*-{
  var map = new $wnd.YMap($doc.getElementById('myveryownmap'));
  map.setMapType($wnd.YAHOO_MAP_REG);
  this.@com.fkereki.mvpproject.client.map1.MapView::yahooMap= map;
  //
  //       You can add controls:
  //
  //       map.addTypeControl();
  //       map.addPanControl();
  //       map.addZoomLong();
  //       map.addZoomShort();
  //
}-*/
;
```

Displaying the map at a given coordinate requires creating a **YGeoPoint** object and using the **drawZoomAndCenter(...)** method. (Notice, once again, that we need a **myself** variable because of closure matters in the **moveMarker(...)** method; see the following code.) After, we can add a marker at the center point of the map, give it an "auto expand" text and show it.

Finally, we must capture clicks on the map to reposition the marker; the **moveMarker(...)** method achieves that: The second parameter stands for the coordinates of the clicked point. Then, we can reset the marker coordinates with **setYGeoPoint(...)** and pan the view so the map will be centered by using **panToLatLon(...)**. Finally, we can call the Java **setCoordinates(...)** method so the updated coordinates will be shown onscreen.

```
private final native void yahooMapDisplay(
    final double lat,
    final double lon,
    final String text) /*-{

  var myself= this;
  var map= myself.@com.fkereki.mvpproject.client.map1.MapView::yahooMap;
  var currentGeoPoint = new $wnd.YGeoPoint(lat, lon);

  map.drawZoomAndCenter(currentGeoPoint, 3);
  map.addMarker(currentGeoPoint,"myveryownmarker");
  map.getMarkerObject("myveryownmarker").addAutoExpand(text);
```

```
map.getMarkerObject("myveryownmarker").openAutoExpand();
$wnd.YEvent.Capture(map, $wnd.EventsList.MouseUp, moveMarker);

function moveMarker(_e, _c) {
  map.getMarkerObject("myveryownmarker").setYGeoPoint(_c);
  map.panToLatLon(_c);
  myself.@com.fkereki.mvpproject.client.map1.MapView::
    setCoordinates(DD)(_c.Lat, _c.Lon);
}

//
// If needed, you could get the current marker coordinates by writing:
//
// var myobj= map.getMarkerObject("myveryownmarker");
// alert("Coords: "+myobj.YGeoPoint.Lat+", "+myobj.YGeoPoint.Lon);
//
}-*/
  ;
}
```

I have used similar logic for applications that worked with geographical data, so the data entry personnel could check whether a store was correctly positioned, and of course, reposition it if needed. You can also use other functions that let you search for a place by giving, say, its street address; check on that for extra flexibility.

Fixed Maps

If you don't need interactive maps and can do with just a image file, Yahoo! Maps also provides a REST API (see http://developer.yahoo.com/maps/rest/V1/) that you can use in a two-step process to get an image built by Yahoo!'s servers.

First, you need to call a service (at http://local.yahooapis.com/MapsService/V1/mapImage) whose answer will be an XML file with a URL in it; you can then assign the URL to an <image> object, and the generated map will be displayed; let's do it first by hand, and then with GWT code. For example, say we want to get an image of the map around the American Museum of Natural History, as in the previous section. We must first connect to http://local.yahooapis.com/MapsService/V1/mapImage?appid=...yourKeyGoesHere...&latitude=40.780411&longitude=-73.974037 and the returned value will be something like the following (slightly abridged and edited) XML string.

```
<?xml version="1.0"?>
<Result xmlns:xsi="http://www.w3.org/2001/XMLSchema-instance">
http://gws.maps.yahoo.com/mapimage?MAPDATA=...encodedMapDataGoesHere...
&amp;mvt=m&amp;cltype=onnetwork&amp;.intl=us&amp;appid=...yourKeyGoesHere...
&amp;oper=&amp;_proxy=ydn,xml</Result>
<!-- ws11.ydn.ac4.yahoo.com
compressed/chunked Mon Jan 18 15:05:10 PST 2010 -->
```

Displaying that URL would provide an image such as shown in Figure 9.4.

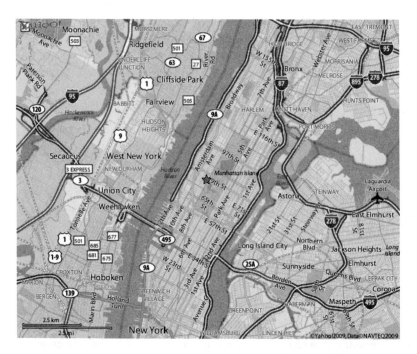

Figure 9.4 Yahoo! Maps also provides a two-step process to get a fixed
map image. © 2010 NAVTEQ. All rights reserved. ©2010 Yahoo! Inc.
YAHOO! and the YAHOO! logo are registered trademarks of Yahoo! Inc.

Now, with the tools we have already been using in previous chapters, getting and displaying such an image becomes not too complicated. The logic that would get the URL
for the map including the American Museum of Natural History (AMNH) would be
along the lines of the following; let's assume this code will go in a Presenter, and that the
corresponding View will have a method enabling the Presenter to set the map's URL.

```
final String YAHOOID = "...yourKeyGoesHere...";
final double AMNHlat = 40.780411;
final double AMNHlon = -73.974037;


xhrProxy.getFromUrl("http://local.yahooapis.com",
    "MapsService/V1/mapImage", "appid=" + YAHOOID + "&latitude="
        + AMNHlat + "&longitude=" + AMNHlon,
    new AsyncCallback<String>() {

        @Override
        public void onFailure(final Throwable caught) {
            environment.showAlert("Couldn't connect to Yahoo Maps");
        }
```

```
@Override
public void onSuccess(final String result) {
  final Document xmlDoc = XMLParser.parse(result);
  final Element root = xmlDoc.getDocumentElement();
  XMLParser.removeWhitespace(xmlDoc);
  final String actualUrl = root.getFirstChild()
      .getNodeValue();

  // set the View's map image URL to actualUrl
  }
});
```

We use the same `xhrProxy` object as earlier (see Chapter 7). Note that the parsed XML object consists only of the root element, with a text node, so we can get the URL by just doing `root.getFirstChild().getNodeValue()`; much easier than in other examples we've already seen! In the `onSuccess(...)` method, you would finish by using the obtained `actualUrl` value, setting the view's image URL to it.

Check the documentation, for there are many more options than the few we used here; for example, instead of using latitude and longitude, you can specify a location by combining several of street, city, state, ZIP, or a free text location description (such as "Albany, NY"). You can also get either a PNG or GIF file, define the map's dimensions, and the zoom level (from 1, meaning street level, to 12, meaning country level).

Note that if all you care for is an image, this sample code shows a simple way of getting it, by building on our previous work. Getting a map requires more work than getting a chart from the Google Chart API (where, as we saw, providing the URL is enough to get the image) but it isn't such a complex method either.

Summary

We have seen how to interact with several popular APIs, in some cases by using just Java code, and in others by mixing in JSNI. GWT applications (or, more generally, Ajax applications) usually mash up information from several places, or use interesting APIs and widgets to provide a nicer experience to the user, and this chapter has shown several ways to do that.

10

Working with Servers

All Internet applications have security concerns, and your GWT application won't be able to elude them. In this chapter we consider important security terms and methods, and then go on to applying them for safe (or, more precisely, *safer*) communications with your server.

The Challenges to Meet

We cannot study possible solutions to security problems without having an understanding of the situations we'll face, so let's start by considering what are our objectives (or what do we mean by security), which tools we may apply, and how to use them with GWT.

This chapter will differ a bit from the rest of the chapters in the book, inasmuch we'll be showing code fragments, which implement the described ideas, rather than whole applications; fortunately, applying the methods shown isn't that hard!

Before Going Any Further

Lest you end with wrong hopes, let's start with a dire warning: Unless you use secure (meaning, SSL communications: `https://` instead of `http://`) there is no way to completely defend your application against a wise hacker with appropriate tools.[1]

In usual "cryptospeak," we talk of two people, Alice and Bob, trying to communicate with each other, possibly over unsafe or unsecure channels of communication. Also, we usually consider the possible existence of several unsavory characters that might want to interfere, such as Eve (an eavesdropper, who wants to see what information is sent back and forth) or Mallory (a more malicious person, who goes beyond mere curiosity, and may even add, modify, or delete packets and programs, or redirect your communications to other servers).

When you use `https://` you can be certain you are connecting to the server you want, and due to the encryption of the point-to-point "tunnel" between your machine

---

1. This solution also has some other problems. For example, code loaded via https:// isn't cached, so end-user performance won't be as good when he comes back to your application.

and the server, nobody can "listen" to the communications between your application and your services. If you don't use this protocol, a hacker might look at the packets that flow between client and server, inspect them, and even modify them at will. He might even modify the JavaScript code you download to your machine, so it will do whatever he wants, unknown to you!

We are going to discuss several ideas that can help against lesser adversaries (for example, the usage of cryptography so Eve cannot read the communications) but remember: Unless you go for full security with SSL, you cannot rest assured that your application won't be hijacked, or your data modified, and that a determined Mallory won't be able to harm you.

Security

Usually, "security" is recognized as equal to the acronym AAA, which stands for Authentication, Authorization, and Accounting, with the following meanings:

- **Authentication:** The system should recognize a valid user.
- **Authorization:** The system should enable specific actions only to certain users.
- **Accounting:** The system should provide a log of used resources, performed tasks, and so on.

Some other meanings are usually added, such as

- **Availability:** Systems should be ready for use, and perform correctly and acceptably.
- **Confidentiality:** Data should be available only to the people who should access it.
- **Integrity:** Data is changed only in allowed ways by allowed people.
- **Non Repudiation:** Users shouldn't perform an action and later deny having performed it.

For the purposes of this chapter, we'll be mainly dealing with Authentication (so only a given set of users will be able to use the application), Confidentiality (so Eve, our eavesdropper, cannot get to the data), and Integrity (so Mallory cannot change, inject, or delete any kind of data updates). Also, when data is signed (and because the signature depends among other things on your password, nobody else could fake it) we are providing a basic Non Repudiation scheme, but that's beyond our intent.

As to Authorization, there are many ways of doing this. Notice, however, that you do have to worry about server-side authorization; never assume that client-side checks are valid, and always consider that the user may be executing tampered-with code (or might have done some tampering himself!) so whichever checks or tests you need to do, must absolutely be done on the server. Finally, there are many Accounting solutions (also a server-side problem), and Availability actually hasn't much to do with GWT.[2]

2. See http://code.google.com/webtoolkit/articles/security_for_gwt_applications.html for a more general description of security problems and solutions.

Ajax Problems

Although "classic" web applications usually remember the state of the application at the server side, Ajax (and thus, GWT) applications tend to do that on the client, to better take advantage of JavaScript code. However, this might tempt a developer to implement security controls at the client side, which is totally insecure. An attacker could modify the code running on his PC while testing for exploitable vulnerabilities, and your server would be receiving data from a tainted source. So, it's worth repeating: *Security controls must be totally implemented, or at least rechecked, on the server.*

As a consequence, never assume that any data or commands received server-side are valid. You should certainly run checks and do validations at the client to provide a more fluid experience to the end user (and in fact we saw such a pattern, PreValidation, in Chapter 6, "Communicating with Your Server") but that won't enable you to skip any controls at the server.[3]

Cryptography

Cryptography has several uses, and we will apply both *encryption* and *hashing*. The first term means transforming a plain text into an unreadable crypto text that can be transformed back into the original only by using an appropriate key, and thus provides for security against Eve, whom we met earlier in this chapter. The second term, *hashing*, refers to a way of producing a fixed-size digest from a given text, in such a way that any changes to the text imply changes in the digest. If you are given a text and a digest, if they do not match, you can be sure there's been some tampering with the data, whereas if there's a match, it's highly likely the text hasn't been modified.[4]

Before we go any further, don't become tempted with the idea of producing your own super-duper-ultra-highly obfuscated cryptographic method; published standard methods (such as AES, RSA, and many more; just google for "Cryptography," and you'll get plenty of references) have withstood analysis, checks, verifications, and attacks, and it's unlikely any method thrown together in a short while can endure the same kind of tests.

Also, do not ever rely on "Security through Obscurity," assuming that the would-be attackers won't guess what you did. In particular, never assume that GWT's code obfuscation will be enough to protect your code; a determined programmer will be able to deduce your algorithms and methods, and you'll be left wide open to all kinds of attacks.

---

3. Note that this doesn't imply coding everything twice; you can easily share tests between client- and server-side code, because everything is written in Java.

4. The standard reference for Cryptography is Bruce Schneier's "Applied Cryptography"; check it at www.schneier.com/book-applied.html, but also read his "Practical Cryptography" (check www.schneier.com/book-practical.html) for real-life practical considerations before you plunge forward applying methods right and left.

Hashing

This said and done, let's start with hashing, because we have already seen the MD5 method in Chapter 8, "Mixing in JavaScript." In that case, our implementation used JSNI; now we need a Java version for the server-side services, and we are going with the JCA (Java Cryptography Architecture)[5] so we can simply write the following short method. Note that MD5 requires a zero-padded 32 bytes long hash, and some published versions of this code omit the final `while` in our code, thus possibly producing an (erroneous) shorter hash.

```
public static String md5(final String text) {
  String hashword = null;
  try {
    final MessageDigest md5 = MessageDigest.getInstance("MD5");
    md5.update(text.getBytes());
    final BigInteger hash = new BigInteger(1, md5.digest());
    hashword = hash.toString(16);
  } catch (final NoSuchAlgorithmException nsae) {
  }

  while (hashword.length() < 32) {
    hashword = "0" + hashword;
  }
  return hashword;
}
```

The preceding code is somewhat cavalier about errors; should a `NoSuchAlgorithm-Exception` be thrown, `hashword` would be null, and the reference to `hashword .length()` would then throw a `NullPointerException`; not very clear, and not very good programming style either!

Let's set up a Security package, with all the methods we'll need; in fact, we'll have different implementations of this package, for client- and server-side coding, but with the same methods. This can be considered an application of the *Façade* design pattern; even if the implementations are different (as in MD5), having the same methods makes for easier coding (only one API to learn) and for testing (the same tests we use for client-side coding can be used server-side.)

Encrypting

Back to cryptography, there are many usable methods, and we are going to use a simple —and fast—one, called RC4 (or also ARCFOUR), which is a symmetric (meaning the same key is used for coding and decoding) algorithm. RC4 is quite efficient and is applied for SSL (secure communications) and WEP. Using RC4 in server-side code is easy, but for client-side coding there isn't such a standard implementation as JCA's.

---

5. Read more on JCA at http://java.sun.com/javase/6/docs/technotes/guides/security/crypto/ CryptoSpec.html.

```
package com.fkereki.mvpproject.client;

import com.google.gwt.user.client.Random;

  private final byte sbox[] = new byte[256];
  private int i;
  private int j;

  // Set up the internal parameters (sbox, i, j) so we can
  // start decoding right away

  public void setUp(final String key) {
    int k;
    byte x;

    for (i = 0; i < 256; i++) {
      sbox[i] = (byte) i;
    }

    final int kl = key.length();
    for (i = 0, j = 0, k = 0; i < 256; i++) {
      j = j + sbox[i] + key.charAt(k) & 0xff;
      k = (k + 1) % kl;

      x = sbox[i];
      sbox[i] = sbox[j];
      sbox[j] = x;
    }

    // Set things up to start coding/decoding

    i = 0;
    j = 0;
  }


  // Assuming everything was set up earlier, encode plaintext. This can
  // be done in stream fashion; sequential calls to this routine will be
  // the same as a single call with a longer parameter. In other words,
  // as Benny Hill had it in a comedy sequence,
  // codeDecode("THE")+codeDecode("RAPIST") equals codeDecode("THERAPIST")

  public String codeDecode(final String plaintext) {
    byte x;
    String r = "";
    final int pl = plaintext.length();
    for (int k = 0; k < pl; k++) {
      i = i + 1 & 0xff;
```

```
    j = j + sbox[i] & 0xff;

    x = sbox[i];
    sbox[i] = sbox[j];
    sbox[j] = x;

    r+= (char)(plaintext.charAt(k) ^ sbox[sbox[i]+sbox[j] &0xff] &0xff);
  }
  return r;
}

// A simple utility method to simplify setting up the key and
// using it for encryption in a single step

public String codeDecode(final String key, final String plaintext) {
  setUp(key);
  return codeDecode(plaintext);
}
}
```

In this case, the code can be used both client- and server-side. Just for variety, let's then reuse it; we have already used JSNI (with MD5) and JCA (again with MD5), so now we'll opt for sharing the same code. Note that the same `codeDecode(...)` method is used for both encoding and decoding.

To always transmit ASCII legible characters (that will make debugging easier!) let's add a pair of utility methods to our Security package. The first, `byteStringToHexString(...)` will convert a String formed by any bytes, to a Hex equivalent; for example, `AtoZ\n` would become `41746f5a0a`, which contains only digits and letters. To revert the effects of this, let's also have `hexStringToByteString(...)`. The source code can be used both client- and server-side, so that means less coding.

```
public class Security {
  public static String byteStringToHexString(final String s) {
    String r = "";
    for (int i = 0; i < s.length(); i++) {
      r += byteToHexChars(s.charAt(i));
    }
    return r;
  }

  // Convert a number (0..255) into its two-character equivalent.
  // For example, 15 returns "0F" and 100 returns "64".
  public static String byteToHexChars(final int i) {
    final String s = "0" + Integer.toHexString(i);
    return s.substring(s.length() - 2);
  }
```

```
public static String hexStringToByteString(final String s) {
  String r = "";
  for (int i = 0; i < s.length(); i += 2) {
    r += (char) Integer.parseInt(s.substring(i, i + 2), 16);
  }
  return r;
}
```

Finally, on occasion we shall need to produce a *nonce*, a cryptographic term that stands for "number used once," but which can actually be any kind of random or time-dependent string. For server-side coding, we can just use code from the Apache Commons Lang component.[6]

```
public static String randomCharString() {
  return RandomStringUtils.randomAlphabetic(32);
}
```

On the other hand, we'll have to whip up our own implementation for client-side coding, because there's no GWT version of `RandomStringUtils`. In any case, it's easy to come up with something like the following.

```
public static String randomCharString() {
  String r = "";
  for (int i = 0; i < 32; i++) {
    r += (char) ('A' + Random.nextInt(26));
  }
  return r;
}
```

We are done; let's now start applying these methods for our GWT security problems.

Stateless Versus Stateful Servers

With usual web systems, all the application "state" is kept at the server, whereas the client is used just to display data and to capture events, which are forwarded to the server. Whenever the server receives an event, it does whatever process is necessary and sends a new page to the client, so the user can see an updated display with the effects of his operation. See Figure 10.1.

More modern (i.e., Ajax) systems turn this scheme upside down. By taking advantage of local JavaScript processing, most events are managed client-side, and RPC is used to send queries or new data to the server. The server by itself is just a service provider; whenever it receives a request from the client, it updates the system database and sends back any results, which will be displayed by the client side logic. See Figure 10.2.

---

6. See http://commons.apache.org/lang/.

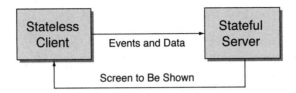

Figure 10.1 In classic web systems, all application state resides at the server, whereas the client is just used for displaying data.

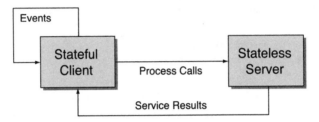

Figure 10.2 Modern web systems take advantage of JavaScript and Ajax calls to bring processing closer to the user.

It can be argued that moving state away from the server helps provide more scalable systems. With fully stateless servers, should you find a bottleneck in server-side processing, you could easily add more servers. With this, clients could connect to any available server, because all the required data would be provided by the client; the server wouldn't have to "remember" anything.

Because of this, we shall be opting for stateless (or, as-little-state-as-possible) server-side coding. This automatically implies that the client-side code will have to identify itself before asking for any processing. The server-side code will have first to validate whether the user is a valid one, and authorize to perform whichever process he might ask, and if everything is OK then proceed with the request and send back the produced results.

To enhance security, both sides (client and server) will have to share a "secret"; that is, information known only to both of them. A client-side easy secret is the user password; however, we cannot just send it over the web connection, for that would be quite risky. We shall recur to creating a special "session key" that will be used for identification and also for encryption and hashing; we shall see this next.

Remembering the secret for each client-side user can be done either with a database or by using HTML sessions. We'll use the first solution (so our servers won't be 100% state free) but that's the only state data that will be kept at the server.

Common Operations

In this section let's consider common operations (such as logging in or changing your password) that require extra care to avoid security risks.

Logging In

We'll start with a typical "what's wrong with this picture?" puzzle and consider the following code, taken from the Login Presenter we saw back in Chapter 4, "Working with Browsers." Remember the somewhat meaningless `getSomething(...)` call? Let's now figure out what it should do. (We should point out that we still haven't said what the servlet should return, but that's not the problem here.[7])

```
loginDisplay.setLoginCallback(new SimpleCallback<Object>() {
  @Override
  public void goBack(final Object result) {
    final String name = LoginFormPresenter.this.getDisplay()
      .getName();
    final String pass = LoginFormPresenter.this.getDisplay()
      .getPassword();

    loginService.getSomething(name, pass,
      new AsyncCallback<String>() {
        ...
      });
  }
});
```

The real problem is that the password is sent "in the clear" to the server. If Eve (our eavesdropping intruder) were to use a sniffer and check all packets sent from your client to the server, she would immediately get a nice user/password pair, which would enable her to fully impersonate a valid user!

It's time for some cryptography, but some methods just won't do. For example, sending a hash of the password instead of the actual password wouldn't work either; Eve (with the aid of Mallory, perhaps) could do a fake login and send the username plus the key hash, and she'd also be in. Sending an encoded password, but using always a fixed key for encoding, would present the same problem. The solution is simple: We will generate a nonce and send

- Username
- Nonce
- Hash of the user password concatenated to the nonce

---

7. For another take on secure logins, see http://code.google.com/p/google-web-toolkit-incubator/wiki/LoginSecurityFAQ.

Unless an intruder knows your password, he cannot produce the correct hash, so this is a safer method. (And, in any case, we shall be adding more protection to our communications, by using signatures.) The code for this would be simple; we'll reuse the MD5 logic we saw back in Chapter 8.[8]

```
loginDisplay.setLoginCallback(new SimpleCallback<Object>() {
  @Override
  public void goBack(final Object result) {
    LoginFormPresenter.this.getDisplay().enableLoginButton(false);

    final String name = LoginFormPresenter.this.getDisplay().getName();
    final String pass = LoginFormPresenter.this.getDisplay()
        .getPassword();
    final String nonce = Security.randomCharString();
    final String hashPassword = Security.md5(nonce + pass);

    loginService.getSessionKey(name, nonce, hashPassword,
        new AsyncCallback<SessionKeyServiceReturnDto>() {
          @Override
          public void onFailure(final Throwable caught) {
            LoginFormPresenter.this.getEnvironment().showAlert(
                "Failed login");
            LoginFormPresenter.this.getDisplay().enableLoginButton(
                true);
            loginSuccessCallback.onFailure(new Throwable());
          }

          @Override
          public void onSuccess(
              final SessionKeyServiceReturnDto result) {

            final String calculatedHash = Security.md5(nonce
                + result.encryptedSessionKey);
            if (result.hash.equals(calculatedHash)) {
              final Security secure = new Security();
              final String sessionKey = secure
                .codeDecode(
                    pass + nonce,
                    Security.hexStringToByteString(
                        result.encryptedSessionKey));
```

8. It has been said that MD5 isn't a good hashing method any longer, and that you should replace it with SHA-1 or better. It can be argued that for these kinds of values, MD5 could be appropriate, but in any case we are more interested in the general logic than on the specific hash function to apply. I went with MD5 because we had already used it earlier in the book, and because its known problems (such as producing two different strings that hash to the same value) do not necessarily apply in this context.

```
            loginSuccessCallback.goBack(new UserPassKeyDto(name,
                pass, sessionKey));
        } else {
            LoginFormPresenter.this.getEnvironment().showAlert(
                "Wrong data - problem in communication!");
            LoginFormPresenter.this.getDisplay()
                .enableLoginButton(true);
            loginSuccessCallback.onFailure(new Throwable());
        }
    }
});
    }
});
```

The preceding code modifies the "Login" button callback in our Login Form. Because we are just trying to log in (this is our first attempt at communicating with the server) there's no shared secret (session key) yet. We shall call the `getSessionKey(...)` method (`getSessionKey(...)` is a better name than `getSomething(...)`, isn't it?) with the user name, a nonce, and a hash of the password concatenated with the nonce. If the server accepts this login (we shall be seeing the server side code in a moment) it will return an encrypted version of the session key, plus a hash code. We use a DTO for this; remember to have it implement `IsSerializable`, and add an empty constructor as we saw in Chapter 6.

```
package com.fkereki.mvpproject.client.dtos;

public class SessionKeyServiceReturnDto
    extends GenericServiceReturnDto {

  public String encryptedSessionKey;

  public SessionKeyServiceReturnDto() {

  }
}
```

The base `GenericServiceReturnDto` class will be used for all data exchanges that require security checking. Notice that we have one only attribute (hash); other attributes will have to be added depending on what your service must return. Also note that none of the secret parameters (user password, session key, and even the nonce) are stored within the DTO; sending them over the wire would be a really dumb move!

```
package com.fkereki.mvpproject.client.dtos;

import com.google.gwt.user.client.rpc.IsSerializable;

public abstract class GenericServiceReturnDto
    implements IsSerializable {
```

```
/*
 * Each extended subclass will add some data. The "hash" field must be
 * calculated using the (non-included) nonce, the other data, and the
 * (non-included) sessionkey.
 */
public String hash;

public GenericServiceReturnDto() {
}
}
```

The client, on receiving the DTO shown here, will have to validate whether the hash coincides with the data, and if so, will decrypt the session key, which was encrypted using the user password plus a nonce. The rationale for using the user password for this encryption is that nobody will be able to decrypt the session key unless he knows the user password. And, the reason for using an extra nonce is that the same key should never be used twice, to avoid some possible attacks.

The required server-side coding is as follows.

```
@Override
public SessionKeyServiceReturnDto getSessionKey(
    final String name,
    final String nonce,
    final String passHash)
    throws FailedLoginException {

final String password = ...get the password for "name" from the db...;

// check the received data by means of the hash
final String calculatedHash = Security.md5(nonce + password);

// if there's a match, create a sessionKey and send it back
if (passHash.equals(calculatedHash)) {
  final String sessionKey = Security.randomCharString()
     .toLowerCase();

  // store the session key from the session
  // (alternative: store the key at the DB)
  final HttpServletRequest request = getThreadLocalRequest();
  final HttpSession session = request.getSession();
  session.setAttribute(SESSION_KEY_ID, sessionKey);

  final Security secure = new Security();
  final String coded = secure.codeDecode(password + nonce,
     sessionKey);
  final String hexCoded = Security.byteStringToHexString(coded);
```

```
final SessionKeyServiceReturnDto sk = new
    SessionKeyServiceReturnDto();

sk.encryptedSessionKey = hexCoded;
sk.hash = Security.md5(nonce + hexCoded);

    return sk;
} else {
    throw new FailedLoginException();
}
}
```

The server starts by calculating the hash it should have received; if there were some meddling with the data or the hash, there won't be a match, and the login attempt will be rejected. On the other hand, if there is a match, the server can be fairly confident that the user at the other end is the correct one; nobody else could have calculated the provided hash, which depended on the password. (And, nice point, nobody can determine the password from the hash; that's a key characteristic of hashes.) After this, the server can just generate a random session key, encrypt it (with the user password concatenated with the received nonce), and send it together with a hash, so the client can recheck the validity of the transmission.

Even if Mallory faked the first call to the server, he wouldn't still have the password (unless he actually "0wn3d" your client machine, and then he could obviously do anything he desired!) and he needs the said password for other steps, as we'll see next. Also, the server could keep a list of client-used nonces and refuse to accept a login with a repeated value, which would deny Mallory's replay attempt.

(In this database, passwords are stored "in the clear," but we could easily plug that potential security hole. We could hash the password before storing it in the users table, and then the user, instead of hashing the nonce plus his password, would hash the nonce plus the hash of his password, and the checking procedure at the server would be similarly changed.)

As a final question, where should the server store the session key it just generated? A logical possibility would be using a server-side session, and write code such as[9]

```
final HttpServletRequest request = getThreadLocalRequest();
final HttpSession session = request.getSession();
session.setAttribute("sessionkey", generatedSessionKey);
```

Retrieving the session key at a later time would merely involve

```
final HttpServletRequest request = getThreadLocalRequest();
final HttpSession session = request.getSession();
return (String) session.getAttribute("sessionkey");
```

Notice that you can use a server-side session to store as many key/value pairs as you want, but we use it just for the session key. The simplest way out, as we mentioned earlier,

---

9. Note that this is pure Java code and actually has nothing to do with GWT.

is using the database itself, and storing the session key along with the user data. (Another, better, possibility would involve using a separate table including a timestamp, the username, the nonce sent by the user, and the session key created by the server. This table would also do as a log for login attempts.) Logic for this is straightforward, so let's move on to more complicated operations.

Changing Your Password

The preceding login code is particular, insofar that the session key cannot be used—mainly because it hasn't been determined yet! Let's now consider other processes, requiring the client to send sensitive data to the server, such as a new password.[10]

Let's first consider our "Change Password" form. The view (done with UIBinder) is simple. See Figure 10.3.

```
<?xml version="1.0" encoding="UTF-8"?>
<!DOCTYPE u:UiBinder SYSTEM "http://dl.google.com/gwt/DTD/xhtml.ent">
<u:UiBinder xmlns:u='urn:ui:com.google.gwt.uibinder'
            xmlns:g='urn:import:com.google.gwt.user.client.ui'
            xmlns:h='urn:import:com.fkereki.mvpproject.client'
            >
  <g:HTMLPanel>
    <h1>ChangePasswordView</h1>
    <table>
      <tr>
        <td><g:Label text="User Name:"/></td>
        <td><g:TextBox u:field='nameTextBox' enabled='false'/></td>
      </tr>
      <tr>
        <td><g:Label text="New Password:"/></td>
        <td><g:PasswordTextBox u:field='passwordTextBox1'/></td>
      </tr>
      <tr>
        <td><g:Label text="Reenter New Password:"/></td>
        <td><g:PasswordTextBox u:field='passwordTextBox2'/></td>
      </tr>
      <tr>
        <td></td>
        <td><g:Button u:field='changePasswordButton' text='Change Password'/></td>
      </tr>
    </table>
  </g:HTMLPanel>
</u:UiBinder>
```

10. It should be repeated here, that it's not likely that you will require such levels of secrecy for all operations; however, if you do, the methods shown here will be adequate. (And if you did require such privacy, you should rather use SSL, encrypt all transmissions in the safest possible way, and forget your problems.)

Figure 10.3 A simple password change form requires hashes and encryption to safely send the new password from the client to the server.

The Display interface is similar to the Login interface and has a setter for the name field, a couple of getters for the password fields, a method for enabling or disabling the Change Password button, a callback for handling the blur events on both password fields, and a callback for the click event of the button.

The corresponding View code is simple, so let's move to the Presenter. We don't want the user to attempt changing his password, unless he has entered it twice, and both data entries match. We can use a common blur handler for both password fields.

```
package com.fkereki.mvpproject.client.changePassword;

// ...imports...

public class ChangePasswordFormPresenter
    extends Presenter<ChangePasswordFormDisplay> {
  public static String PLACE = "change";

  LoginServiceAsync loginService;

  SimpleCallback<String> loginSuccessCallback;

  public ChangePasswordFormPresenter(
      final String params,
      final ChangePasswordFormDisplay loginDisplay,
      final Environment environment) {

    super(params, loginDisplay, environment);
    loginService = getEnvironment().getModel().getRemoteLoginService();

    final SimpleCallback<Object> commonBlurHandler =
      new SimpleCallback<Object>() {
      @Override
      public void goBack(final Object result) {
        final String pass1 = ChangePasswordFormPresenter.this
            .getDisplay().getPassword1();
```

```
          final String pass2 = ChangePasswordFormPresenter.this
             .getDisplay().getPassword2();
          final boolean canLogin = !pass1.isEmpty() & pass1.equals(pass2);
          ChangePasswordFormPresenter.this.getDisplay()
             .enableChangePasswordButton(canLogin);
      }
   };
   loginDisplay.setPasswordBlurCallback(commonBlurHandler);
   commonBlurHandler.goBack(null);
```

Initializing the form is quite straightforward. Notice we require some new methods in the Environment object: We'll store in it the current user (whose name we show in a read-only field), the current password (which the user entered in the login form), and the current session key (which was obtained when the user logged in.)

```
   final String currentUser = environment.getCurrentUserName();
   final String currentKey = environment.getCurrentSessionKey();
   final String currentPass = environment.getCurrentUserPassword();


   loginDisplay.setName(currentUser);
```

The only part missing from the code is the click handler for the Change Login button. We get the new password from the form, generate a nonce, and use it plus the user (current) password and the session key to encrypt the new password. Adding a hash (to avoid data tampering), we call the `changePassword(...)` method. If the password change is successful, we have to change the password in the environment; otherwise, the server (which already has the new password) wouldn't decrypt future encrypted data.

```
   loginDisplay
       .setChangePasswordCallback(new SimpleCallback<Object>() {
        @Override
        public void goBack(final Object result) {
          ChangePasswordFormPresenter.this.getDisplay()
             .enableChangePasswordButton(false);

          final String pass1 = ChangePasswordFormPresenter.this
             .getDisplay().getPassword1();

          final Security sc = new Security();
          final String nonce = Security.randomCharString();

          final String encryptedPass1 = sc.codeDecode(nonce
             + currentPass + currentKey, pass1);

          final String visibleEncryptedPass1 = Security
             .byteStringToHexString(encryptedPass1);
```

```
final String hashPassword = Security.md5(nonce
    + visibleEncryptedPass1
    + environment.getCurrentSessionKey());

loginService.changePassword(currentUser,
    visibleEncryptedPass1, nonce, hashPassword,
    new AsyncCallback<Void>() {
      @Override
      public void onFailure(final Throwable caught) {
        ChangePasswordFormPresenter.this.getEnvironment()
            .showAlert("Failed change");

        ChangePasswordFormPresenter.this.getDisplay()
            .enableChangePasswordButton(true);
      }

      public void onSuccess(final Void result) {
        ChangePasswordFormPresenter.this.getEnvironment()
            .showAlert("Password was changed");

        ChangePasswordFormPresenter.this.getEnvironment()
            .setCurrentUserPassword(pass1);

        ChangePasswordFormPresenter.this.getDisplay()
            .enableChangePasswordButton(true);
      }
    });
  }
});
  }
}
```

The scheme showed in this case can be used for any kind of data exchange. For example, if we had a service that sent back sensitive data, it would encrypt it (using the user password, the session key, and a nonce), and add a hash. The client would then have to recalculate the hash, and if it matched, then it would decrypt the data and use it.

Summary

All Internet applications can be vulnerable to malicious third parties, and thus you'll have to take security in consideration whenever you program with GWT. (Also, read the reference mentioned in footnote 2 on security; there are many ways to take in a user.) Fortunately, the required steps are simple and easy to apply. On the other hand, it's a bit sad to notice that unless you go with the https:// solution, anything you plan or do might be eventually subverted; for example, the user could be tricked into connecting to a malicious server!

11

Moving Around Files

Sending files to a server, or receiving a file from a server, is a common requirement, and GWT allows you to do so, but you'll have to use tools we haven't yet seen. In this chapter we'll study these matters, see how to provide feedback to the user as the process runs, and even get to use different ways of communicating with the server, complementing the methods we already studied.

Uploading Files

Given the browser restrictions on client-side file handling (meaning, basically you cannot do anything at all with files!) uploading any files to a server requires more "classical" web programming, like submitting forms to send the data; we won't be able to apply any of GWT or Ajax techniques to work otherwise.

We'll start with a simple file upload form, then consider the server-side servlet that will receive and process it, and finally move on to study how to give feedback to the user while this whole job is being done.

An Upload Form

Let's work with an as-easy-as-possible upload form, with absolutely no frills. (See Figure 11.1.) I named the form `FileUpload`, so the UiBinder code is `FileUploadView.ui.xml`.

We could have several file upload fields, if we wanted to send up many files at the same time, just as with any web page.[1] (And to prepare for this, the server-side code will include a loop, so it could receive any number of files; see next.)

---

1. With the upcoming HTML 5 new features, you could allow for drag-and-drop selection of files, and apply JSNI to do some JavaScript local processing, but you cannot depend on that right now because it's not widely implemented. To learn more about this, see the latest draft at http://dev.w3.org/html5/spec/Overview.html for more data on the `<input type="file">` new element and on drag-and-drop methods.

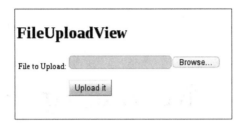

Figure 11.1 A no-frills file upload form. We could as easily upload several files at the same time.

The interesting point is that the only way to submit files to a server is through a form, and thus we'll have to enclose the `FileUpload` widgets within a `FormPanel`. Another important point is that you must give each `FileUpload` widget a name; otherwise, you won't be able to process those files server-side.[2]

```xml
<?xml version="1.0" encoding="UTF-8"?>
<!DOCTYPE ui:UiBinder SYSTEM "http://dl.google.com/gwt/DTD/xhtml.ent">
<u:UiBinder xmlns:u='urn:ui:com.google.gwt.uibinder'
            xmlns:g='urn:import:com.google.gwt.user.client.ui'
            xmlns:h='urn:import:com.fkereki.mvpproject.client'
            >
  <g:FormPanel u:field="uploadForm">
    <g:HTMLPanel>
      <h1>FileUploadView</h1>
      <table>
        <tr>
          <td>
            <g:Label text='File to Upload:' />
          </td>
          <td>
            <g:FileUpload u:field="fileToUpload" name="uploadedfile" />
          </td>
        </tr>
        <tr>
          <td></td>
          <td>
            <g:Button u:field="uploadButton" text='Upload it' />
          </td>
        </tr>
      </table>
    </g:HTMLPanel>
  </g:FormPanel>
</u:UiBinder>
```

2. Forgetting this is easy and will lead to producing a zero-length list in the file processing servlet, when you do `upload.parseRequest(request)`... guess how I know?

You will also have to set three **FormPanel** parameters (or your upload will fail) and I opted to do this in the View code, though it could be argued that setting them from the Presenter would be better because it would allow applying JUnit testing as in Chapter 13, "Testing Your GWT Application":

- Set the form's Action to the path for your file processing servlet.
- Set the encoding to Multipart.
- Set the method to POST; you cannot send files otherwise.

This form's Display interface will provide a getter for the filename (so we can check whether to submit the form), a callback to handle the click the Upload File button, a callback to process (and possibly cancel, if some condition isn't satisfied) the Submit event that will be fired by the button, another callback to handle the Submit Complete event (which is fired when the submission is done), and a method to actually submit the form.

```
package com.fkereki.mvpproject.client.fileUpload;

import com.fkereki.mvpproject.client.Display;
import com.fkereki.mvpproject.client.SimpleCallback;
import com.google.gwt.user.client.ui.FormPanel;

public interface FileUploadDisplay
    extends Display {

  String getFileToUploadName();

  void setSubmitCallback(SimpleCallback<FormPanel.SubmitEvent> scb);

  void setSubmitCompleteCallback(
      SimpleCallback<FormPanel.SubmitCompleteEvent> scb);

  void setUploadClickCallback(SimpleCallback<Object> scb);

  void submitForm();
}
```

The corresponding view is in **FileUploadView.java**:

```
package com.fkereki.mvpproject.client.fileUpload;

// ...imports...

public class FileUploadView
    extends View
    implements FileUploadDisplay {
```

```java
@UiTemplate("FileUploadView.ui.xml")
interface Binder
    extends UiBinder<FormPanel, FileUploadView> {
}

@UiField FormPanel uploadForm;
@UiField FileUpload fileToUpload;
@UiField Button uploadButton;

SimpleCallback<SubmitCompleteEvent> onSubmitCompleteCallback;
SimpleCallback<SubmitEvent> onSubmitCallback;
SimpleCallback<Object> onUploadClickCallback;

private static final Binder binder = GWT.create(Binder.class);

public FileUploadView() {
  final FormPanel dlp = binder.createAndBindUi(this);
  initWidget(dlp);

  uploadForm.setAction("/mvpproject/fileprocess");
  uploadForm.setEncoding(FormPanel.ENCODING_MULTIPART);
  uploadForm.setMethod(FormPanel.METHOD_POST);
}

@Override
public String getFileToUploadName() {
  return fileToUpload.getFilename();
}

@UiHandler("uploadForm")
public void onSubmitComplete(final SubmitCompleteEvent event) {
  onSubmitCompleteCallback.goBack(event);
}

@UiHandler("uploadForm")
public void onSubmitForm(final SubmitEvent event) {
  onSubmitCallback.goBack(event);
}

@Override
public void setSubmitCallback(final SimpleCallback<SubmitEvent> scb) {
  onSubmitCallback = scb;
}

@Override
public void setSubmitCompleteCallback(
    final SimpleCallback<SubmitCompleteEvent> scb) {
```

```
    onSubmitCompleteCallback = scb;
  }

  @Override
  public void setUploadClickCallback(final SimpleCallback<Object> scb) {
    onUploadClickCallback = scb;
  }

  @Override
  public void submitForm() {
    uploadForm.submit();
  }

  @UiHandler("uploadButton")
  void uiOnUploadClick(final ClickEvent event) {
    onUploadClickCallback.goBack(null);
  }
}
```

Let's now go to the Presenter code, which actually does the work.

```
package com.fkereki.mvpproject.client.fileUpload;

// ...imports...

public class FileUploadPresenter
    extends Presenter<FileUploadDisplay> {
  public static String PLACE = "upload";

  public FileUploadPresenter(
      final String params, final FileUploadDisplay fileUploadDisplay,
      final Environment environment) {

    super(params, fileUploadDisplay, environment);

    fileUploadDisplay
      .setUploadClickCallback(new SimpleCallback<Object>() {

        @Override
        public void goBack(final Object result) {
          if (getDisplay().getFileToUploadName().isEmpty()) {
            getEnvironment().showAlert(
                "You must pick a file to upload.");
          } else {
            getDisplay().submitForm();
          }
        }
      });
```

```
fileUploadDisplay
    .setSubmitCallback(new SimpleCallback<SubmitEvent>() {

        @Override
        public void goBack(final SubmitEvent result) {
            // you could check for special conditions
            // if the event cannot proceed, then do:

            // result.cancel();

            // As an alternative, these checks could go
            // in the button click method.
        }
    });

    fileUploadDisplay
        .setSubmitCompleteCallback(new
          SimpleCallback<SubmitCompleteEvent>() {

            @Override
            public void goBack(final SubmitCompleteEvent result) {
                // do something when the file process is done
            }
        });
    }
}
```

We aren't including any feedback here while the file is being uploaded; we'll get to that later, and it will involve adding some code to the Submit event handler.

A File Processing Servlet

Now, let's turn to the server-side file processing servlet. (Of course, this code could also be a PHP script, for example, because we are dealing with standard HTML form submission; let's keep to Java to go along with GWT's orientation.) Get and add the Apache Commons `commons-fileupload` and `commons-io` jars to your application, and then you'll be able to easily get and process the uploaded files.[3]

You'll also have to modify the `web.xml` file for your project, to include the information on your servlet. In a rapt of inspiration, I named the servlet `fileProcess`, and thus I added the following lines to the said XML file:

```
<servlet>
    <servlet-name>fileProcess</servlet-name>
    <servlet-class>com.fkereki.mvpproject.server.FileProcess</servlet-class>
</servlet>
```

3. See http://commons.apache.org/ for this.

```
<servlet-mapping>
    <servlet-name>fileProcess</servlet-name>
    <url-pattern>/mvpproject/fileprocess</url-pattern>
</servlet-mapping>
```

Our servlet code is as follows. For now, we'll just care about the doPost(...) method; we'll later use the doGet(...) method to provide feedback to the user.

```
package com.fkereki.mvpproject.server;

// ...imports...

public class FileProcess
    extends HttpServlet {

  @Override
  protected void doPost(
      final HttpServletRequest request,
      final HttpServletResponse response)
      throws ServletException,
        IOException {

    final FileItemFactory factory = new DiskFileItemFactory();
    final ServletFileUpload upload = new ServletFileUpload(factory);

    try {
      final List<FileItem> itemsList = upload.parseRequest(request);
      for (final FileItem item : itemsList) {
        if (!item.isFormField()) {
          final InputStream input = item.getInputStream();
          final FileOutputStream output = new FileOutputStream(
              "/tmp/dummy");

          final byte[] buf = new byte[1024];
          int len;
          while ((len = input.read(buf)) > 0) {
            output.write(buf, 0, len);
          }
          output.close();
          input.close();
        }
      }
    } catch (final FileUploadException e) {
      throw new ServletException(e.getMessage());
    }
  }
}
```

We are just receiving the file and saving it to /tmp/dummy—probably not quite useful in a true-life system! The code uses the Commons API; there's nothing GWT-specific in there. This kind of programming is actually quite classic non-Ajax servlet code; for example, you could have also provided parameters to the servlet by using hidden fields or form fields, if desired. You could even have access to the session and apply all the usual web processing methods you knew before using GWT.[4]

As to the code itself, note there's a loop that processes all form items, discarding mere fields, to process all the uploaded files. (This would allow you to process several files at once.) You can use the getSize(...) method to get the file total size (and possibly discard too large files), and getName(...) to get the original file name, among other methods.

Providing Feedback to the User

If you are uploading large files, or if their process can take some time, it would be better from the user's point of view if you were to provide him with some kind of feedback. However, when most (if not all) servlet containers receive a request, they store it internally in their entirety before invoking your code; thus, you won't be able to provide any useful feedback to the user: It would just jump from 0% to 100% with no in-between moments.[5]

Given this restriction, let's at least work on providing some feedback during the actual file process. We could store information on the advance of our code during the processing loop (the session would be a simple solution) and send it back to the user with the doGet(...) method. We'd change the main file writing part of our code like this:

```
final byte[] buf = new byte[1024];
final long size= item.getSize();
int len;
int processed = 0;
while ((len = input.read(buf)) > 0) {
  output.write(buf, 0, len);
  processed += len;
  request.getSession().setAttribute("processed",
      processed + "/" + size);
}
```

We use processed to keep count of how many bytes have been read, and we store the total length of the file in size. Finally, we set up a string such as 1024/22960 (meaning, 1024 bytes read out of 22960) and store it in the processed attribute of the session, so the user can query it. Of course, we could easily ramp the level of the feedback information and provide more data, but this will do for an example. We must also

4. In fact, we will be doing this in order to provide feedback.

5. Check the ProgressListener interface for more on this; you can find usage documentation at http://commons.apache.org/fileupload/using.html.

write the `doGet(...)` method, which shall just access the session and return the progress information just stored.

```
@Override
protected void doGet(
    final HttpServletRequest request,
    final HttpServletResponse response)
    throws ServletException,
      IOException {

  response.getOutputStream().print(
      (String) request.getSession().getAttribute("processed"));
}
```

How should the client get and use this information? Let's first consider how to call the servlet and do a GET and then move on to other considerations. As we are not working with RPC, we'll have to use the `RequestBuilder` class to do direct Ajax calls. Possibly in the Submit event code at the Presenter, you would add something such as

```
final RequestBuilder builder = new RequestBuilder(
    RequestBuilder.GET, "/mvpproject/fileprocess");

builder.setCallback(new RequestCallback() {

  @Override
  public void onError(
      final Request request,
      final Throwable exception) {

    // warn on error...
  }

  @Override
  public void onResponseReceived(
      final Request request,
      final Response response) {

    // use response.getText() to get the service returned value
    // and then use it to provide feedback to the user
  }
});
```

Given this, you would do a GET by simply writing

```
try {
  builder.send();
} catch (final RequestException e) {
  // warn the user if the call failed
}
```

How and when would you use this code? I'll leave the details up to you, but the simplest way would be creating a `Timer` (at the Submit event) and scheduling it to run, say, every 2 seconds (2000 milliseconds).[6] At the Submit Complete event, you would `cancel(...)` the timer. The Timer's `run(...)` method would do the GET with the preceding code and use the returned value to update some label or process bar on the form.

Downloading Files

After all the work we did to upload files, the counterpart, downloading a file, is an anticlimax; the code is quite simple, and the only possible complications could lay server-side, to produce the required result.[7]

We shall see two ways of getting a file; either by posting the form (as with the file upload example) or by using a more classic link.

A File Download Form

As earlier, let's go with a simple form. (See Figure 11.2.) We'll provide our (simple, make believe) servlet with three parameters; it would be just as easy to include more, or to add hidden fields to the form.

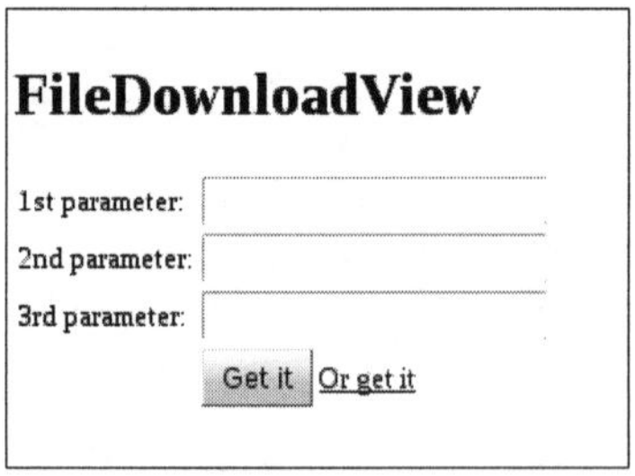

FileDownloadView

1st parameter: _____
2nd parameter: _____
3rd parameter: _____
Get it | Or get it

Figure 11.2 This form will invoke a servlet, which will produce a text file;
real-life applications would get a PDF, a spreadsheet, or the like.

The `FileDownloadView.ui.xml` file is similar to the one we used for uploads; let's just see part of it, including the third parameter, the button, and the link.

---

6. Even better, schedule it to run once, and when it runs, have the timer schedule itself again in 2 more seconds, so you'll avoid creating a bunch of pending requests should there be some kind of slowdown.

7. For example, if you want to produce reports in several different formats, you might want to consider JasperReports (see http://jasperforge.org/) or Pentaho (at www.pentaho.com/), but note that using these tools won't have anything to do with GWT; it's a pure server-side coding effort.

```
<tr>
  <td>
    <g:Label text='3rd parameter:' />
  </td>
  <td>
    <g:TextBox u:field="parameter3" name="parameter3" />
  </td>
</tr>
<tr>
  <td></td>
  <td>
    <g:Button u:field="downloadButton" text='Get it' />
    <g:Anchor u:field="downloadLink" text='Or get it' />
  </td>
</tr>
```

The Display interface will provide getters for the three parameters, methods for setting the callbacks for the button and link click handlers, a setter for the destination (href) of the link, and methods for setting the Submit event handler and for actually submitting the form.

```
package com.fkereki.mvpproject.client.fileDownload;

// ...imports...

public interface FileDownloadDisplay
    extends Display {

  String getParameter1();
  String getParameter2();
  String getParameter3();

  void setDownloadClickCallback(SimpleCallback<Object> scb);

  void setDownloadLinkClickCallback(SimpleCallback<Object> scb);

  void setLinkHref(String href);

  void setSubmitCallback(SimpleCallback<FormPanel.SubmitEvent> scb);

  void submitForm();
}
```

The View code (`FormDownloadView.java`) is simple, and we can skip it. Let's just consider the constructor, which sets the form parameters. Note that this time, we use a GET method instead of a POST, and we invoke a different servlet, `fileproduce`, which we'll be seeing next:

```
public FileDownloadView() {
  final FormPanel dlp = binder.createAndBindUi(this);
  initWidget(dlp);

  downloadForm.setAction("/mvpproject/fileproduce");
  downloadForm.setMethod(FormPanel.METHOD_GET);
}
```

To finish, let's consider the Presenter code. Setting callbacks is similar to the upload code; the only interesting part is the link click callback. In it, we have to get the form parameters, encode them appropriately so they can be sent to the server, and dynamically create the destination for the link.

```
package com.fkereki.mvpproject.client.fileDownload;

// ...imports...

public class FileDownloadPresenter
    extends Presenter<FileDownloadDisplay> {
  public static String PLACE = "download";

  public FileDownloadPresenter(
      final String params,
      final FileDownloadDisplay fileDownloadDisplay,
      final Environment environment) {

    super(params, fileDownloadDisplay, environment);

    fileDownloadDisplay
        .setDownloadLinkClickCallback(new SimpleCallback<Object>() {

          @Override
          public void goBack(final Object result) {
            final String param1 = URL.encode(getDisplay()
                .getParameter1());
            final String param2 = URL.encode(getDisplay()
                .getParameter2());
            final String param3 = URL.encode(getDisplay()
                .getParameter3());

            getDisplay()
                .setLinkHref(
                    "/mvpproject/fileproduce?parameter1=" + param1
                        + "&parameter2=" + param2 + "&parameter3="
                        + param3);
          }
        });
```

```
        // set the other callbacks
    }
}
```

With this code, either by clicking the button (which will do a classic form submission) or on the link, the user will invoke a remote servlet, which will generate a file.

A Sample File Producing Servlet

In a real-life application, you would be invoking a servlet that would most likely produce some kind of report or spreadsheet, but for this example let's go for something rather more trivial and just send back a text file including the received form parameters as its contents.

This is straightforward server-side Java programming; the only points you must remember is setting its content type and disposition.[8] The rest of the `doGet(...)` method is simple; we just output the received parameters to the request `OutputStream` and close it.

```
package com.fkereki.mvpproject.server;

// ...imports...

public class FileProduce
    extends HttpServlet {

  @Override
  protected void doGet(
      final HttpServletRequest request,
      final HttpServletResponse response)
      throws ServletException,
        IOException {

    // media type (or, more modern, content type)
    //
    // text/plain application/msexcel

    final ServletOutputStream output = response.getOutputStream();
    response.setContentType("text/plain");
    response.setHeader("Content-Disposition",
        "attachment; filename=somefile.txt");
    output.println("Received parameters:");
    output.println(request.getParameter("parameter1"));
    output.println(request.getParameter("parameter2"));
    output.println(request.getParameter("parameter3"));
    output.close();
  }
```

8. See RFC 2046 at www.ietf.org/rfc/rfc2046.txt for more on this.

For generality, we can let the servlet answer to POST methods in the same way than to GETs.

```
@Override
protected void doPost(
    final HttpServletRequest request,
    final HttpServletResponse response)
    throws ServletException,
      IOException {

  doGet(request, response);
}
}
```

Now, running the form and clicking the button or link will call the servlet, produce a `somefile.txt` text file, and give you the option to open or download it. See Figure 11.3.

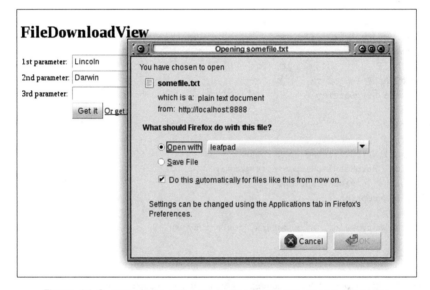

Figure 11.3 Clicking on either the button or the link does a call to the servlet that produces a simple text file as output.

It's most important to note that in this example, we have been mostly using time-tried web programming techniques and not much GWT-original code. (If, for example, you wanted to display the contents in a separate window, you would just add `target="_blank"` to the link's destination; pure classic HTML!) Also, you need not invoke a servlet; it would have been equally simple (just a matter of changing destinations) to interact with PHP or Python scripts; the client-side code doesn't care, and the server-side programming need not know that it is talking to a GWT client.

Summary

In this chapter we studied both how to upload and download files from a server. These processes required using forms and Ajax, so we got to complement the server-communication techniques seen in previous chapters. We also interacted with common servlets, proving GWT can coexist in a more classic Java-oriented server-side architecture.

Internationalization and Localization

Developing applications that can be used in different countries, with different languages, requires applying specific techniques, but GWT simplifies dealing with internationalization (i18n) and localization (l10n) matters. In this chapter we'll examine the relevant tools, and also how to apply them to UiBinder designed forms.

If you are developing an application that will potentially be used worldwide, instead of being restricted to an Intranet, you will have to take into account multiculture and multilanguage aspects, so your software is still usable.

Since having several separate versions for each required language (or, worse, for each locale; remember American English isn't the same as British English, for example) can soon become quite unwieldy, you'll want to use methods that allow developing and maintaining just one code base.

GWT provides i18n support with its `Constants` and `ConstantsWithLookup` interfaces allowing you to work with string literals in different languages, and with the `Messages` interface, which adds singular/plural considerations, as well as to work with UiBinder.

Finally, in terms of l10n, GWT lets you deal with different currency or date formats, allowing you to more completely adapt your application to specific groups of users, and that will be the last theme in this chapter.[1]

Internationalization (i18n)

Let's start by considering how to provide appropriate texts for users in different countries. We'll first give a quick overview to Java's standard resource bundles, and then move

---

1. By the way, if you don't know where i18n and l10n come from, i18n refers to the fact that there are 18 letters between the initial *i* and the final *n* in "internationalization," and likewise for l10n and "localization."

to the `ConstantsWithLookup` and `Messages` GWT interfaces, which will let us use those bundles in a quite efficient way.[2]

All i18n methods require the same libraries, so no matter which one you decide to use, you'll have to add the line `<inherits name="com.google.gwt.i18n.I18N"/>` to your `gwt.xml` configuration file.

Resource Bundles

In standard Java programming, internationalization is usually done by means of resource bundles: `.properties` files with locale-specific data. Although this data might be anything (numbers, dates, whatever) most usually we'll just deal with strings. Each string is identified by a "key," which must remain constant across different resource bundles. Basically, in your code you will (mostly indirectly, sometimes directly) refer to this key so your program will be locale-independent, inasmuch as what string will be shown shall depend on which locale resource bundle you use.

GWT supports generic resource bundles (strings that will be shown if no other more specific locale is chosen), language resource bundles (for example, English or Spanish versions of your strings), and even country-specific resource bundles (such as British English, or Mexican Spanish). You should have a generic bundle file, plus one or more language bundles, plus possibly some country specific bundles. All keys should appear in the generic bundle file. If a certain key appears in several bundles, country strings have priority over language strings, and the latter have priority over the generic ones. For example, suppose we are given these bundles (whose names shall be explained presently).

Transport.properties	Transport_en_GB.properties	Transport_es.properties
flight=airplane	flight=aeroplane	flight=avión
vehicle=car		vehicle=automóvil
underground=subway	underground=tube	underground=subterráneo
sea=ship		sea=barco

In this case, a British user who wanted to use the underground would get a message about the *tube*; Spanish users would get references to the *subterráneo*; everybody else (including other non-British English speakers) would get the *subway* standard reference. (GWT considers English as the standard language.) Note that you don't have to repeat keys in all files; all British users would get *car* for vehicle, for example, because they don't have a specific string value for that key.

You should always provide a basic, standard reference (though you don't need to use a resource bundle for this, because you can do with annotations; see the following) plus

2. If you also have to support RTL (right-to-left) languages such as Arabic or Hebrew, using the techniques in this chapter won't be enough, for you'll also have to change the visual theme; see http://code.google.com/webtoolkit/doc/latest/DevGuideUiCss.html#themes for more on this.

resource bundles for each language you plan to support, eventually even going as far as to provide files for specific countries.

Resource bundles must be named with the interface name (see next) optionally followed by an underscore and a lowercase two-character language specification, and possibly another underscore and an uppercase two-character country code.[3]

A final reminder: Resource bundles must be written in UTF-8 if you require foreign letters or accents. Be sure to include the line

```
<meta http-equiv="content-type" content="text/html; charset=UTF-8">
```

in your `.html` file, and also to configure your resource bundle editor to use this character set.[4]

Using Constants

The `Constants` and `ConstantsWithLookup` interfaces bind, at compile time, the provided resource bundles with your provided code, to produce locale-specific versions of the code. (We'll be seeing the specific code generator mechanism in a short while.) Whenever the user browses to your application, the loader code determines your browser type (as we mentioned in Chapter 4) and your locale, and then loads the compiled version of your system that matches those two parameters. (As we saw earlier, this is as efficient as it gets, for you download only code that suits your situation perfectly, instead of a large suit-everybody version, with support for all browsers and all languages, even if you don't require them.) We will first use the simpler `Constants` interface, and then see why and when we would prefer the other one.[5]

For a simple example, say you wanted to greet a user. You could have a generic message and a more specific one, along the (not very original!) lines of

```
genericHello=Hello there!
specificQuery=How are you today?
```

For British speakers you might change the first line to `Hullo there!` (do note the spelling of the first word) whereas for Spanish users you would provide something with plenty of special characters, along the lines of

```
genericHello=¡Hola!
specificQuery=¿Cómo estás hoy?
```

3. The language codes are taken from the ISO 639-1 standard (see www.infoterm.info/standardization/iso_639_1_2002.php) whereas country codes (which we already used in Chapter 6) are from ISO 3166-1.

4. For example, in Eclipse you should go to Edit, Set Encoding and pick UTF-8; otherwise, your file won't match expectations and results will look weird, to say the least.

5. Note that constants need not be Strings (for you can also provide Boolean, float, integer, and so on constants) but as far as internationalization goes, this is by far the most common case.

To use these files, let's extend the `ConstantsWithLookup` interface. (We could as easily have extended `Constants`, but as I want to later show dynamic string lookup, I went with `ConstantsWithLookup`.) If we opted to call it `Greet`, the `Greet.java` file could be

```
package com.kereki.testi18n.client;

import com.google.gwt.i18n.client.ConstantsWithLookup;

public interface Greet
    extends ConstantsWithLookup {

  String genericHello();

  String specificQuery();
}
```

Because your interface was named `Greet`, your resource bundles should be named `Greet.properties`, `Greet_en_GB.properties` and `Greet_es.properties` with the contents previously listed; the first would be the generic catch-all, whereas the second would be applied to British users, and the third one for Spanish ones. These bundles must be at the same directory where the source file for your interface resides.

Finally, you must let the compiler know about which languages will be supported, by editing the `gwt.xml` file and adding

```
<extend-property name="locale" values="en" />
<extend-property name="locale" values="en_GB" />
<extend-property name="locale" values="es" />
```

We can test this internationalization by writing just a pair of lines.

```
final Greet greet = GWT.create(Greet.class);
Window.alert(greet.genericHello() + " " + greet.specificQuery());
```

The first line uses deferred binding to create the appropriate class (depending on the locale of the browser) and the second line displays the required texts.[6]

If you run this code without any further ado, you'll get a `Hello there! How are you?` message. If you want to test the other locales, you can either add a line such as

```
<meta name="gwt:property" content="locale=es">
```

to your `.html` file (which will set the default language for your application to Spanish) or add the parameter `locale=es` to the URL in your browser; any of these solutions would produce a `¡Hola! ¿Cómo estás?` alternative message. The first solution is best for large scale testing, whereas the URL one (which takes precedence over the other solution) is preferred for quick tests.

---

6. For extra efficiency, you should create the `greet` object just once, and then always refer to it; the Singleton design pattern comes to mind, and is a perfect fit for this situation.

Some Annotations Tricks

You need not have a generic resource bundle, for you can use annotations to provide default values—and that's better from the point of view of documentation and usage. For example, we might want to have a string describing the kind of users to whom the specific locale version applies. By adding

```
@DefaultStringValue("English speakers")
String kindOfUsers();
```

to the `Greet.java` file, you would be defining a new text, which by default would be `English speakers`, without the need for a `Greet.properties` entry. (You would, however, have to add `kindOfUsers=British speakers` to the `Greet_en_GB.properties` file and `kindOfSpeakers=Hablantes de Español` to `Greet_es.properties`.) Having the default value in the same interface file helps programmers understand the meaning of the strings, without resorting to checking other bundles for tips or hints.

For extra clarity, your keys need not match the methods names. By using the `@Key(...)` annotation, you can specify which is the actual key used in the `properties` file. You could write

```
@Key("day.morning")
@DefaultStringValue("morning")
String morning();

@Key("day.afternoon")
@DefaultStringValue("afternoon")
String afternoon();
```

This would require adding, in the Spanish resource bundle, lines such as

```
day.morning=Mañana
day.afternoon=Tarde
```

(Note that we used `@DefaultStringValue(...)` to avoid having a generic `.properties` file, as shown earlier.) The keys could be structured so as to allow a more logical ordering, whereas the interface methods can keep using simple names.

Translating Error Codes

The preceding code works just fine for texts that are created client-side, but what would you do with, say, an error message that was originated server-side? An i18n aware application that will display error messages only in English isn't a very good international application! There are two solutions to this problem; you could also use standard internationalization techniques server-side, or you could send error codes instead of error texts, and have the codes translated into texts client-side. The first technique has nothing to do with GWT, so we'll skip it, but let's consider now the `ConstantsWithLookup` interface to solve the problem client-side.

This interface adds methods that let you seek the value corresponding to any given key. With the `Constants` interface, the mapping between keys and methods is static; `ConstantsWithLookup` adds a dynamic way of getting the required values.

For a simple example, if we change our `Greet` class to extend `ConstantsWithLookup` (and change nothing else) then the two following lines would produce the same result:

```
Window.alert(greet.kindOfUsers());
Window.alert(greet.getString("kindOfUsers"));
```

The standard pattern of usage would be

- Define constants to represent status or error messages.

- Modify your remote servlets, so they will return those constants instead of strings.

- Use (at the client side) a `ConstantsWithLookup` class to translate the constants into localized strings.

You might be tempted to always use this kind of interface, but to understand when to use each of the two constants interfaces, let's examine the produced JavaScript code. The compiler makes short work of straight calls; for example, by compiling the application with *Pretty* style (see Chapter 15, "Deploying Your Application") we can see that the en_GB version of the code produces our greeting message to British users by simply doing:

```
$wnd.alert('Hullo there! How are you today?');
```

On the other hand, to fulfill dynamic requests, code such as the following will be generated, including all possible strings. (This is logical because there's no way to tell which key you might ask for.) Even though the code is efficient and uses a cache to avoid re-doing searches, it still must include every possible key in your GWT code.

```
function $getString(this$static, arg0){
  var target;
  target = dynamicCast($get_1(this$static.cache, arg0), 1);
  if (target != null) {
    return target;
  }
  if ($equals_1(arg0, 'specificQuery')) {
    $put(this$static.cache, 'specificQuery', 'How are you today?');
    return 'How are you today?';
  }
  if ($equals_1(arg0, 'genericHello')) {
    $put(this$static.cache, 'genericHello', 'Hullo there!');
    return 'Hullo there!';
  }
  if ($equals_1(arg0, 'kindOfUsers')) {
    $put(this$static.cache, 'kindOfUsers', 'British English Speakers');
    return 'British English Speakers';
  }
```

```
    throw $MissingResourceException(new MissingResourceException, "Cannot find
constant '" + arg0 + "'; expecting a method name");
    }
```

So, to get the smallest possible output code, you might consider using a `Constants` object for the strings you generate client-side, plus a `ConstantsWithLookup` object exclusively to deal with server-side codes.

Messages

So far, we have been considering static (i.e., unvarying) messages, most appropriate for captions, warnings, and the like, but applications also require dynamic, varying messages that are built up from fixed and changing elements, such as an *"Hasta la vista..."* message, to be completed appropriately, as in *"Hasta la vista, Baby."* (Of course, this need for variable messages also should take into account locales, so the message could be *"Auf wiedersehen..."* or *"Au revoir..."* for Germans or Frenchmen.) GWT supports these localized, variable texts by means of the `Messages` interface.

This interface is very much like the `Constants` and `ConstantsWithLookup` interfaces we saw earlier (you also invoke it in the same way, by using `GWT.create(...)`) and works by defining keys and strings, with the most important differences that the string values you provide can include special placeholders, and that the methods you write can accept arguments that will be substituted for the placeholders.

Let's create a simple `MyMessages` interface, which we can use to provide good-bye messages. The format for placeholders is the standard Java `MessageFormat` style: Parameters to be substituted start at 0, so the single parameter in our `sayGoodbye(...)` method will replace all `{0}` occurrences within the string.[7] Let's also produce message showing the year of birth and current age, just to show how to replace more parameters, and how to work with other data types.

```
package com.kereki.testi18n.client;

// ...imports...

@DefaultLocale("en")
public interface MyMessages
    extends Messages {

  @DefaultMessage("I was born in {0} so now I''m {1} years old.")
  String sayAge(int year, int age);

  @DefaultMessage("Good- bye, {0}")
  String sayGoodbye(String whom);
}
```

7. See http://java.sun.com/j2se/1.5.0/docs/api/java/text/MessageFormat.html for more on this.

We are following here the idea of including default values within the interface code to simplify future editing. (Pay particular attention to the doubled-up single quote in the `sayAge(...)` string.) For British users, we would have a `MyMessages_en_GB.proper-ties` file with, possibly, a line reading

```
sayGoodbye=Goodbye, {0}!
```

(note the lack of a hyphen in "Goodbye," and no alternative string for `sayAge(...)`) whereas Spanish users would require a `MyMessages_es.properties` resource file with

```
sayGoodbye=¡Hasta la vista, {0}!
sayAge=Tengo {1} años porque nací en {0}
```

(The only reason for showing the age first and the birth year second is to prove it can be done; you need not use the parameters in ascending order.)

Now, although `sayAge(2000,10)` produces a perfectly fine `I was born in 2000 so now I'm 10 years old`, a call such as `sayAge(2009,1)` produces a queer result: `...now I'm 1 years old`. However, the `Messages` interface provides a way around that. Let's see first how the code looks and then provide the explanations.

We'll write a new `sayAge2(...)` method fixing the plural problem. You must provide a generic plural case (`...I'm {1} years old`) and then add the special cases that, depending on the used language, may apply when the number is zero or one.[8]

```
@DefaultMessage("I was born in {0} so now I''m {1} years old.")
@PluralText({"one","I was born in {0} so now I''m just one year old." })
String sayAge2(int year, @PluralCount int age);
```

Note the `@PluralCount` annotation, which indicates which parameter is related to plurals; in this case, we want to treat the parameter indicated as {1} as the special one. In English, zero is treated as plural (`...I'm 0 years old`) so you just need a special case for one (`...I'm just one year old`—we need not actually show the 1!). The corresponding Spanish resource bundle would include

```
sayAge2=Tengo {1} años porque nací en {0}
sayAge2[one]=Tengo un año porque nací en {0}
```

You would provide similar rules for Italian, German, or Portuguese as spoken in Portugal. For Portuguese as spoken in Brazil (or for French) rules vary, because zero is considered singular.

```
sayAge2=Eu sou {1} anos de idade porque eu nasci em {0}
sayAge2[one]=Eu sou um ano de idade porque eu nasci em {0}
sayAge2[none]= Eu sou zero ano de idade porque eu nasci em {0}
```

You must apply the rules pertaining to the specific locale; you cannot, for example, provide a special "zero" case for English, because the standard rules say it's to be treated

---

8. For some languages, such as Arabic, there are special plural forms for number two and even for small numbers, but for most (if not all) western languages, the only special cases you'll have to consider are zero and one.

as a plural. If you want to check which rules apply for each language, there's no official source other than the actual GWT Java code; check it out[9] and then examine the `DefaultRule*java` files at the `trunk/user/src/com/google/gwt/i18n/client/impl/plurals/` directory.

UiBinder Internationalization

Let's end this chapter by considering how to translate complete pages. Of course, you could build screens up field by field and text by text, using the methods in previous sections to provide the required translations. You would probably be better off without using UiBinder, but you could make it work.

This solution, however, wouldn't solve all the possible i18n considerations: For example, whereas in western countries the family name follows the first name, in eastern countries (such as Japan, China, and Korea) it's the other way round: the family name comes first, and the first name follows. If you wanted to reorder two `TextBox`es representing the family and first names to comply with custom, you would have to add some extra coding.

GWT provides a `Messages`-based way to apply internationalization to UiBinder forms that, even though it isn't as polished as the rest of the tools, can be used with little effort.[10] Let's first examine a simple screen (see Figure 12.1) with some text intermingled with fields.

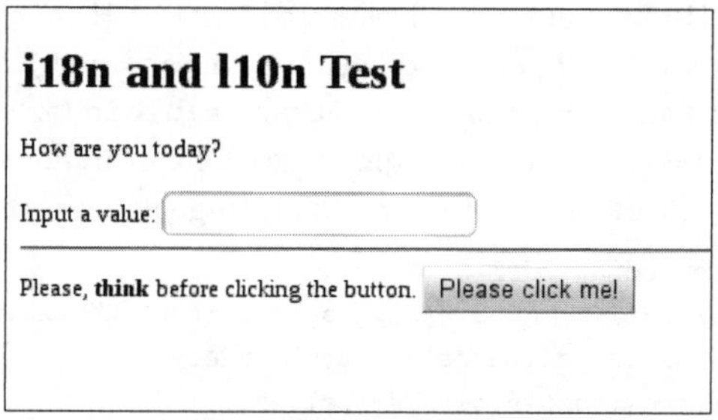

Figure 12.1   A nonsense form for UiBinder-based internationalization

Let's summarize the whole process in advance. To internationalize a UiBinder form, you will have to add several elements to the form XML code. These elements will identify the parts of the form that need translation and provide placeholders for fields and other nonvarying components. When you compile your project, a resource bundle will be generated for your form, with a line for every item that must be translated, in

9. See http://code.google.com/webtoolkit/makinggwtbetter.html#checkingout for instructions on this.

10. The fact that this solution is still lacking some polish can be verified by reading the discussion at the bottom of http://code.google.com/p/google-web-toolkit/wiki/UiBinderI18n and the follow-up thread at http://code.google.com/p/google-web-toolkit/issues/detail?id=4355.

`Messages` style. To finish the job, you will have to provide translations for each language you want to support; you will probably require a team of (human) translators for this task.[11] When the form is shown, UiBinder will use a hidden `Messages` interface to translate all onscreen terms.

Now, let's get to details. The standard `ui.xml` file for the form would have along the lines of

```
<?xml version="1.0" encoding="UTF-8"?>
<!DOCTYPE ui:UiBinder SYSTEM "http://dl.google.com/gwt/DTD/xhtml.ent">
<u:UiBinder xmlns:u='urn:ui:com.google.gwt.uibinder'
  xmlns:g='urn:import:com.google.gwt.user.client.ui'>
  <g:HTMLPanel>

    <div>How are you today?</div>
    <br />
    Input a value: <g:TextBox />
    <hr />
    Please, <b>think</b> before clicking the button.
    <g:Button u:field="aButton" title="Produce some kind of result">
        Please click me!
    </g:Button>
  </g:HTMLPanel>
</u:UiBinder>
```

To use UiBinder's i18n facilities, you have to add several elements to the preceding file, and the complete file (we'll get to explanations in a moment) should become as follows. First, you need to add some boilerplate at the `<u:uibinder>` element, so the necessary methods will be invoked and i18n binding will happen. The only attribute you might want to change (if English isn't your default language) is `defaultLocale`.

```
<?xml version="1.0" encoding="UTF-8"?>
<!DOCTYPE ui:UiBinder SYSTEM "http://dl.google.com/gwt/DTD/xhtml.ent">
<u:UiBinder xmlns:u='urn:ui:com.google.gwt.uibinder'
  xmlns:g='urn:import:com.google.gwt.user.client.ui'
  u:defaultLocale="en"
  u:generateFormat='com.google.gwt.i18n.rebind.format.PropertiesFormat'
  u:generateKeys="com.google.gwt.i18n.rebind.keygen.MD5KeyGenerator"
  u:generateLocales="default">
```

HTML elements need no special notation. General text, however, should be enclosed in a `<u:msg>` element so it will be recognized as something to be translated. The `key` attribute (equivalent to the `@Key(...)` annotation) will be used in the resource bundle to identify the enclosed string. You need not specify keys, but in that case GWT will generate them with a MD5 based method; personally, I prefer using my own, more understandable, keys, but to each his own!

---

11. Of course, Google Translate could (some day) be integrated into this task....

The `description` attribute appears as a comment in the file to help translators by giving some context. HTML elements within a text are recognized, as in `<b>think</b>`.

```
<g:HTMLPanel>

  <div>
    <u:msg key="example.salute" description="Greeting">
      How are you today?
    </u:msg>
  </div>

  <br />

  <u:msg>
    Input a value: <g:TextBox />
  </u:msg>

  <hr />

  <u:msg key="reconsideration" description="Urge to reconsider">
    Please, <b>think</b> before clicking the button.
  </u:msg>
```

You will usually also require translating other terms, such as tooltips or image descriptions. Each such attribute shall be enclosed in a `<u:attribute>` element, which must include the `name` of the attribute, an optional `description` as an aid to the translator, and an optional `key`. In case a word might have two or more meanings (the common example is `orange`, which might be a color or a fruit) you can also add a `meaning` attribute (such as `meaning="the fruit"`) so the translator can discern which translation to use.

```
    <g:Button u:field="aButton" title="Produce some kind of result">
      <u:attribute key="button.title"
        name="title" description="tooltip text for button" />
      <u:msg key="button.text" description='Button text'>
        Please click me!
      </u:msg>
    </g:Button>


  </g:HTMLPanel>
</u:UiBinder>
```

When you compile your code, you must include the `-soyc` parameter.[12] (An alternative is including the `-extra` parameter, and specify a directory for the output translation files.) After the code is compiled, a file will be created within the `extras` directory, with a name

12. We will be touching on the possible compile parameters in more detail in Chapter 15, when we deal with code splitting. For now, you'll just have to accept the need for them!

such as `com.kereki.testi18n.client.ExampleMyUiBinderImplGenMessages`
`.properties`—in my case, I was working with the `com.kereki.testi18n` package,
and the `Example.ui.xml` file was in the `client` subpackage. The contents of this file
will look like the following, though I reordered some lines for clarity:

```
# Generated from
  com.kereki.testi18n.client.ExampleMyUiBinderImplGenMessages
# for locale default

# Description: Greeting
example.salute=How are you today?

# 0=arg0 (Example: <span>), 1=arg1 (Example: </span>)
3251F2DD00D79AD3E05D89C06E60F1AA=Input a value\: {0}{1}

# Description: Urge to reconsider
reconsideration=Please, <b>think</b> before clicking the button.
# Description: Button text
button.text=Please click me\!

# Description: tooltip text for button
button.title=Produce some kind of result
```

Let's walk through this. For the first salute, a straight line (`example.salute=How`
`are you today?`) in the style of what we have already seen, was produced.

The line asking to input a value shows what happens if you don't enter a key; a MD5
based value (`3251F2DD00D79AD3E05D89C06E60F1AA`) was used instead. Also, notice that
placeholders were created for the `TextBox`; don't worry about the fact that there are two
placeholders for a single field—it's just the way internationalization sometime works
with UiBinder.

The `think` line shows that HTML elements were passed through, without change; a
translator would be able to keep them. And, finally, note that two lines were produced
for the text and tooltip of the button.

What do you do now? The generated file must be copied to the same directory
as the ui.xml file, and renamed—but the renaming rules are also somewhat
awkward; my `Example.ui.xml` file required a Spanish resource bundle named
`ExampleMyUiBinderImplGenMessages_es.properties` as follows:

```
# Generated from
  com.kereki.testi18n.client.ExampleMyUiBinderImplGenMessages
# for locale default

# 0=arg0 (Example: <span>), 1=arg1 (Example: </span>)
3251F2DD00D79AD3E05D89C06E60F1AA=Entre un valor\: {0}{1}

# Description: Button text
button.text=¡Por favor, oprímame\!
```

```
# Description: tooltip text for button
button.title=Genera algún tipo de resultado

# Description: Greeting
example.salute=¿Cómo está hoy?

# Description: Urge to reconsider
reconsideration=Por favor, <b>piense</b> antes de oprimir el botón.
```

Running the same application with `locale=es` added (see Figure 12.2) produced a wholly translated output… except for the `H1` title, which I forgot to include in the `ui.xml` file! I decided to let this error be, as a reminder of the possible problems you will likely find.

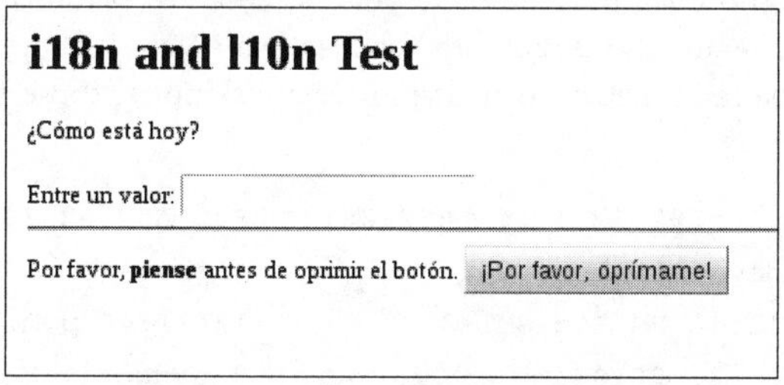

Figure 12.2 The same form, but translated automatically into Spanish.

As I said, UiBinder-based internationalization does work, but you'll have to agree that the work here isn't as straightforward as earlier. (The need for actually compiling the application with an extra parameter to boot, and the strange names for the resource bundles, come to mind.) Documentation isn't complete (and sometimes even wrong; I had to work out some of the previous details by perusing forum threads or by studying the GWT source code itself) and it's possible that there will be changes in the near future, so be careful when using this facility.[13]

Localization (l10n)

Localization is a concept akin to internationalization (but far easier to implement) that has to do with dates, time, and numbers representation, rather than with strings translation. After all the work required for full internationalization, the comparable localization tasks will seem like an anticlimax, for you can use it out-of-the-box without any specific adaptation.

---

13. The current version of the documentation is at http://code.google.com/webtoolkit/doc/latest/DevGuideUiBinderI18n.html; check it for extra use cases, or for changes in functionality.

Although you could roll out your own date and number formats (by using a `Constants` interface, for example) GWT provides specialized resource bundles for most locales, which take care of all needed conversions to and from dates and numbers. Roughly speaking, you could compare GWT's date and number formatting functionality to Java's own `java.text.SimpleDateFormat` and `java.text.DecimalFormat` packages.[14]

For example, if you want to get the current date in "short" format, you can simply write

```
String currentDate=
  DateTimeFormat.getShortDateFormat().format(new Date())
```

and the correct locale format would be applied. For example, in the US (`locale=en`) you would get something such as `4/2/10`, but with `locale=en_GB` then `02/04/2010` would be produced; notice that in European fashion, the day comes before the month.[15] The following table shows all possible predefined `Date` and `Time` formats for `locale=en` and `locale=es`. There are also `DateTime` formats, which are just the concatenation of the corresponding `Date` and `Time` formats, so we are skipping those for brevity.

toString	`Fri Apr 02 12:11:44 UYT 2010`	`Fri Apr 02 12:11:44 UYT 2010`
Full Date	`Friday, April 2, 2010`	`viernes 2 de abril de 2010`
Full Time	`12:11:44 PM Etc/GMT+3`	`12:11:44 p.m. Etc/GMT+3`
Long Date	`April 2, 2010`	`2 de abril de 2010`
Long Time	`12:11:44 PM UTC-3`	`12:11:44 UTC-3`
Medium Date	`Apr 2, 2010`	`02/04/2010`
Medium Time	`12:11:44 PM`	`12:11:44`
Short Date	`4/2/10`	`02/04/10`
Short Time	`12:11 PM`	`12:11`

By the way, the needed data was produced with this code.

```
final Date today = new Date();
GWT.log(today.toString());
GWT.log(DateTimeFormat.getFullDateFormat().format(today));
GWT.log(DateTimeFormat.getFullTimeFormat().format(today));
GWT.log(DateTimeFormat.getLongDateFormat().format(today));
GWT.log(DateTimeFormat.getLongTimeFormat().format(today));
GWT.log(DateTimeFormat.getMediumDateFormat().format(today));
```

14. If you want to learn about all formatting possibilities, check out http://google-web-toolkit .googlecode.com/svn/javadoc/2.0/com/google/gwt/i18n/client/DateTimeFormat.html and http://google-web-toolkit.googlecode.com/svn/javadoc/2.0/com/google/gwt/i18n/client/ NumberFormat.html.

15. If you want to see the specific rules applied for each locale, download the GWT source code, and see the files at `trunk/user/src/com/google/gwt/i18n/client/constants` directory.

```
GWT.log(DateTimeFormat.getMediumTimeFormat().format(today));
GWT.log(DateTimeFormat.getShortDateFormat().format(today));
GWT.log(DateTimeFormat.getShortTimeFormat().format(today));
```

If you need your own format (say you want to produce dates in the ISO 8601 standard format, such as 2010-04-02) you can use the getFormat(...) method and provide your own pattern string. The following code would produce the desired ISO format.

```
DateTimeFormat formatIso = DateTimeFormat.getFormat("yyyy-MM-dd");
String dateIso = formatIso.format(new Date());
```

There are many pattern codes, as in the following table. Note that they are practically the same as in Java[16]

- G provides the era, AD or BC.
- y provides the year; yyyy would be 2010, but yy would be just 10.
- M provides the month: MMMM would be the full name (April), MMM a shorter version (Apr), MM the left-padded with zeroes number (04), and M the number (4).
- d provides the day in the month.
- H provides the hour in 24-hours format (0–23), whereas k provides it in 1–24 format.
- h provides the hour in AM/PM format (1–12), whereas K provides it in 0–11 format.
- m provides the minute in the hour (0–59).
- s provides the second in the minute (0–59).
- S provides the milliseconds.
- E provides the day of the week, in text; EEEE would be the full name (Friday), and EEE a shorter version (Fri).
- a provides the AM/PM marker.
- a single quote is used to escape text, as in 'Date=', and if you want an actual quote in the text, you'll have to write it twice as in 'O''clock'.

For all numbers, if you specify the code twice, you'll get a left-padded with zeroes number: HH would produce 09, whereas H would just produce 9.

Finally, you can also use formats to parse strings into Date objects. For example, if we had the ISO format string 1809-02-12 (the birth date of Abraham Lincoln and Charles Darwin, which we saw some chapters ago, in Figure 8.1) and wanted to produce a Date object, we should write

```
DateTimeFormat formatIso = DateTimeFormat.getFormat("yyyy-MM-dd");
Date lincolnDarwin = formatIso.parse("1859-02-12");
```

16. See http://java.sun.com/docs/books/tutorial/i18n/format/simpleDateFormat.html for the possible codes. Java adds the D, F, W, and w codes (standing for the day in the year, the day in the week, the week in the year, and the week in the month) but lacks the z and v codes shown in the table.

You can also use the `parseStrict(...)` method, which is more careful; whereas a date such as February 30th would be accepted by `parse(...)` and turned into March 2nd, `parseStrict(...)` would throw `IllegalArgumentException` instead.

Similarly, `NumberFormat` provides currency, percent, integer, and float formats, according to locale rules; for example, a comma is used to separate thousands in the US (thus, `2,010`) but in Spanish a dot is substituted instead (so, `2.010`). The basic predefined formats, for `locale=en` and `locale=es`, are as follows.

Currency	$22,919.60	Arg$22.919,60
Decimal	22,919.6	22.919,6
Percent	2,291,960%	2.291.960%
Scientific	2E4	2E4

The code that produced this output was merely

```
double number = 22919.60;
GWT.log(NumberFormat.getDecimalFormat().format(number));
GWT.log(NumberFormat.getPercentFormat().format(number));
GWT.log(NumberFormat.getScientificFormat().format(number));
GWT.log(NumberFormat.getCurrencyFormat().format(number));
```

You can immediately see there's a problem with currencies; for example, `Arg$` isn't the currency symbol either for Spanish, nor for Argentine.[17] You could write `getScientificFormat("UYU")` to get the Uruguayan currency format,[18] but it returns `Ur$22.919,60`; once again, a wrong symbol.

You can also specify your own formats, by using the following codes to create a format string.

- 0 stands for any digit. # also stands for any digit, but if it represents a zero at the left of the number, a space is shown instead.[19]
- The dash (–) stands for the minus sign.
- The period stands for whatever character is used in your country for the fraction separator, and the comma stands for the thousands separator. For example, in Uruguay the period stands for a comma, while the comma stands for a period... rather confusing!

17. See www.xe.com/symbols.php for a list of currency symbols.

18. The used codes seem to be based on those of ISO 4217, which includes USD for the US Dollar, EUR for the Euro, and GBP for the British Pound, for example. However, there are many countries missing from the list used by GWT.

19. If you were to format James Bond's secret agent number with format "000", you'd correctly get "007", but if you used "###" as a format, you'd get "   7" instead, with two leading spaces.

- E (for "Exponent") is used to separate the mantissa from the exponent, in scientific notation.
- % is used to show that the number is to be formatted as a percentage, and thus multiplied by 100.
- A single quote is used to escape text, as with Dates.

For example, you could format a number to be displayed in 15 columns, with an optional trailing sign, with NumberFormat.getDecimalFormat("###,###,##0.00-"). Finally, you can also use the parse(...) method to transform a string into a number, like in

```
double number = NumberFormat.getDecimalFormat().parse("1234.56");
```

GWT will throw NumberFormatException if the number cannot be parsed.

Summary

Designing an application for international use requires more work and preparation than doing a simple single-locale one. However, GWT provides reasonably simple i18n and more straightforward (almost in the "no assembly required" category) l10n tools that let you get the job done with no great complexity.

13

Testing Your GWT Application

Testing, and in particular, fully automated testing, is an important part of the GWT development cycle. In this chapter we'll study ways of doing so in optimal ways, starting with unit tests and ending with integration and acceptance testing.

Why Testing?

The idea of testing software is fairly obvious,[1] but the GWT philosophy is based on testing everything automatically, without anybody's intervention, as an aid to bug prevention and detection at the earliest time.[2] The Google Testing Blog (at http://googletesting .blogspot.com/) goes as far as including the motto *"Debugging sucks; Testing Rocks"* at the top of the page. Another saying is "If it's not tested, it's broken"; untested code can (and must be assumed to) contain any number of bugs.

Automatic testing lies at the heart of techniques such as test-driven development (TDD) and methodologies like Scrum[3] and Extreme Programming (XP).[4] The main idea is to develop code, with a method based on repetitions of a short development cycle loop:

- First you write an (obviously failing) automated test case for a new functionality. This isn't a waste of time; if a test for a yet-unwritten function should pass, then something is obviously very wrong with your test...
- Then you write code that implements the said functionality and passes the test. It goes without saying that all previous tests should also pass; your code shouldn't break other code!

1. Though now and then everybody is tempted to skip testing, because "it's just so small a change, nothing could go wrong!"
2. If you examine GWT's own source code, you'll find lots and lots of the kind of tests we'll be developing in this chapter.
3. See www.scrumalliance.org/ for more on Scrum.
4. See www.extremeprogramming.org/ for a good introduction to XP.

- And finally, you refactor the code so that it meets acceptable standards. Getting the code to work, and then enhancing it (while using the recently written test to ensure as far as possible that the refactoring doesn't break anything) is easier than trying to get the code to work and be elegant at the same time.[5]

Advantages of Automatically Tested Code

Automated tests encourage better, simpler, code designs; help against common problems such as regressions (reintroducing an earlier bug while modifying some seemingly unrelated code); and inspire more confidence in the quality of the produced software, which can be shown to pass lots of tests, proving that at least it provides some desired level of functionality.

Developers with good TDD practice are more likely to focus on what's actually required (the YAGNI principle, standing for You Ain't Gonna Need It) and simplicity (think KISS, or Keep It Simple, Stupid) because they only develop what's actually needed to pass the tests, not worrying about unrequired functionality or unjustified enhancements. Also, they are more likely to detect bad designs, side effects, or obscure code, because all these conspire against automated testing.

Automated tests also serve, at a certain level, as documentation. Everybody knows that you can never have too many examples, and each test is a living example showing how to use a class, what kind of parameters to provide, and which results you should get.

We'll consider three types of testing for GWT programs:

- Unit Tests, which apply to specific classes or methods, testing them one at a time, independently of other classes and methods. These tests must be as fast as possible, so you won't balk at running them and won't require a browser.

- Integration Tests, which apply, for example, to specific forms or services and imply using a browser for the tests. These tests are slower, but test functionality closer to the user's requirements.

- Acceptance Tests, which are specifically focused on use cases and are oriented to verifying the functionality of the system as a whole. These tests are usually the slowest and largest, and require the most setup and preparation, because they try out the workings of the complete system.

We'll use common tools (such as JUnit or Selenium) for some of these tests and GWT specific extensions (GWTTestCase) for others.

And if a Bug Appears?

A basic theorem of Computing Theory states that testing can never prove the absence of errors but only their presence. Before going any further, let's consider a practical ques-

---

5. Martin Fowler's page on Refactoring at www.refactoring.com/ is a must-see.

tion: what would you do if a bug surfaces in your code? (Yes, even though you may test and test and test, bugs almost surely remain in your code.) No matter how tempted you may be, what you won't do is run away to patch your source code: There's a more important problem to fix: namely, that your test code isn't obviously good enough, for it let a bug go past!

The first step, after you understand how the error came to be, is to write a new test case that will simulate the situation that led to the error, and thus logically fail. Then, *and only then,* try to fix the code and run the test suite again; your recently added test should now pass, but more important, you now have better tests for the future. It is obvious that your original tests missed some conditions; your new ones at least take care of one problem, and that kind of bug won't reappear.

Unit Testing with JUnit

Many Java programmers already use JUnit for testing their code, but what's most interesting is the fact that you can also use it to test GWT code, despite its compilation into JavaScript. JUnit[6] is a member of the global xUnit family, whose members allow automatic testing for code written in languages as diverse as Smalltalk (SUnit), PHP (PHPUnit), HTTPUnit (web pages and services), and JSUnit (JavaScript). Its current version is 4.8.1, and you'll have to get the required `jar` file, as we mentioned in Chapter 2, "Getting Started with GWT 2."

With earlier versions of GWT, you had to create the appropriate project structure with the `jUnitCreator` command-line tool, but now the required directories and files are automatically created with the project.[7] The standard structure has a `test` directory at the same level as `src`. You can parallel the project structure from `src/.../client` into a `test/.../client` directory; having the test code and the tested code in the same package will help with visibility matters, but won't hamper creating the application, because by default only code in `src/client` gets compiled.

A Basic JUnit Example

So as to get in gear for more complicated testing, let's at first consider how to test the `KeyValueMap` class we used to store parameters for forms in Chapter 4, "Working with Browsers." (Don't fret if this example doesn't have anything to do directly with forms; we'll presently get to testing such code.) As that class is at `src/com/fkereki/mvpproject/client/KeyValueMap.java`, our test code will reside at `test/com/fkereki/mvpproject/client/KeyValueMapTest.java`; note the usual naming convention for our test class. For ease of understanding, let's review the original class code.

---

6. See http://junit.org/.

7. At least, when you use the Eclipse plugin. If you use `webAppCreator`, you'll have to pass the `-junit` parameter to it.

```java
package com.fkereki.mvpproject.client;

// ...imports...

public class KeyValueMap
    extends HashMap<String, String> {

  private static final long serialVersionUID = 5225712868559413562L;

  public KeyValueMap() {
    this("");
  }

  public KeyValueMap(final String params) {
    initializeWithString(params);
  }


  public final void initializeWithString(final String params) {
    clear();
    if ((params != null) && !params.isEmpty()) {
      String[] args = params.split("&");
      for (String element : args) {
        int equalIndex = element.indexOf("=");
        if (equalIndex == -1) {
          put(element, "");
        } else {
          put(element.substring(0, equalIndex), element
              .substring(equalIndex + 1));
        }
      }
    }
  }

  @Override
  public String toString() {
    String result = "";
    String separator = "";
    for (String key : keySet()) {
      result += separator + key + "=" + get(key);
      separator = "\n";
    }
    return result;
  }
}
```

To test this class, we might write code such as the following. All the `@Test` marked methods will be run, but the order cannot be defined. We could use the `setUp(...)` and `tearDown(...)` methods to prepare the environment for the whole set of tests, but we won't be needing them in this particular example.

```
package com.fkereki.mvpproject.client;

// ...imports...

public class KeyValueMapTest {

  @Before
  public void setUp()
      throws Exception {
  }

  @After
  public void tearDown()
      throws Exception {
  }
```

A first test would verify whether a `KeyValueMap`, initialized with an empty string, is empty.[8]

```
@Test
public void testKeyValueMap() {
  final KeyValueMap kvm0 = new KeyValueMap("");
  assertTrue(kvm0.isEmpty());
}
```

We could then move on to testing `KeyValueMap` objects, initialized with one or more *key=value* pairs, to check if they have the correct sizes and contents.[9]

```
@Test
public void testKeyValueMapString() {
  final KeyValueMap kvm1 = new KeyValueMap("lincoln=1865");
  assertEquals(1, kvm1.size());

  final KeyValueMap kvm2 = new KeyValueMap("lincoln=1865&darwin=1882");
  assertEquals(2, kvm2.size());
  assertTrue(kvm2.containsKey("lincoln"));
```

8. Some people prefer naming the test so it says what it will test (and possibly even what results it would expect) such as `testKeyValueMapWithEmptyString(...)` and `testKeyValueMapWithEmptyStringShouldReturnEmpty(...)`—I go for shorter names, but to each his own poison!

9. There are two Assert classes; see http://stackoverflow.com/questions/291003/differences-between-2-junit-assert-classes for more on picking one.

```
    assertTrue(kvm2.containsKey("darwin"));
    assertEquals("1865", kvm2.get("lincoln"));
    assertEquals("1882", kvm2.get("darwin"));
}
```

The `toString(...)` method also requires some tests. Note that we don't check the complete string, because we cannot be sure about in which order the keys will be returned. (And, in fact, we do not actually care about the order.) Be careful not to write "fragile" tests, which fail even when we haven't changed anything that should impact them.[10]

```
@Test
public void testToString() {
    final KeyValueMap kvm0 = new KeyValueMap("");
    assertEquals("", kvm0.toString());

    final KeyValueMap kvm1 = new KeyValueMap("lincoln=1865");
    assertEquals("lincoln=1865", kvm1.toString());

    final KeyValueMap kvm2 = new KeyValueMap(
        "lincoln=1865&darwin=1882&einstein=1955");
    final String kvmst2 = kvm2.toString();
    assertTrue(kvmst2.contains("lincoln=1865"));
    assertTrue(kvmst2.contains("darwin=1882"));
    assertTrue(kvmst2.contains("einstein=1955"));
    assertTrue(kvmst2.contains("\n"));
}
}
```

Running the code (with Eclipse, select the test directory, right-click it, and select Run As, and then JUnit Test) produces the much desired green bar that shows all tests ran as hoped. (See Figure 13.1.) If you had more tests in the directory, they would have been executed as well. You can create a suite of your own,[11] but the automatic way (running all `@Test` annotated methods) is easier.

If you changed, say, the first lines in `testKeyValueMapString` to read (note the wrong size check) as follows:

```
public void testKeyValueMapString() {
    final KeyValueMap kvm1 = new KeyValueMap("lincoln=1865");
    assertEquals(5, kvm1.size());
```

then the test run would have produced a different result, a red bar, and an explanation of the failed test, showing what was expected and what was actually seen. See Figure 13.2 for such a failure.

---

10. See http://xunitpatterns.com/Fragile%20Test.html for a discussion on this; in particular, the "Sensitive Equality" section directly applies to our example.

11. See http://junit.org/apidocs/junit/framework/TestSuite.html for an explanation of Test Suites.

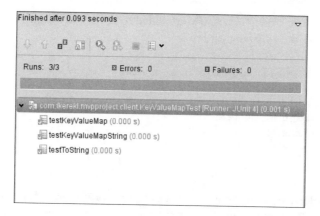

Figure 13.1 If all tests run as desired, you'll get a green bar, plus a report showing which tests were run, and some timing details.

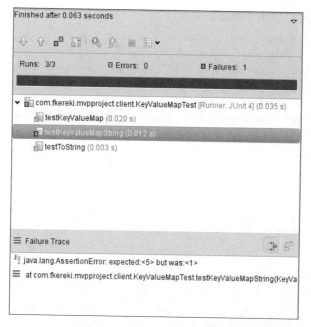

Figure 13.2 A wrong test produces a red bar instead and an explanation of the failed condition.

Other JUnit methods of interest (and the names are quite self-documented) include `assertArrayEquals(...)`, `assertNull(...)` and `assertNotNull(...)`, `assertSame(...)` and `assertNotSame(...)`, and `assertTrue(...)` and

`assertFalse(...)`, among others. If you wanted to test an exception, you could use
`fail(...)` as per the following pattern.[12]

```
Try {
  // do something that should raise an exception
  fail();
} catch (TheExpectedException e) {
  // OK, this should be the case
} catch (Exception e) {
  // oops, an unexpected exception
  fail();
}
```

If the code doesn't produce the expected exception, or if it produces an unexpected
one, the `fail(...)` calls will produce a red bar.

However, a question pops up: How thorough was our test? Let's get to this before
moving on to more complex cases.

Test Coverage with Emma

There are several measures of to which degree you have tested your code, and the most
basic one is called Statement Coverage, which answers the question "Has every sentence
in the program been executed at least once?" Statement coverage is presented as a percentage, from 0% (you haven't actually tested anything!) to 100% (all the parts in your
code have been exercised at least once.)[13]

For Eclipse GWT programming, you can use the EclEmma plugin, which produces a
visual map showing with colors what parts of your tested code were or weren't executed,
after any test run.[14]

Let's apply it to the test we just developed; was it complete, did we miss anything?
After installing the plugin, a new option appears in the menu. Select your test directory,
right-click it, and pick Coverage As, JUnit Test, and you'll get a report showing how
much of your code was run, and a view of the source code highlighting in green the
executed parts, and in the red the missed ones. See Figure 13.3. [15]

---

12. In JUnit 4 (but not with GWTTestCase) you could also write `@Test(expected=
TheExpectedException)` and do away with the `try...catch` block.

13. Though this is not a sufficient condition to ensure testing thoroughness, it should be clear that
if your tests haven't managed to execute a given sentence, that particular sentence could actually
be anything, and you wouldn't notice. Not having 100% coverage permits errors; however, don't read
this as "100% coverage guarantees no errors"!

14. See www.eclemma.org for more on this.

15. Note that depending on the current versions of the plugin, you might have to patch it according
to instructions on http://code.google.com/webtoolkit/doc/latest/DevGuideTestingCoverage.html.
This may change in the future, so check it out carefully before proceeding.

```
/**
 * Standard constructor; produces an empty KeyValueMap.
 */
public KeyValueMap() {
    this("");
}

/**
 * Create a KeyValueMap, and initialize it with the params string.
 *
 * @param params
 *            A string with URL-like parameters (see below)
 */
public KeyValueMap(final String params) {
    initializeWithString(params);
}

/**
 * Initialize a KeyValueMap with a parameters URL-like string.
 *
 * @param params
 *            A string formatted like param1=value1&param2=value2&... It is
 *            assumed that the value has been appropriately escaped.
 */
public final void initializeWithString(final String params) {
    clear();
    if ((params != null) && !params.isEmpty()) {
        String[] args = params.split("&");
        for (String element : args) {
            int equalIndex = element.indexOf("=");
            if (equalIndex == -1) {
                put(element, "");
            } else {
                put(element.substring(0, equalIndex), element
                    .substring(equalIndex + 1));
            }
        }
    }
}
```

Figure 13.3 A statement coverage run shows that our tests actually
missed trying out two parts of the code, the empty KeyValueMap()
constructor and the first `put(...)` call in the
`initializeWithString(...)` method.

EclEmma noted that not all the `KeyValueMap` code had been tested, and the result is correct: We missed trying out the basic parameter-less constructor, and we also didn't try initializing an object with a string such as `curly&larry&moe&stooges=3`, which would store empty values for the first three keys. We can fix this by adding a few more tests, such as the following.

```
@Test
public void testKeyValueMapNoParameters() {
    final KeyValueMap kvm = new KeyValueMap();
    assertTrue(kvm.isEmpty());
}
```

```
@Test
public void testKeyValueMapNoValues() {
  final KeyValueMap kvm = new KeyValueMap("curly&larry&moe&stooges=3");
  assertEquals(4, kvm.size());

  assertTrue(kvm.containsKey("curly"));
  assertTrue(kvm.containsKey("larry"));
  assertTrue(kvm.containsKey("moe"));
  assertTrue(kvm.containsKey("larry"));

  assertEquals("", kvm.get("curly"));
  assertEquals("", kvm.get("larry"));
  assertEquals("", kvm.get("moe"));
  assertEquals("3", kvm.get("stooges"));
}
```

Rerunning the coverage test now produces a round 100% score for our class, so we can be more satisfied about our testing. However, note that while low coverage values do point to inadequate testing, high coverage values do not guarantee the absence of errors and are probably not cost-effective. (For example, trying to produce all possible runtime exceptions can be a hard job, and direct code examination may prove to be better.) Usually, values around 80% to 90% are expected, but you shouldn't go overboard with this; when tests start getting complicated, try to focus more on coding more clearly and finding bugs than on achieving higher coverage values.[16]

What we have seen up to now is standard fare for JUnit programmers, and it's easy to see how it would apply to server-side code, or to such methods as previously shown, which do not deal with users, input fields, graphic objects, and the like. How would we apply JUnit to such code? Let's turn to MVP code, which is far more interesting.

Testing MVP Code

It might not be obvious at the beginning, but there are many reasons why you couldn't directly test GWT form code with JUnit. First, JUnit depends on reflection, and GWT compiled code doesn't provide it, so that's a showstopper. If your code runs JavaScript (maybe through JSNI, as in Chapter 8, "Mixing in JavaScript," or by using some DOM or History methods, as in Chapter 4) then JUnit won't be able to deal with it; it can work only with stand-alone Java code, which cannot run JavaScript. Using any DOM-related methods is also a no-no; JUnit doesn't have access to a browser, so that code couldn't even be executed. Finally, using GWT.Create(...) also won't work, leaving out

---

16. See www.bullseye.com/minimum.html for a good study on this and for actual requirements for several industries.

RPC and many other GWT features.[17] So, how do you get to test any forms with JUnit? We already saw the answer in Chapter 5, "Programming the User Interface"; MVP lets you separate concerns by testing the important Presenter code (based on pure Java) and leaving for later the mostly trivial View code.

Testing with Mock Objects

You can get around all the preceding limitations if your code is 100% functional, with no side effects, and deals with the rest of the system only through its input parameters. We are going to use a well-known technique and use *mock objects* to simulate and verify all the interactions between the tested object and the rest of the system.

Going back to an already mentioned example, how would you test a method that shows a `Window.alert(...)` message, in a fully automatic way, with no other tools but Java? A method that produces such an alert is breaking the stated rule given: It is accessing and using something (namely, `Window` static methods) that it didn't receive as a parameter. Another example: How would you test code that sends "tweets," or that makes online payments? These two examples are even worse; whenever you tested your program, it would start annoying people everywhere with test tweets, or freely making orders and spending your money!

If, however, your object under test had received an object, itself with a method that could simulate (but not actually do) the desired behavior, then your code would be testable. (The object under test would use the received object, and the latter could afterward let us know whether it was called, with which parameters, in what order, and so.) The received object would probably not do any kind of real work (thus, it's actually a *mock* object) but rather "keep score" so we can later see what happened.

Of course, writing many of these mock objects would be quite a chore. Moreover, if we need to run several different tests on the same object, then we would probably need several sets of the same mock objects; that much programming would more likely make you do without testing!

There are several kinds of objects used in testing other than mocks, according to the usual Software Engineering literature; let's briefly consider some of those, in growing scale of complexity.[18]

---

17. This isn't actually 100% true; there are some cases that can be tested despite what was asserted in the text. If your code can be tested even with a null object (that is, receiving null instead of an actual object) you can surround a `GWT.create(...)` call with `GWTMockUtilities.disarm()` and `GWTMockUtilities.restore()` calls, and no object will be created. Of course, you won't be able to run all kind of tests if the object is null, but for some restricted tests it could be a good aid.

18. Sometimes, all these objects are generically called "test doubles," for they replace real objects in the same way as a "stunt double" replaces an actor for some scenes in a movie.

- *Dummy* objects are passed around only to fill parameter lists but never are actually used.

- *Stubs* provide "canned" answers to calls. The possibilities range from constant answers (the method always returns the same value) to matching the received value to a predefined list to decide what value to return.

- *Fake* objects actually do work, but usually with some restrictions, such as using RAM for storing data instead of a database. Developing these objects can be as hard as developing the actual classes themselves.

What we are dealing with, mock objects, are objects preprogrammed with expectations specifying the calls that are to be made upon them, and the values they should return. For our tests, both stubs and mock objects could do as well, but in the first case we must do the verifications (was the method called? What values did it receive?) by ourselves, whereas in the second case, the mock library takes care of that. Just for the sake of making the difference clear, we'll use both stubs and mocks in our MVP tests.

EasyMock

EasyMock can construct objects for interfaces by using Java's proxy mechanism. It can also work with objects through a special class extension. (We are working with classes, such as `Environment`, so we shall at least part of the time require this extension.) Because of how expectations are recorded, it's likely that refactoring your code won't affect your EasyMock based tests, which is a good advantage.[19]

Let's test a login presenter, the last one we built before using UiBinder. (UiBinder itself neither helps nor hampers our testing, because it's View-oriented, and we are testing Presenter code.) We last saw this in Chapter 5; let's remember what our Presenter code looked like:

```
package com.fkereki.mvpproject.client.login2;

// ...imports...

public class LoginFormPresenter
    extends Presenter<LoginFormDisplay> {
  static String PLACE = "login";

  LoginServiceAsync loginService;
  SimpleCallback<String> loginSuccessCallback;
```

19. Some other similar mocking libraries (which even use a similar way for specifying expectations) are Mockito (at http://mockito.org/) and jMock (at www.jmock.org/). As usual, "you makes your choices, and you takes your chances."

```
public LoginFormPresenter(
    final String params, final LoginFormDisplay loginDisplay,
    final Environment environment,
    final SimpleCallback<String> callback) {

  super(params, loginDisplay, environment);
  loginSuccessCallback = callback;
  loginService = getEnvironment().getModel().getRemoteLoginService();

  final SimpleCallback<Object> commonBlurHandler =
      new SimpleCallback<Object>() {

    @Override
    public void goBack(final Object result) {
      final String name = LoginFormPresenter.this.getDisplay()
          .getName();
      final String pass = LoginFormPresenter.this.getDisplay()
          .getPassword();
      final boolean canLogin = !(name.isEmpty()) & !(pass.isEmpty());
      (LoginFormPresenter.this.getDisplay())
          .enableLoginButton(canLogin);
    }
  };
  loginDisplay.setNameBlurCallback(commonBlurHandler);
  loginDisplay.setPasswordBlurCallback(commonBlurHandler);

  loginDisplay.setName("federico");
  loginDisplay.setPassword("");
  commonBlurHandler.goBack(null);

  loginDisplay.setLoginCallback(new SimpleCallback<Object>() {
    @Override
    public void goBack(final Object result) {
      final String name = LoginFormPresenter.this.getDisplay()
          .getName();
      final String pass = LoginFormPresenter.this.getDisplay()
          .getPassword();

      LoginFormPresenter.this.getDisplay().enableLoginButton(false);

      loginService.getSomething(name, pass,
          new AsyncCallback<String>() {
            public void onFailure(final Throwable caught) {
              LoginFormPresenter.this.getEnvironment().showAlert(
                  "Failed login");
```

```
                   LoginFormPresenter.this.getDisplay().enableLoginButton(
                       true);
                   loginSuccessCallback.onFailure(new Throwable());
               }

               public void onSuccess(final String result) {
                   loginSuccessCallback.goBack(result);
               }
           });
       }
     });
   }
}
```

As is, our code is good for testing, because

- It interacts with a remote servlet to do the login but gets the needed reference by means of the provided Environment parameter rather than directly accessing an actual server.

- It shows some alerts, but it also does it through the received Environment parameter, allowing us to check whether alerts were produced but without stopping the test waiting for user interaction.

- It works with the View in MVP fashion, but it doesn't directly deal with widgets or handlers, rather going through the View interface. Furthermore, the View is received as a parameter by the Presenter constructor, which is also good (because the actual View interacts with the DOM and with JavaScript code, which would prohibit the kind of tests we are striving for).

We will test the Presenter by providing several mock objects; for example, one such object will simulate connecting to the server and trying a login, a second will make do as if it had shown an alert, whereas yet a third one will stand for the View, and fake all calls from the Presenter and also invoke all its blur and click methods. Just for the sake of showing different ways of working, we shall mock most of the objects with EasyMock but use a stub for the remote login and the successful log callback.

We shall do a simple login attempt test. We shall simulate that the user enters a password, then clicks on the login button, and the service will approve the attempt. We are going to implement our own mock login service object, which will use a `wasCalled` variable to record that the service was truly called, and two more variables (`calledName` and `calledPass`) to store the received values, so we can later test what they actually were. Boolean variable `didReturn` will be used to check whether the Presenter did or didn't call the successful login callback.[20]

---

20. The name `LoginFormPresenter2Test` has to do with our testing the second version of the `LoginFormPresenter`, from Chapter 5.

```
package com.fkereki.mvpproject.client.login2;

// ...imports...

public class LoginFormPresenter2Test {
  boolean didReturn = false;
  boolean wasCalled = false;
  String calledName = "";
  String calledPass = "";
```

Now, let's write our test. We shall be using EasyMock objects for the Environment, for the Model that the Environment will be asked to return, and for the View; we create all these with `createMock(...)`. If we cared for the strict sequence of calls (more on this later) we would have rather used `createStrictMock(...)`, and if we didn't care to provide return values for all calls and could stand returning standard values (zeroes, nulls, and falses), `createNiceMock(...)` would have been appropriate.

```
  @Test
  public void testLoginPresenter1() {

    final Environment environmentMock = createMock(Environment.class);

    final Model modelMock = createMock(Model.class);

    final LoginFormDisplay loginViewMock =
      createMock(LoginFormDisplay.class);
```

As promised, we'll create the login service mock object by hand, just to show it can be done—and that it's probably more work than needed! For example, we must code otherwise unneeded methods (which will `fail(...)` if called, so we'll notice the unexpected call). We must also record whether we were called, and fail the test if the login service happens to be called more than once, because in this particular test we are assuming the login will be successful.

```
    final LoginServiceAsync loginServiceMock = new LoginServiceAsync() {
      @Override
      public void changePassword(
          final String name,
          final String encryptedNewPassword,
          final String nonce,
          final String parametersHash,
          final AsyncCallback<Void> callback) {

        fail(); // this shouldn't be called!
      }
```

```
@Override
public void getSessionKey(
    final String name,
    final String nonce,
    final String passHash,
    final AsyncCallback<SessionKeyServiceReturnDto> callback) {

  fail(); // this shouldn't be called!
}

@Override
public void getSomething(
    final String name,
    final String pass,
    final AsyncCallback<String> callback) {

  if (wasCalled) {
    fail();
  } else {
    wasCalled = true;
    calledName = name;
    calledPass = pass;
  }
}
};
```

Now, let's start setting our expectations. From what we know about the Presenter, it shall require getting a reference to the underlying Model object; our Environment must expect a getModel(...) call and return modelMock. Likewise, modelMock must expect a call asking for the remote login service object and must return our hand-build loginServiceMock. If any of these calls fails to happen, or happens more than once, the test will fail.

```
expect(environmentMock.getModel()).andReturn(modelMock);
expect(modelMock.getRemoteLoginService()).andReturn(
    loginServiceMock);
```

The Presenter will also call setNameBlurCallback(...) and similar methods so the View will know what to call on blur and click events. We must store whatever values are provided for callbacks, to use them later when needed. EasyMock provides the Capture<...> class and capture(...) methods to simplify this oft-required task. When the corresponding methods are invoked, the received parameters will get stored.

```
final Capture<SimpleCallback<Object>> nameBlurCapture =
    new Capture<SimpleCallback<Object>>();
```

```
final Capture<SimpleCallback<Object>> passwordBlurCapture =
  new Capture<SimpleCallback<Object>>();
final Capture<SimpleCallback<Object>> callbackCapture =
  new Capture<SimpleCallback<Object>>();

loginViewMock
    .setNameBlurCallback(EasyMock.capture(nameBlurCapture));
loginViewMock.setPasswordBlurCallback(EasyMock
    .capture(passwordBlurCapture));
loginViewMock.setLoginCallback(EasyMock.capture(callbackCapture));
```

Now, from what we know, the Presenter will initialize the name field with `"federico"` (guess why?) and will empty the password field. The following two lines set up expectations for the mock objects, which will later be verified.

```
loginViewMock.setName("federico");
loginViewMock.setPassword("");
```

We know that at the beginning, the Presenter will check the values of the name and password fields and therefore decide whether to enable or disable the login button. When the `getName(...)` method gets called, we want it to return `"federico"` (because nobody modified it); likewise, `getPassword(...)` should return an empty string, and thus we should expect the Presenter to disable the login button. If you want to test an exception, you could use `andThrow(...)` instead of `andReturn(...)`.[21]

```
expect(loginViewMock.getName()).andReturn("federico");
expect(loginViewMock.getPassword()).andReturn("");
loginViewMock.enableLoginButton(false);
```

When we construct the Presenter object, we must provide it with a callback, which the Presenter should call when the login succeeds. We could do something along the lines of

```
final SimpleCallback<String> callbackMock = new
    SimpleCallback<String>() {

  @Override
  public void goBack(final String result) {
    assertFalse(didReturn);
    didReturn = true;
  }
};
```

---

21. EasyMock also provides more elaborate matchers, such as `anyObject(...)`, `anyString(...)`, `anyInt(...)`, and so on, which accept any parameter of the said type; `notNull(...)`, which accepts any non-null value; and `matches(...)`, which can be used for pattern matching the received value. You can use these matchers on a parameter-by-parameter basis.

Back to the test expectations, we shall be simulating that the user entered a password, and the password blur method will be fired. We know the presenter will have to check both the name and password fields to decide whether to enable the login button, and this time it will pass a `true` value.

```
expect(loginViewMock.getName()).andReturn("federico");
expect(loginViewMock.getPassword()).andReturn("eduardo");
loginViewMock.enableLoginButton(true);
```

Now, because all pieces are in place, and all expectations were set, let's get the ball rolling. The `replay(...)` method puts all objects in expect/check mode, so whenever they get called, parameters will be tested, values will be returned, all according with our setup.

```
EasyMock.replay(modelMock);
EasyMock.replay(loginViewMock);
EasyMock.replay(environmentMock);
```

Creating the Presenter object starts the replay. We can right away check whether it provided a non-null callback for clicks on the login button and if it stored the `loginServiceMock` we provided.[22]

```
final LoginFormPresenter lp = new LoginFormPresenter("",
        loginViewMock, environmentMock, callbackMock);

assertTrue(callbackCapture.getValue() != null);
assertTrue(lp.loginService != null);
assertTrue(lp.loginService == loginServiceMock);
```

Calling the password blur handler simulates the data entry, and calling the login button handler simulates the final click.

```
passwordBlurCapture.getValue().goBack(null);
callbackCapture.getValue().goBack(null);
```

Now, all we have to do to finish our tests is check whether our handmade mock objects were actually called as expected.

```
    assertTrue(didReturn);
    assertTrue(wasCalled);
    assertEquals(calledName, "federico");
    assertEquals(calledPass, "eduardo");
  }
}
```

---

22. This isn't that usual; normally, we just test things that are available through a declared interface... but why not? Having the test class and the tested class in the same package allows for these kind of "inner checks."

All the other checks, such as if a method were called unexpectedly, or with unexpected parameters, are done by EasyMock, so it's still possible that the test will fail, even if it didn't produce an error so far.

Using EasyMock is a great way to simplify your tests, and gives you enough latitude to provide for the most complicated test situations. (Note, for example, how much shorter and easy to understand were our EasyMock tests than our hand-written login service mock?) If you manage to set up the Presenter tests with EasyMock, the usually most complex parts of your applications will be easily tested, and at full speed, which doesn't happen with the browser-based tests we shall be considering in the next sections.

Integration Testing with GWTTestCase

JUnit tests can be applied only to server-side code and to part (hopefully, most) of the client-side code. However, this is not enough; you should test, for example, whether a complex view actually does what it should do, or if a remote service can actually be called and produce the correct results. For all these tests, you need to simulate your actual environment, for the code runs in a browser.

`GWTTestCase` acts like a bridge between JUnit and GWT. Previous versions of GWT used actual browsers to run unit tests, but since 2, `HtmlUnit` is used as a built-in browser. As `HtmlUnit` is written in Java, you can debug GWT tests in development mode, which is an advantage. Also, you can test the results of integrating several classes (including classes that require JavaScript) and find problems that might have escaped you if you only did browser-less testing.

On the negative side, because it's not an actual browser, there can be subtle problems; you will have to use Selenium or similar tools for doing tests on actual compiled code. Also, delays are more significant, because a development mode shell has to be started, and the actual runs will also take longer if you communicate with a server. Finally, you won't be able to mock objects automatically with EasyMock or the like, which require some Java features such as reflection, that aren't available with GWT; you'll have to do that work by yourself.

Setup is also a bit more complex; you have to include the source directories in the Class path; see Figure 13.4.

Let's study a couple of examples of this kind of testing and check both a View and a Remote Servlet.

Testing a View

We've tested a login presenter; let's now do some tests of the login view. You could try to do all kinds of tests (layout, rendering, events, callbacks, and more) but remember to think in terms of economy and focus on the most important tests!

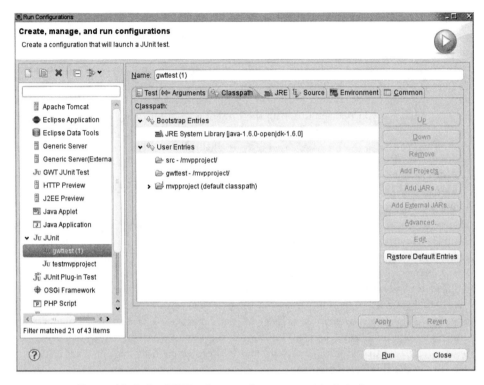

Figure 13.4 For GWTTestCase testing, you must include the source
directories in the Classpath; click on Advanced... then Add Folder to do so.

As a reminder, the code to be tested was

```
package com.fkereki.mvpproject.client.login2;

// ...imports...

public class LoginFormView
    extends View
    implements LoginFormDisplay {

  AsyncCallback<Object> loginCallback;
  AsyncCallback<Object> nameBlurCallback;
  AsyncCallback<Object> passwordBlurCallback;

  final TextBox nameTextBox = new TextBox();
  final TextBox passwordTextBox = new PasswordTextBox();
  final Button loginButton = new Button("Log in");
  final FlexTable flex = new FlexTable();
  final DockPanel dock = new DockPanel();
```

```
public LoginFormView() {
  // add a click handler to the login button
  // add a blur handler to the name and password fields
  // set up all fields onscreen and "init" the widget
}

@Override
public void enableLoginButton(final boolean b) {
  loginButton.setEnabled(b);
}

@Override
public final String getName() {
  return nameTextBox.getValue();
}

@Override
public final String getPassword() {
  return passwordTextBox.getValue();
}

@Override
public final void setLoginCallback(final SimpleCallback<Object> acb) {
  loginCallback = acb;
}

@Override
public final void setName(final String s) {
  nameTextBox.setValue(s);
}

@Override
public void setNameBlurCallback(final SimpleCallback<Object> acb) {
  nameBlurCallback = acb;
}

@Override
public final void setPassword(final String s) {
  passwordTextBox.setValue(s);
}

@Override
public void setPasswordBlurCallback(final SimpleCallback<Object> acb) {
  passwordBlurCallback = acb;
}
}
```

Our test class must now extend `GWTTestCase`. Note we use the same package as the original view's, so we can take advantage of visibility rules.

```
package com.fkereki.mvpproject.client.login2;

// ...imports...

public class LoginFormViewGWTTest
    extends GWTTestCase {
```

We use a pair of Boolean variables to learn whether specific callbacks were invoked. (Previously we did a similar thing.)

```
boolean loginWasCalled;
boolean blurWasCalled;
```

All `GWTTestCase` instances must include a `getModuleName(...)` that just returns the complete name of the unit to be tested.

```
@Override
public String getModuleName() {
  return "com.fkereki.mvpproject.Mvpproject";
}
```

With all this out of the way, let's start our testing. After creating the View object, we must set its callbacks, but note that they don't actually do anything, but just record they were called.[23]

```
@Test
public void testLoginView() {
  final LoginFormView lv = new LoginFormView();

  final SimpleCallback<Object> blurCB = new SimpleCallback<Object>() {

    @Override
    public void goBack(final Object result) {
      blurWasCalled = true;
    }
  };

  lv.setNameBlurCallback(blurCB);
  lv.setPasswordBlurCallback(blurCB);

  lv.setLoginCallback(new SimpleCallback<Object>() {
```

---

23. GWTTestCase is derived from JUnit 3, so the `@Test` annotations aren't actually necessary; instead, test methods should begin with "test." I have followed *both* conventions in the text, so when GWTTestCase catches up with JUnit 4, my code will be ready.

```
    @Override
    public void goBack(final Object result) {
      loginWasCalled = true;
    }
  });
```

Now, we can start using the View's methods and check if they work as expected. The first tests actually use the real fields; you could argue that you shouldn't get down to this level and access any widgets (but rather work only through interfaces) but in any case you'll have to, in order to fire click and blur events. Also, there's no other way to test whether the login button was actually enabled or disabled.

```
    lv.nameTextBox.setValue("urk");
    lv.passwordTextBox.setValue("ork");
    assertEquals("urk", lv.getName());
    assertEquals("ork", lv.getPassword());

    lv.setName("federico");
    lv.setPassword("");
    assertEquals("federico", lv.getName());
    assertEquals("", lv.getPassword());

    lv.enableLoginButton(false);
    assertFalse(lv.loginButton.isEnabled());
    lv.enableLoginButton(true);
    assertTrue(lv.loginButton.isEnabled());
```

Testing events require some DOM manipulation. Note the `DomEvent.fireNativeEvent(...)` method, which is quite interesting.

```
    final Document doc = com.google.gwt.dom.client.Document.get();
    final NativeEvent evt1 = doc.createBlurEvent();
    DomEvent.fireNativeEvent(evt1, lv.nameTextBox);
    assertTrue(blurWasCalled);

    blurWasCalled = false;
    DomEvent.fireNativeEvent(evt1, lv.passwordTextBox);
    assertTrue(blurWasCalled);

    final NativeEvent evt2 = doc.createClickEvent(0, 0, 0, 0, 0, false,
        false, false, false);
    DomEvent.fireNativeEvent(evt2, lv.loginButton);
    assertTrue(loginWasCalled);
  }
}
```

If wanted, you could have linked the view to an actual presenter and provided an actual Model to work with, and so on. You shouldn't, however, try to do a full acceptance test because tools such as Selenium make shorter work out of that.

Testing a Servlet

Our previous test didn't require a servlet, but at some time you'll have to write such tests. (Otherwise, how would you detect mismatched parameters, a wrong setup, or any other such problems?) The main problem here is the need for a wait, because RPC works asynchronously. If you just did a RPC and then went on to test results, you would fail, because they wouldn't have arrived.

Let's test a pair of methods in the World servlet. Note that for this, you must have preloaded the database with countries, states, and cities (as we saw in Chapter 6, "Communicating with Your Server"). You should probably be running your own database; you wouldn't want to run tests against production data, would you? Also, you'll have to modify the `gwt.xml` file a bit to include the path to the servlet.

```
<servlet path='/world'
    class='com.fkereki.mvpproject.server.WorldServiceImpl'/>
```

The start of our test class is similar to the one we just saw for a view.

```
package com.fkereki.mvpproject.client.rpc;

//...imports...

public class WorldServiceGWTTest
    extends GWTTestCase {

  final Model model = new Model();

  @Override
  public String getModuleName() {
    return "com.fkereki.mvpproject.Mvpproject";
  }
}
```

As a minimal test, we could try getting back all cities in Soriano, a department (region code 17) in Uruguay (country code `UY`) and verify whether "Darwin" is included in the list. (We already saw this city in Chapter 6; also see Figure 13.6 farther on in this chapter.) Although this test is clearly not enough, the most important part is the `delayTestFinish(...)` call, so the servlet will have time to return, and the `finishTest(...)` call after the servlet callback. Also, note that the result tests must be verified in the callback.

```
@Test
public void testGetCities() {
  model.getCities("UY", "17", 0, 1000,
      new SimpleCallback<LinkedHashMap<String, ClientCityData>>() {
        @Override
        public void goBack(
            final LinkedHashMap<String, ClientCityData> result) {
```

```
        assertTrue(result.size() > 0);
        assertEquals("Darwin",
            result.get("darwin").cityAccentedName);
        finishTest();
      }
    });
```

```
  delayTestFinish(5000); // 5 seconds
}
```

The test for countries is almost the same.

```
@Test
public void testGetCountries() {
  model
      .getCountries(new SimpleCallback<LinkedHashMap<String, String>>() {
        @Override
        public void goBack(final LinkedHashMap<String, String> result) {

          assertTrue(result.size() > 0);
          assertTrue(result.containsKey("UY"));
          finishTest();
        }
      });

  delayTestFinish(5000);
  }
}
```

Because of the servlet delays, you shouldn't do more than one call at once. (In some freak situations, the second call might finish before the first one, and results would be totally unexpected.) If you need do a second RPC, include it in the callback for the first call. To wrap this up, let's verify what I said about the delays. (See Figure 13.5.)

Running these tests took about 49 seconds; the greater part of that was internal GWT setup work. It's a fact that with `GWTTestCase` you can test parts and interactions of your code that you would miss otherwise, but because of the longer times, do try to test as much of the code with pure JUnit and leave special tests for `GWTTestCase`.

Acceptance Testing with Selenium

With the tools we have already seen, it should be clear that you could test most of your application, if not all (file uploads can get tricky, for example), using a mixture of JUnit (for server-side code, and for nonvisual parts of client-side code) and GWTTestCase (for the visual parts of your code). However, let's give a quick look at an oft-used tool, Selenium, that helps writing and running tests for a complete web application. Though we won't be getting in full detail (Selenium is quite vast, with dozens of commands) we'll show how to use it and some caveats you should take into account.

Figure 13.5 GWTTestCase testing usually requires much longer setup
times, though the tests themselves may be fast.

Three different software pieces compose Selenium, but we'll mostly consider the first
one, which lets you create and run tests individually; however, you'll probably sooner or
later decide that the other two tools, which have to do with automating large scale tests
on different browsers, are also of interest.

- Selenium IDE is a Firefox add-on that provides a simple interface for building and
  running tests, either on its own or as part of complete test suites. You can record
  your actions and checks, and store them as a script that can be played back. If you
  want, you can even write your tests from scratch (the test language is actually quite
  simple) but the IDE helps a lot.

- Selenium RC (Remote Control) enables you to use Java and other programming
  languages for extending your tests. Selenium IDE can run only static (i.e., predefined) tests; if you want to iterate through a result set or do arithmetic or other
  tests, you can program them in Java while using Selenium commands to get the
  data, for example. Using a programming language would also allow setting up a
  complex environment before running the actual tests. Also, Selenium RC enables
  you to run tests on browsers that are not supported by the IDE. Thus, you get to
  use Selenium as a "starter kit," and then do the rest of your work in Java, with all
  its development tools.

- Selenium Grid enables you to run several instances of Selenium RC at the same
  time, even under different operating systems and with different browsers. This is
  more useful for large series of tests, which can be run in parallel.

You should use Selenium only on the compiled application (see Chapter 15,
"Deploying Your Application") as the last ("acceptance") kind of test. Reading between
lines, this already suggests a first consideration; you shouldn't probably start with

Selenium until you are fairly confident that the user interface won't be changing too much; otherwise, you might have to redo the completed tests almost from scratch.

A Very Simple Example

Let's remember our City Browsing form. If we browsed to "Uruguay," and picked "Soriano" department, the first 20 cities would be as shown in Figure 13.6.

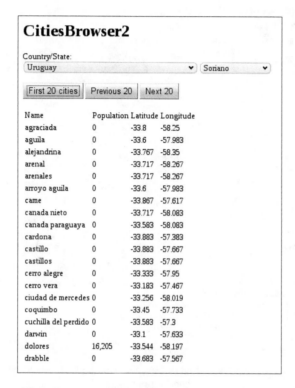

Figure 13.6 The cities browsing form will be tested with Selenium.

Given the data we loaded, a possible test would be

- Open the correct URL.
- Wait for the country data to come in.
- Click on it, and select Uruguay.
- Wait again for the states data.
- Click it, and select Soriano.
- Click the First 20 Cities button.

- Wait for the table to get populated.
- Check that "darwin" appeared in the list.

You can use Selenium to record these actions and tests, and if you opt to run the test, you'll get a green result. (See Figure 13.7.) You can save this test, and later run it as a part of a general suite.

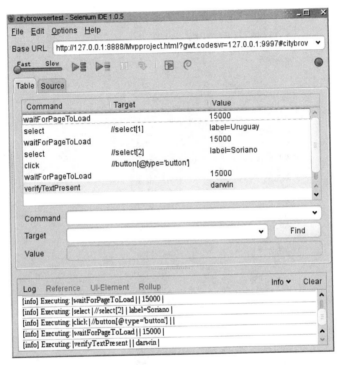

Figure 13.7 Running our short test produces a green result; everything checked out okay.

Note that you had little to type or specify to create and run this test; you could also have managed with GWTTestCase, but this is easier to set up, and furthermore you can run it in different browsers and under different operating systems.

There are far more options available for testing, including the possibility of writing your own tests and wait conditions in JavaScript, so you could, for example, test if the list of Uruguayan departments is 19 elements long, or whether the United States shows 50 states. Check the Selenium documentation for a complete list of commands.[24]

24. You can find it at http://seleniumhq.org/docs/04_selenese_commands.html#chapter04-reference.

What Can Go Wrong?

We just scratched the surface of Selenium with our previous example, but let's anyway consider several problems that you might find.

The most important point is that the logic Selenium uses to decide what locator to use for a given screen object frequently causes problems, because simple or trivial changes in the form may cause Selenium to refer to a different field. The best solution is to assign your own IDs with `DOM.setElementAttribute(someWidget.getElement(), "id", "theNewId")`; and use it as the locator.[25] However, note that this can quickly become tiresome.[26]

GWT applications are (by definition) heavy on DHTML and Ajax, meaning that most of the time, the interface gets created dynamically, depending on data received from the server. You should get used to including `waitFor...` Selenium commands, because otherwise your tests will run too fast, missing widgets or values it should find.

As a plus, you can add extra functionality to Selenium by either writing your own extensions, or by using already developed ones.[27] (You can even do unstructured testing with `goto` statements. How about that, in modern times?) Other extensions help working with frames and windows, so even if you at first cannot run the tests you want, you can probably manage by means of extending Selenium, or using Selenium RC.

Summary

We have seen three different methods for automatic testing of GWT applications: a specific one, GWTTestCase, and two generic ones: JUnit and Selenium. Although you won't be able to use Selenium until your application is stable (which, on the other hand, isn't such a problem because Selenium is geared toward acceptance tests, and you don't run those if the application is only halfway there!) the complete trio of tools do provide a strong base for your tests.

---

25. An alternative: Consider using the `ensureDebugId(...)` method; read http://google-web-toolkit.googlecode.com/svn/javadoc/2.0/index.html?com/google/gwt/user/client/ui/UIObject.html for more on this.

26. Unhappily, you won't be able to assign the id attribute with UIBinder.

27. You can find a repository of such extensions at http://wiki.openqa.org/display/SEL/Contributed+User-Extensions, whereas instructions for writing your own are at http://release.seleniumhq.org/selenium-core/1.0/reference.html#extending-selenium.

## 14

Optimizing for Application Speed

You can never have a too speedy application, and in this chapter we'll consider design patterns that let you take advantage of spare time, and measuring tools that let you find out where your application is spending most of its processing time. The combination of both these programming techniques and benchmarking tools will enable you to optimize your application in often surprising ways.

We are going to consider several ways to speed up your application. We'll start with some design patterns that will enable your application to use background processing to provide or process data more quickly. We'll also be including the new GWT 2 bundles, which let you save time by sending several kinds of data from the server to the client in a single trip. And finally, as more general solutions, we'll also introduce several benchmarking tools that will let you detect bottlenecks in your application.

Design Patterns for Speed

Let's start by stating our goals clearly. We want to consider design patterns that will allow greater speed from the user's point of view. In truth, we are not saying the patterns will make the application faster, but at least that it will *seem* faster to the user; an important difference! As always, it will be a matter of trade-offs; we use some extra (client) memory, but we can skip doing repeated calls to the server, or we speculate and get some data from the server just in case the user wants it.

Given our preceding definition, the prevalidation pattern (that we saw in Chapter 6, "Communicating with Your Server") could equally as well have been included here, because it allows faster feedback and better usability. Yet again the same could be said of the code splitting feature we'll see in the next chapter, for it allows a much faster load process, that is balanced, to be sure, with some delays down the line.

Caching

GWT usually makes your application perform better, but there is one area in which it can actually make performance worse: caching. Whenever your browser requests data (such as a page) from a server, it first looks into its own cache, to check whether it already has the data. If the required results are found in memory, the browser will forego calling the server and just provide the data from the cache. (Of course, several conditions must be fulfilled before something is kept in the cache, but that's not relevant here.) The problem here is that whenever GWT calls a remote servlet, it implements the RPC by means of a noncacheable Ajax call, so even if your program asks for the same data over and over again, the browser won't store it in its cache and will require it anew from the server every time.

If your application requires the same (constant) data that it has already received earlier, you could enhance performance by setting up a local cache of your own, bypassing the browser's one. The pattern of usage would require, before calling the server, to check if the asked-for data is already in the cache, and if so, just skip the call. There are two points to consider:

- Never use a cache for information that changes often.
- If you are using a cache for information that can go stale over time, consider using a timestamp so that you'll avoid using old data.[1]

The general pattern for using a cache would be as follows.

```
Class_with_cache:
  Define class attributes for the cache
  Set the cache to empty initially


Whenever data are required:
  Check if the asked for data are already in the cache
  If so,
    Get the data from the cache, and return it
  Otherwise,
    Use RPC, Ajax, or whatever, to get the data
    On callback:
      Put the data in the cache, and return it
```

Let's illustrate this pattern with our `CountryState` object, which we used in our cities browsing form in Chapter 6. The simplest application of this pattern has to do with the `countryCode` ListBox. In this case, we can make do with a `static` object in which to store the received country list; whenever we ask for the countries list, we first check if the list is already loaded, and if so, we just return it. Changes in the Model class code are minimal with regard to the code we saw earlier in the book. (In Chapter 6 we had mentioned that it would be better if no other part of the application knew the actual

1. This is, in essence, how browsers manage their own internal caches.

details of how to connect to any service. Using methods such as `getCountries(...)` effectively encapsulates those details and furthermore allows optimizations as we shall see.)

```
static LinkedHashMap<String, String> countriesCache = null;

public void getCountries(
    final AsyncCallback<LinkedHashMap<String, String>> cb) {

  if (countriesCache == null) {
    getRemoteWorldService().getCountries(
        new AsyncCallback<LinkedHashMap<String, String>>() {
          @Override
          public void onFailure(final Throwable caught) {
            // ...error...
          }

          @Override
          public void onSuccess(
              final LinkedHashMap<String, String> result) {
            countriesCache = result;
            cb.onSuccess(result);
          }
        });
  } else {
    cb.onSuccess(countriesCache);
  }
}
```

The countries cache is null at the beginning. The first time you call `getCountries(...)`, the resulting list will be stored in the cache, and all further calls will just produce the data from there, with no delays.

Working with states is just a tad more complex, because we'll have to use some kind of collection; storing just the states from a single country wouldn't do. Whenever we get asked for the states of a given country, we must check if `statesCache` already contains that country as a key; if so, we already got the data and don't have to go to the server. This code is also in the Model.

```
static LinkedHashMap<String, LinkedHashMap<String, String>> statesCache =
    new LinkedHashMap<String, LinkedHashMap<String, String>>();

public void getStates(
    final String country,
    final AsyncCallback<LinkedHashMap<String, String>> cb) {

  if (!statesCache.containsKey(country)) {
    getRemoteWorldService().getStates(country,
        new AsyncCallback<LinkedHashMap<String, String>>() {
```

```
        @Override
        public void onFailure(final Throwable caught) {
          // ...error...
        }

        @Override
        public void onSuccess(
            final LinkedHashMap<String, String> result) {

          statesCache.put(country, result);
          cb.onSuccess(result);
        }
      });
  } else {
    cb.onSuccess(statesCache.get(country));
  }
}
```

If you are worried about total RAM requirements, you could apply some kind of LRU (least recently used) logic and just store states for the more recently used, say, 10 or 20 countries.

The same kind of change could be applied to the cities fetching logic, and the changes are relatively minor. The only point deserving attention is the way we build up the cache key by concatenating the country, state, and start position parameters, separated by colons.[2]

```
/*
 * The cache key is COUNTRY:REGION:STARTING_CITY_NUMBER and the associated
 * value is a LinkedHashMap<String,ClientCityData>
 */
static LinkedHashMap<String, LinkedHashMap<String, ClientCityData>>
  citiesCache = new LinkedHashMap<String,
    LinkedHashMap<String, ClientCityData>>();
```

The rest of the code follows the same pattern we used earlier. Let's include it so we can add more changes to it in the following section.

```
public void getCities(
    final String country,
    final String state,
    final int pStart,
    final int pCount,
    final AsyncCallback<LinkedHashMap<String, ClientCityData>> cb) {

  if (!country.isEmpty() && !state.isEmpty()) {
```

2. We are assuming here that pCount is always constant. If this weren't true, handling the cache would just be a tad harder, but we need not care about the details for this example.

```
     if (!citiesCache
         .containsKey(country + ":" + state + ":" + pStart)) {

    getRemoteWorldService().getCities(country, state, pStart,
        pCount,
        new AsyncCallback<LinkedHashMap<String, ClientCityData>>() {

            // ...onFailure() definition...

            public void onSuccess(
                final LinkedHashMap<String, ClientCityData> result) {

                citiesCache.put(country + ":" + state + ":" + pStart,
                    result);
                cb.onSuccess(result);
            }
        });
    } else {
        cb.onSuccess(citiesCache.get(country + ":" + state + ":"
            + pStart));
    }
  }
}
```

Now, we'll study other patterns that we could apply in that case, to speed up sequences of consecutive calls.

Prefetching

Whenever your client-side application is going to need lots of data from the server, you'll have to implement some kind of chunking or paging, and that means the user will have to wait for each new "batch" of data. If you could foretell which data a user was going to require, you could use Ajax mechanisms and "get ahead of the game," getting the data from the server before actually required, and thus providing a much more responsive interface. Of course, you cannot always guess what the user will finally ask for, so you must take into account the possibility that you'll guess wrongly and get some unneeded data; that is a certain risk that you must balance with the sure delays that the user will have to endure if you opt to not *prefetch*.

Prefetching just means trying to anticipate your user needs and call for data before the user actually requires it. However, you must be careful with this pattern: If you just go overboard by prefetching everything in sight, you'll just make things worse! Since the times of limited-speed, dial-up modems, all browsers have limited the maximum allowed number of client-to-server connections. (As a matter of fact, that limitation even got included as part of the HTTP version 1.1 standard, which reads *"A single-user client SHOULD NOT maintain more than 2 connections with any server or proxy."*) If you make several requests for data to your server, you should assume that at most only two of them will go out (in parallel) while the rest will be queued for even longer-than-usual delays.[3]

The simplest pattern for prefetching is as follows:

```
Class_with_cache_and_prefetching:
  Define class attributes for the cache
  Set the cache to empty initially

Whenever data are required:
  Check if the asked for data are already in the cache
  If so,
    Get the data from the cache, and return it
  Otherwise,
    Use RPC, Ajax, or whatever, to get the data
    and also to prefetch extra data

    On callback:
      Store the data in the cache
      If data were needed (as opposed to prefetched)
        Return it
```

We can apply this kind of logic to the cities browser application. We will implement a cache along the lines shown in the previous section, but we will also be storing extra data as a prevision for the future. Note in particular that the first check at the cache looks for cities starting at position **pStart+pCount**; if the user steps through the data consecutively, that will mean that the required data will already be loaded in memory.[4]

```
public void getCities(
    final String country,
    final String state,
    final int pStart,
    final int pCount,
    final AsyncCallback<LinkedHashMap<String, ClientCityData>> cb) {

  if (!country.isEmpty() && !state.isEmpty()) {

    if (!citiesCache.containsKey(country + ":" + state + ":"
        + (pStart + pCount))) {

      getRemoteWorldService().getCities(country, state,
          pStart + pCount, pCount,
```

---

3. Modern browsers have upped the limit from the original value of two, but the principle remains the same: You shouldn't hog all communication "just in case," and should the user be working with a browser that allowed a smaller number of connections than you expected, performance would suffer.

4. Once again, we are assuming pCount never changes.

```
new AsyncCallback<LinkedHashMap<String, ClientCityData>>() {
    public void onFailure(final Throwable caught) {
        // ...error...
    }

    public void onSuccess(
        final LinkedHashMap<String, ClientCityData> result) {

        citiesCache.put(country + ":" + state + ":"
            + (pStart + pCount), result);
    }
});
    }
```

The rest of the code is exactly the same as in the cache-only version, which we saw at the end of the previous section.

```
if (!citiesCache
    .containsKey(country + ":" + state + ":" + pStart)) {

    // ...as in the "cache only" version...
    }
    }
}
```

Note that the code works by doing two calls: the first to prefetch some data and load the cache, and the second to provide the actually asked-for data. Of course, the calls are done only if the involved data aren't already in the cache.

If you foresee the possibility of the user browsing many different countries and states, applying some kind of limits to the cache would prove to be wise; a simple though possibly a bit too extreme solution would be going through the whole cache and simply purging any data coming from a country other than the one the user is currently examining.

As is, the user will experiment a certain delay when he calls for the first group of cities, but then, if he just takes a little while before asking for the next page, he will notice no delays at all, for the required data will have already been brought from the server to the client.

For even more impressive results, whenever the "states" listbox value changes, you could add a call such as the following, so the first cities (that is, when start is zero) for the given country and state would already be loaded even before the user clicked on the First Cities button. (See the cities browsing Presenter, from where this was taken.) Note that the callback doesn't do anything![5]

---

5. Why so many get(...) calls? You have to go through the Environment to get at the Model and then ask it to get cities from the server. For the RPC parameters, the Presenter needs the Display to get the Country and State widget, and then get the Country (or State) from it.

```
getEnvironment().getModel().getCities(
   getDisplay().getCountryState().getCountry(),
   getDisplay().getCountryState().getState(),
   0, CitiesBrowserView.CITIES_PAGE_SIZE,
   new SimpleCallback<LinkedHashMap<String, ClientCityData>>() {
     @Override
     public void goBack(
         LinkedHashMap<String, ClientCityData> result) {
       // ...do nothing!
     }
   });
```

If you are feeling even more adventurous, you could wait just a bit before getting the cities, just in case the user changes its mind and picks a different state; you'll probably want to use a timer, as we will be using in the next section though for different purposes.

Thread Simulation

Consider any CPU-intensive task, such as parsing and processing large amounts of XML, or displaying lots of data on screen. If a process takes too long, the end user will be shown a message such as Internet Explorer's "Stop running this script? A script on this page is causing Internet Explorer to run slowly. If it continues to run, your computer may become unresponsive" or Firefox's own "A script on this page may be busy, or it may have stopped responding. You can stop the script now, or you can continue to see if the script will complete." What's worse, if the user actually pays heed to the warning, he will stop the wayward script, and thus cancel your GWT application!

Using threads would be a standard solution for this problem, but GWT won't allow it, because JavaScript provides just a single thread of execution, implying that compiled threaded code wouldn't work as expected. Ajax would also provide a solution, if you required server-side processes but is no good for your client-side problem.

Luckily, there are two solutions for this problem: You could use timers and parcel your script in several small pieces, or you can go one step better, and use GWT's own *deferred commands*, which actually provide even better performance. Let's apply both of them to showing the cities data in our cities browsing application.

A Timer-Based Solution

JavaScript provides simple timers, and GWT provides an equivalent `Timer` class, with a `schedule(...)` method that works in similar fashion like JavaScript's `setTimeOut(...)` method.

The idea for this solution is to do just a bit of work and store values so the process can seamlessly continue after a timeout, but freeing the CPU in the meantime. Of course, before resuming the process, check if the process needs to go on; the user might have changed the country or state, or paged forward and backward, and it wouldn't do if your application ignored that, and kept showing old data.

The general pattern is as follows:

```
define a class that extends Timer:
  define attributes so it can save its parameters
  define attributes so it can save local variables from run to run
  define attributes so it can save form field values

  on construction:
    save the received parameters
    initialize local variables for the process
    save the current form field values

  run() method:
    if the current form field values match the saved values:
      execute some process, updating the local variables
      if there's still more work to be done
        schedule another process in a short while

whenever you want to simulate a thread with a timed method:
  create an object of the new class above, with appropriate parameters
  execute its run() method
```

Let's apply this pattern to our cities browsing example, and in particular, to the logic that actually displays the cities' data onscreen.[6] Most of the code will be left as was, so we shall just highlight the main points. Also (and this supports some things we said about MVP) note that only the Presenter needs any changes.

```
package com.fkereki.mvpproject.client.citiesBrowser3;

// ...imports...

public class CitiesBrowserPresenter
    extends Presenter<CitiesBrowserDisplay> {
  public static String PLACE = "citybrowse";
```

We shall implement a *Command* pattern[7] by extending the `Timer` class. (Note we are referring to the GWT one at `com.google.gwt.user.client.Timer` and not to the standard `java.util.Timer` class.) The cities' display process will be parceled into several short, spaced processes, so the end user will feel the browser to be "more responsive."

```
  private class TimedCitiesDisplay
      extends Timer {

    final NumberFormat nf = NumberFormat.getDecimalFormat();
    LinkedHashMap<String, ClientCityData> citiesList = null;
```

6. Okay, this particular code is fast enough so you could do without this pattern, but on the other hand, it provides a simple way of showing how to apply this optimization scheme.

7. See http://c2.com/cgi/wiki?CommandPattern for a fuller description.

```
Iterator<String> currentCity = null;
int currentRow = 0;
```

We shall store the original country, state, and start position, because the user could change to a different country or state, or advance to a different set of cities, and it wouldn't do to keep displaying the old data. Before we get to display anything, we'll make sure it matches what the user is seeing onscreen.

```
String originalCountry = null;
String originalState = null;
int originalStart = 0;
```

This method will be used to display a whole page of cities. We shall be using an iterator to step through the list of cities; it will be the link between a part of the process and the next part. We shall also update the three variables we mentioned in the previous paragraph, and display Loading... texts before anything else gets shown. (Of course, this presupposes that displaying just that text is much faster than displaying the whole city data; if not, you would be just exchanging a delay for another!)

```
public TimedCitiesDisplay(
      final LinkedHashMap<String, ClientCityData> pCitiesList) {
   citiesList = pCitiesList;
   currentCity = pCitiesList.keySet().iterator();
   currentRow = 0;

   originalCountry = getDisplay().getCountryState().getCountry();
   originalState = getDisplay().getCountryState().getState();
   originalStart = currentStart;

   displayEmptyCities(0, "Loading...");
}
```

The run(...) method will display a few cities, and if there are any other remaining ones (see the someMore variable) it will schedule a new process that will continue with the current display. Should there have been any change (different country, state, or start position) the process just won't do anything, and it won't schedule a new run either. The CITIES_AT_A_TIME constant defines how many cities will get shown per run (another constant, CITIES_DELAY_IN_MS, is used to specify how many milliseconds apart is a run from the next) and the currentRow variable is used to count the rows, for display purposes.

```
@Override
public void run() {
  boolean someMore =
      originalCountry.equals(
        getDisplay().getCountryState().getCountry())
      && originalState.equals(
        getDisplay().getCountryState().getState())
      && originalStart == currentStart;
```

```
      for (int i = 0; someMore && i < CITIES_AT_A_TIME; i++) {
        if (currentCity.hasNext()) {
          final ClientCityData cd = citiesList.get(currentCity.next());
          currentRow++;
          getDisplay().setCityData(currentRow, cd.cityName,
              nf.format(cd.population), nf.format(cd.latitude),
              nf.format(cd.longitude));
        } else {
          /*
           * If there are no more cities, display empty lines
           * (a fast process) and disable the next timer call
           */
          displayEmptyCities(currentRow, "");
          someMore = false;
        }
      }

      /*
       * If there are still some more cities to display,
       * schedule a new display process in a short while.
       */
      if (someMore) {
        schedule(CITIES_DELAY_IN_MS);
      }
    }
  }

  static final int CITIES_AT_A_TIME = 10;
  static final int CITIES_DELAY_IN_MS = 250;
```

Here things start getting back to normal, and the rest of the original Presenter code is pretty much unchanged, except for the `getAndDisplayCities(...)` that now uses our `TimedCitiesDisplay` class.

```
  void getAndDisplayCities() {
    if (currentStart < 0) {
      currentStart = 0;
    }

    displayEmptyCities(0, "Loading...");
    getEnvironment().getModel().getCities(
        getDisplay().getCountryState().getCountry(),
        getDisplay().getCountryState().getState(), currentStart,
        CitiesBrowserView.CITIES_PAGE_SIZE,
        new SimpleCallback<LinkedHashMap<String, ClientCityData>>() {
          @Override
          public void goBack(
              final LinkedHashMap<String, ClientCityData> result) {
```

```
            new TimedCitiesDisplay(result).run();
        }
    });
  }
}
```

We can see this solution caught just between runs of our timed process in Figure 14.1.[8]

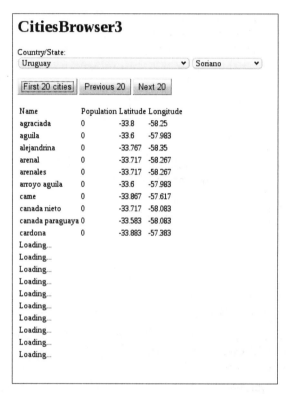

Figure 14.1 A part of the cities list has already been shown, and a timer-based command will fire shortly, to continue the display.

This is a solution much along the lines of "classic" JavaScript programming, but GWT actually provides an even better alternative, as we shall see in the next section.

A Deferred Command-Based Solution

Deferred commands are a GWT-specific feature, which make for an even better solution. These commands are queued for execution when the CPU is free, so if you do a small

---

8. A small confession is in order: I had to set CITIES_DELAY_IN_MS to a far larger value so that I could use my screen capture program and get the shown image.

part of the process, and use a deferred command to resume processing, GWT will run it as soon as possible, for a better throughput. (With the timer-based solution, if the user isn't actually doing anything, the time between runs of the display process will simply be wasted.) The general pattern of usage for this solution would be as follows.

```
define a class that extends IncrementalCommand:
  define attributes so it can save its parameters
  define attributes so it can save local variables from run to run
  define attributes so it can save form field values

  on construction:
    save the received parameters
    initialize local variables for the process
    save the current form field values

  on execute() method:
    if the current form field values match the saved values:
      execute some process, updating the local variables
      if there's still more work to be done
        return true, so it will run again shortly afterwards
      otherwise,
        return false (the job is done)
    otherwise,
      return false (situation changed)

whenever you want to simulate a thread with a deferred command:
  create an object of the new class above, with appropriate parameters
  use the addCommand() to add your new object to the processing queue
```

Back to the code, once again we'll leave most of our Presenter unchanged. For the `Timer`-based solution, note that now we use `IncrementalCommand` instead. However, if you compare both this version and the one in the previous section, you'll find more coincidences than differences.

```
package com.fkereki.mvpproject.client.citiesBrowser4;

// ...imports...

public class CitiesBrowserPresenter
    extends Presenter<CitiesBrowserDisplay> {
  public static String PLACE = "citybrowse";

  private class DeferredCitiesDisplay
      implements IncrementalCommand {
    final NumberFormat nf = NumberFormat.getDecimalFormat();
    LinkedHashMap<String, ClientCityData> citiesList = null;
    Iterator<String> currentCity = null;
    int currentRow = 0;
```

```
String originalCountry = null;
String originalState = null;
int originalStart = 0;

public DeferredCitiesDisplay(
    final LinkedHashMap<String, ClientCityData> pCitiesList) {

  citiesList = pCitiesList;
  currentCity = pCitiesList.keySet().iterator();
  currentRow = 0;

  originalCountry = getDisplay().getCountryState().getCountry();
  originalState = getDisplay().getCountryState().getState();
  originalStart = currentStart;

  displayEmptyCities(0, "Loading...");
}
```

Now we have an `execute(...)` method instead of a `run(...)` one, but the actual code is pretty much unchanged. Whenever the `execute(...)` method is run, if it returns `true`, it means it has to be run again; if it returns `false`, the command is considered to be done, and execution will cease.

```
public boolean execute() {
  boolean someMore = originalCountry.equals(getDisplay()
      .getCountryState().getCountry())
    && originalState.equals(getDisplay().getCountryState()
      .getState()) //
    && originalStart == currentStart;

  for (int i = 0; someMore && i < CITIES_AT_A_TIME; i++) {
    if (currentCity.hasNext()) {
      final ClientCityData cd = citiesList.get(currentCity.next());
      currentRow++;
      getDisplay().setCityData(currentRow, cd.cityName,
          nf.format(cd.population), nf.format(cd.latitude),
          nf.format(cd.longitude));
    } else {
      displayEmptyCities(currentRow, "");
      someMore = false;
    }
  }

  return someMore;
}
}
```

Of course, we must change `getAndDisplayCities(...)` so it will use our new `DeferredCommand` class; the difference is in the last executable sentence shown here.

```
void getAndDisplayCities() {
  if (currentStart < 0) {
    currentStart = 0;
  }

  displayEmptyCities(0, "Loading...");
  getEnvironment().getModel().getCities(
      getDisplay().getCountryState().getCountry(),
      getDisplay().getCountryState().getState(), currentStart,
      CitiesBrowserView.CITIES_PAGE_SIZE,
      new SimpleCallback<LinkedHashMap<String, ClientCityData>>() {
        @Override
        public void goBack(
            final LinkedHashMap<String, ClientCityData> result) {

          DeferredCommand
            .addCommand(new DeferredCitiesDisplay(result));
        }
      });
  }
}
```

In terms of the user experience, this solution may feel much like the Timer-based one, but display will actually be faster and smoother. If the user isn't interacting with the browser, successive runs will be scheduled as soon as possible, taking the most advantage of the available CPU power.

Bundling Data

Since GWT 1.4, you could use "image bundles" to improve application load performance, by making fewer calls to the server to get whichever images were required for your site. We already mentioned earlier in this chapter that your client page won't be able to do any number of simultaneous calls to the server, and this implies that if your application requires many images or icons, there will be a delay while the browser queues all calls to the server. (You could use Speed Tracer or any other of the tools that we will study later in this chapter to see the sequence of short load times in action.)

This is not the only problem. Because the kind of images you will use will surely be small (you wouldn't want to be downloading large files in any case, would you?) then HTTP will add a not trivial-sized overhead; it could even surpass the size of a given icon! And, even if your pictures won't be changing (just how often do you redesign your icons?) the browser will have to do a request to check whether the cached image may be considered still fresh.

The `ImageBundle` interface provided a way to solve all these problems by building a single package out of many files, and providing access to it through a Java object, in a way similar to the use of the `Constants` i18n interface that we saw in Chapter 12, "Internationalization and Localization."[9] This interface has now been deprecated, and replaced by `ClientBundle`, which allows including other types of files, not necessarily images.[10] A `ClientBundle` interface can give access to:

- `DataResource` elements, which provide an URL that enables getting the file contents at runtime.

- `TextResource` elements provide access to the contents of a text file, which are included in the compiled file.

- `ExternalTextResource` elements are similar to `TextResource` ones, but the text is obtained at runtime via Ajax.

- `CssResource` lets you inject CSS files into your application.[11]

- Finally, `ImageResource` is the familiar type for `ImageBundle` users; it provides access to an image.

Let's work out a simple example, using several of the types mentioned. I downloaded several of the images used in Google's GWT web site and also created a PDF out of the `ClientBundle` documentation page.[12] I listed a directory's contents into text files (in long and short formats) to provide more variety.

The first part is creating an interface, as when working with Constants.

```
package com.kereki.clientbundles.client;

// ...imports...

public interface SampleResource
    extends ClientBundle {
```

We can take advantage of a `static` variable to use this interface as a Singleton.

```
public static final SampleResource RESOURCE = GWT
    .create(SampleResource.class);
```

Now, as in i18n work (see Chapter 12) you must define a method for each file you want to access. The `@Source(...)` annotation is used to specify the file's name; by default, they are to be placed in the `client` directory. Note that i18n applies here; if you specify a file named `something.txt`, and your locale is `es_UY`, GWT will first look for `something_es_UY.txt`, then for `something_es.txt`, and finally for `something.txt`.

---

9. Web programmers know this technique as *CSS sprites* and that was what GWT applied internally.

10. As with constants, you also have a `ClientBundleWithLookup` interface, which allows getting resources by name.

11. This is actually an understatement; see http://code.google.com/webtoolkit/doc/latest/DevGuideClientBundle.html#CssResource for other extra functionalities.

12. See http://code.google.com/webtoolkit/doc/latest/DevGuideClientBundle.html for the original.

```
@Source("gwt_large_logo.png")
public ImageResource gwtLargeLogo();

@Source("gwt_small_logo.png")
public ImageResource gwtSmallLogo();

@Source("download_gwt.png")
public ImageResource gwtDownload();

@Source("learn_more.gif")
public ImageResource gwtLearnMore();

@Source("read_the_docs.gif")
public ImageResource gwtReadTheDocs();

@Source("ClientBundleDoc.pdf")
public DataResource clientBundleDocumentation();

@Source("detailed_list.txt")
public TextResource longListing();

@Source("short_list.txt")
public ExternalTextResource shortListing();
}
```

Using this bundle is easy. Let's just create a single page that will show all icons, the PDF file, and both listings. The final page will look as shown in Figure 14.2.

The code for this application is quite simple; I didn't worry much about elegance! First, we create some panels: a vertical one for general layout and a horizontal one for the icons.

```
package com.kereki.clientbundles.client;

// ...imports...

public class Clientbundles
    implements EntryPoint {

  @Override
  public void onModuleLoad() {
    final VerticalPanel vp = new VerticalPanel();
    final HorizontalPanel hp1 = new HorizontalPanel();
    hp1.add(new Image(SampleResource.RESOURCE.gwtLargeLogo()));
    hp1.add(new Image(SampleResource.RESOURCE.gwtSmallLogo()));
    hp1.add(new Image(SampleResource.RESOURCE.gwtDownload()));
    hp1.add(new Image(SampleResource.RESOURCE.gwtReadTheDocs()));
    hp1.add(new Image(SampleResource.RESOURCE.gwtLearnMore()));
    vp.add(hp1);
```

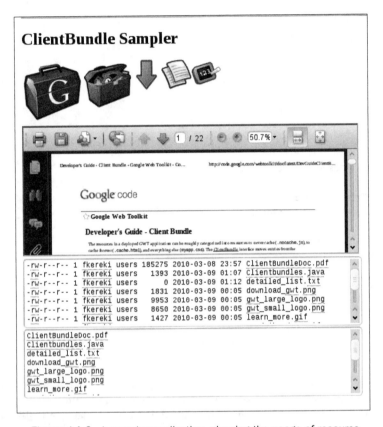

Figure 14.2 A sampler application, showing the usage of resource bundles to display some images, a PDF file, and text files by two different means.

Using a `DataResource` is simple; we will create a `Frame` and load it with the PDF file we created.

```
final Frame showPdf = new Frame(SampleResource.RESOURCE
    .clientBundleDocumentation().getUrl());
showPdf.setSize("540px", "200px");
vp.add(showPdf);
```

For a `TextResource`, it's even easier, for you can directly access its text with the `getText(...)` method.

```
final TextArea showListing1 = new TextArea();
showListing1.setText(SampleResource.RESOURCE.longListing()
    .getText());
showListing1.setSize("540px", "100px");
vp.add(showListing1);
```

Things become a bit more complicated with `ExternalTextResource` types, for you must do an Ajax call to get the file's contents, and that also allows for errors and exceptions. We initialize an area with a `Loading...` text, and after showing it, we get the file text with a `getText(...)` call, which requires a `ResourceCallback<TextResource>` object. In its `onSuccess(...)` method, we'll actually load the text into the screen widget; otherwise, we'll report a failure.

```
final TextArea showListing2 = new TextArea();
showListing2.setText("Loading...");
showListing2.setSize("540px", "100px");
vp.add(showListing2);

RootPanel.get().add(vp);

try {
  SampleResource.RESOURCE.shortListing().getText(
      new ResourceCallback<TextResource>() {
        public void onError(final ResourceException e) {
        }

        public void onSuccess(final TextResource r) {
          showListing2.setText(r.getText());
        }
      });
  } catch (final ResourceException e) {
    showListing2.setText("Failure!");
  }
}
}
```

As a final step, you will have to add the line `<inherits name="com.google.gwt .resources.Resources" />` to your gwt.xml file.

Using bundles is obviously a judgment call; you will exchange speed for size because your generated code will be larger. (The converse of this is code splitting, which we will analyze in Chapter 15, "Deploying Your Application.") However, if you do require many (hopefully small) files, you will discover that the speed advantages during normal execution (and the faster future visits, due to the cached data) justify the somewhat larger initial download time.

Speed Measurement Tools

The preceding patterns we saw are to be used at source code level, knowing that they will produce speed improvements. Let's now examine tools that will let you analyze the actual running code, to determine where your application is actually spending its time, and which are the causes of your possible slowdowns.

We will consider several browser general (meaning they could also be used for non-GWT applications) measurement tools. Personally, I find no "top" tool, so I regularly use all of them. It's likely they will converge over time, but for the time being they don't exactly offer the same functionality or suggestions.[13]

Speed Tracer

Speed Tracer is the first of our "browser general measurement tools" we spoke about earlier. It is provided as an extension for the Google Chrome that enables you to find performance problems in any web application by enabling you to visualize and analyze low level metrics.[14]

This tool will show you a graphic picture indicating clearly where your application spends most time and will also pinpoint specific problems and provide suggestions for fixing them.

Installing Speed Tracer isn't hard[15] but you must remember to add the `--enable-extension-timeline-api` parameter when you open Google Chrome. Using it is simple; just navigate to the page you want to analyze, and click the green stopwatch button to start capturing events and times; the red button will stop the data capture. I analyzed an actual (i.e., in production) small GWT application. See Figure 14.3.

The graphic at the top shows you the "peaks" of processing, with the corresponding timeline. You can focus on a specific period by dragging the selection bars, or by clicking and dragging. This should be the first information you study, because it can help focus on the "hot spots"; the tall, wide areas, and in particular, the short vertical marks that pinpoint specific problems. (Height stands for activity, so the rule to apply is simple: High is bad, low is good.) You can hover the mouse over a spot to get details on the particular event. If you are interested in only certain types of events, click the magnifying glass, and a filter bar will appear and let you specify your selection criteria.

If you select the Network view, you can see what resources (downloaded images, called services, and so on) were actually used. (See Figure 14.4.) You get a separate timeline for each resource. Also, if there is a hint or suggestion, a severity-color-coded icon (red=serious problem; orange=warning; green=hint) appears next to each resource, matching vertical marks in the timeline. By clicking a line you can get even more detailed information.

---

13. If you are willing to modify your project's source code to get runtime statistics, you might want to consider the "Lightweight Metrics System" at http://code.google.com/webtoolkit/doc/latest/DevGuideLightweightMetrics.html used with `gwt-debug-panel` at http://code.google.com/p/gwt-debug-panel/. Setting it up requires several steps, and then you also have to add appropriate calls at the places you want to measure, but on the positive side, it will provide you with information you couldn't get otherwise.

14. See http://code.google.com/webtoolkit/speedtracer/.

15. See http://code.google.com/webtoolkit/speedtracer/get-started.html#downloading.

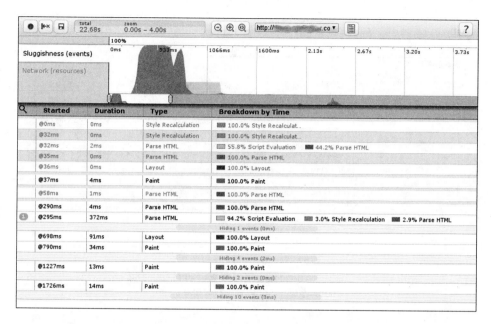

Figure 14.3 Speed Tracer's "Sluggishness" report shows you where time was spent and what was being done.

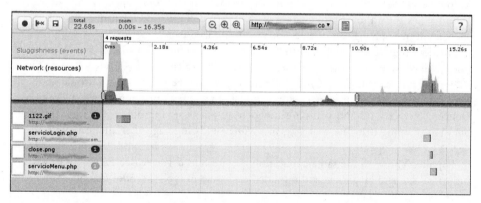

Figure 14.4 In Network mode, you can see what resources were used and their timeline.

Finally, Speed Tracer also offers a Hints mode, in which it highlights your page's "speed bumps" and possibly suggests appropriate measures. See Figure 14.5.

Speed Tracer is the most recent newcomer, but the information it provides is quite to the point and can help getting extra speed.

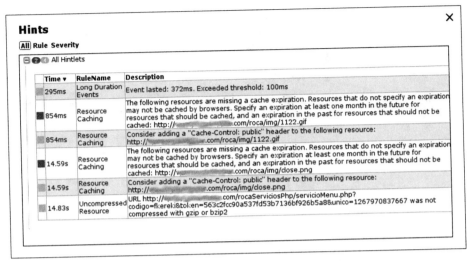

Figure 14.5 The Hints document shows your application speed bumps
and suggests some ways around them.

YSlow

YSlow (as in "Why Slow?") is a plugin for Firefox's Firebug, developed by the people at
Yahoo![16] It's geared toward suggesting ways of improving the performance of your
application by applying sets of rules for well-optimized pages.

After starting YSlow (which is itself included in Firebug) you can pick which set of
rules to apply (currently there are three sets—small sites and blogs, Classic V1, and YSlow
V2—involving 22 rules) and by clicking them you can see which rules it would apply.[17]
You can even create your own set; for example, if you aren't planning to use a Content
Delivery Network (CDN) you can simply create a new set (possibly based in an existing
one) but skipping that rule; that way, you will avoid being nagged all the time with the
"get a CDN" suggestion.

I applied YSlow to the same application as with Speed Tracer (see Figure 14.6) with
the "small site and blogs" set, and it graded each rule in typical school fashion, from "A"
(excellent) to "F" (fail).

Clicking each rule produces an explanation of the problem, a brief suggestion of the
steps you should take to solve the problem, and a Read More link to a fuller description
of the rule, what it implies, and how to fix the particular problem.

16. See http://developer.yahoo.com/yslow/ for more on this tool.

17. See http://developer.yahoo.com/performance/rules.html for the latest version of the rules that
YSlow applies.

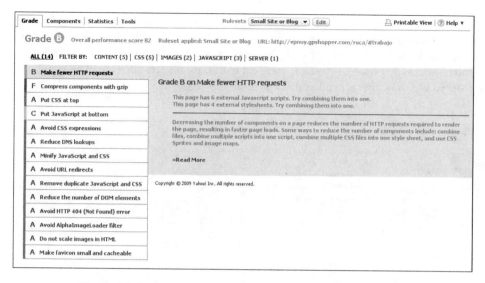

Figure 14.6 YSlow grades your application on up to 22 rules and
suggests measures you should take to optimize it.

Next to the Grade tab, you get the Components tab (see Figure 14.7) that shows all
the types of resources your application uses (HTML, CSS, and JavaScript files, plus
images and icons, and more) with detailed information as to their size, whether they
were compressed, the URL they came from, their Expires date, and so on. You can click
the magnifying glass icon to get even more detailed information on the specific resource.

▲ TYPE	SIZE (KB)	GZIP (KB)	COOKIE RECEIVED (bytes)	COOKIE SENT (bytes)	HEADERS	URL	EXPIRES (Y/M/D)	RESPONSE TIME (ms)	ETAG
⊟ doc (1)	0.9K								
doc	0.9K				🔍	http://...com /roca/	no expires	88	"1af0045-3cf-474f917740200"
⊟ js (6)	319.8K								
js	5.3K				🔍	http://...com /roca/roca.nocache.js	no expires	362	"1af003b-1506-474f917740200"
js	14.9K	4.4K			🔍	http://maps.google.com /maps?...	no expires	1216	
js	193.4K	69.3K			🔍	http://maps.gstatic.com /intl/en_us/mapfiles /208a/maps2.api/main.js	2011/3/7	1216	
js	8.5K				🔍	http://...com /roca/js/md5.js	no expires	355	"1af004d-217a-474f917740200"
js	64.8K				🔍	http://...com /roca/js/prototype.js	no expires	354	"1af004c-fd64-474f917740200"
js	32.7K				🔍	http://...com /roca/js/effects.js	no expires	353	"1af004b-7fc0-474f917740200"
⊞ css (4)	17.2K								
⊟ image (1)	12.3K								
image	12.3K				🔍	http://...com /roca/img/1122.gif	no expires	1142	"1af0068-3037-474f917740200"

Figure 14.7 The Components tab shows you all the server resources
that were required by your application.

You can get a resume of the information in the Components tab, by selecting the Statistics tab. This produces a display (see Figure 14.8) with two pie charts showing what would be loaded with an empty cache browser, or what would be loaded if the cache had been already primed. If you are using expiration parameters correctly, the second chart would show that much less data has to be downloaded.

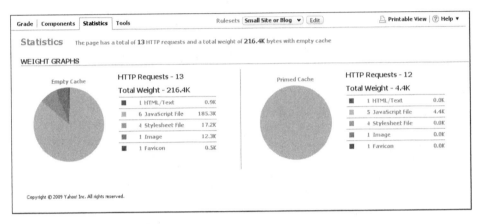

Figure 14.8 The Statistics tab shows you how much data would be downloaded with an empty or primed cache.

Finally, the Tools tab provides many options, some of which are of interest.

- JSLint runs this analyzer[18] on all your JavaScript code. Note that it won't be useful for most of your code—the GWT generated part—and you will probably be able to use it only for external libraries. As the JSLint creators point out, "JSLint will hurt your feelings" but its suggestions are worth it.

- All JS Minified lets you see the JavaScript code, as it would look if minified. GWT takes care of doing it for its own code, so once again you will only use this for external libraries.

- All Smush.it runs this Yahoo! tool[19] that can apply a lossless transformation to reduce the size of your image files without affecting their quality, letting you download equivalent optimized versions of them.

- Printable View presents all the information in the Grade, Components, and Statistics tabs in a single printable page.

YSlow thus offers not only a good analysis of your page, but also suggests ways of fixing whatever problems it found, even providing sometimes (as with JavaScript minification and image optimization) the full solutions you require.

18. See www.jslint.com/ for more on JSLint.

19. See http://developer.yahoo.com/yslow/smushit/ for information on how Smush.it works.

Page Speed

Google's own Page Speed[20] is another Firebug plugin, in some aspects quite similar to YSlow, but worthy enough of your attention; in fact, I usually apply both, to make sure I'm not missing anything.

For Page Speed to analyze a page, you'll have to start FireBug, pick Page Speed, and click Analyze Performance. The main result it will provide is a page score, from 0 to 100, which reflects the quality (in terms of the predefined rules) of your application. See Figure 14.9.

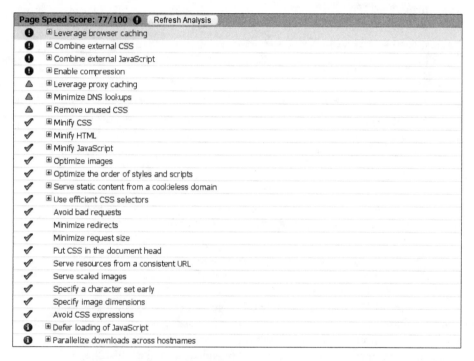

Figure 14.9 Page Speed grades your application from 0 to 100 and points out its problematic areas in terms of unsatisfied web design rules.

Each rule includes an icon (red for serious problems, yellow for warnings, green for approved parts, and blue for information) and by clicking on the plus sign next to the icon, you can get a more detailed explanation of the problem and a suggestion as to the required fix.[21] See Figure 14.10.

20. See http://code.google.com/speed/page-speed/ for the Page Speed site.

21. See http://code.google.com/speed/page-speed/docs/rules_intro.html for the list of applied rules.

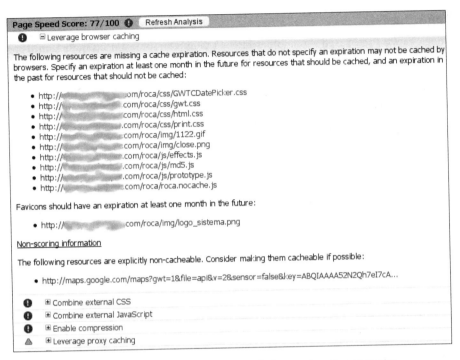

Figure 14.10 Clicking a rule provides further explanation as to the
problem and a suggestion or fix.

The Page Speed menu bar provides a Performance tab (whose results we have already seen) and a Resources tab. The latter shows you all the resources (images, files, and more) that were downloaded from the server, with further information as to URL, size, and so on. (See Figure 14.11.) You should study this page, and check whether most of the fixed resources could be loaded from the cache, and if files are being compressed; not satisfying these conditions would negatively impact the performance of your application.

Finally, a Page Speed Activity extra tool is provided (see Figure 14.12) that produces a detailed timeline showing all the requests to the server, color coded by type, and with bars proportional to their actual times. Having many of these bars roughly at the same time would indicate the need for joining files together (possibly by using bundles) or for caching, whereas long bars could possibly point out server delay problems or too long processes.

As we said, Page Speed is quite similar to YSlow (and even to Speed Tracer, though that runs on a different browser) but being able to apply different sets of rules and taking different measurements is the equivalent of going to several different doctors to confirm a diagnosis, so I'd insist on using all tools, even if at times there is some considerable overlap between them.

	Status	Type	File Size	Transfer Size
⊞ http://████████.com/roca/	200	doc	975 bytes	975 bytes
⊞ http://████████.com/roca/img/logo_sistema.pn	200 (cache)	favicon	567 bytes	567 bytes
⊞ http://████████.com/roca/roca.nocache.js	200	js	5.3kB	5.3kB
⊞ http://████████.com/roca/js/md5.js	200	js	8.4kB	8.4kB
⊞ http://████████.com/roca/js/prototype.js	200	js	63.3kB	63.3kB
⊞ http://████████.com/roca/js/effects.js	200	js	31.9kB	31.9kB
⊞ http://maps.google.com/maps?gwt=1&file=api&v=2&se	200	js	14.6kB	4.4kB
⊞ http://maps.gstatic.com/intl/en_us/mapfiles/208a/map	200	js	188.9kB	67.7kB
⊞ http://████████.com/roca/css/gwt.css	200	css	7kB	7kB
⊞ http://████████.com/roca/css/html.css	200	css	6kB	6kB
⊞ http://████████.com/roca/css/GWTCDatePicker.	200	css	3.5kB	3.5kB
⊞ http://████████.com/roca/css/print.css	200	css	334 bytes	334 bytes
⊞ http://maps.gstatic.com/intl/en_us/mapfiles/transparer	200	image	95 bytes	95 bytes
⊞ http://████████.com/roca/img/1122.gif	200	image	12.1kB	12.1kB
⊞ http://████████.com/roca/img/close.png	200	image	762 bytes	762 bytes
⊞ http://████████.com/roca/A9CB52440B2DD8250	200	iframe	458.5kB	458.5kB
⊞ http://████████.com/rocaServiciosPhp/servicioL	200	other	36 bytes	36 bytes
⊞ http://████████.com/rocaServiciosPhp/servicioᴺ	200	other	1.1kB	1.1kB
		18 resources	**803.2kB**	**671.9kB**

Figure 14.11 The Resources tab provides information on every request
to the server.

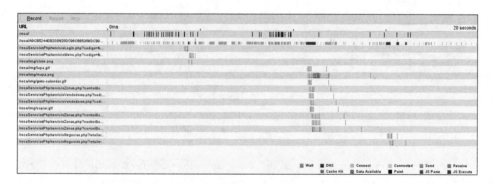

Figure 14.12 The Page Speed Activity lets you analyze a timeline for your
application, detecting bottlenecks and too many concurrent calls.

JavaScript Debuggers

Let's finish the analysis of browser-based tools with JavaScript's own debuggers. Firefox's
Firebug, which we have already seen, has a Net panel that can produce a detailed list of
all events and resources invoked by your application (see Figure 14.13). This isn't as good
as Speed Tracer's analysis, for example, but it can do as a starting point.

In a similar vein, you could use Safari's debugger, or Opera's DragonFly debugger (see
Figure 14.14), which can also produce a detailed timeline of events. Of course, because
you cannot at the time use Opera for GWT Development mode, it's less likely that you
would want to use this browser.

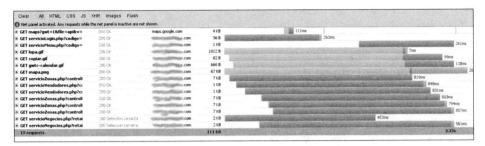

Figure 14.13 Firefox's Firebug debugger includes a Net tab, which shows all events and their durations.

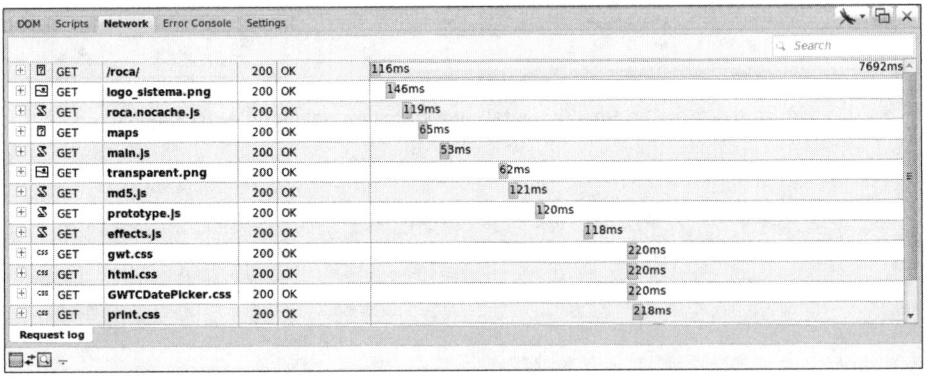

Figure 14.14 Opera's DragonFly debugger can also help; the only problem is that you cannot use Opera for GWT development.

Debuggers aren't specifically geared toward optimization, but on the other hand, they are always available as you do your development, so why miss using them?

Summary

We have seen three ways of enhancing the performance of your application: design patterns, some GWT 2 new features, and browser speed measurement tools. By combining all these solutions, you can find bottlenecks, detect slowdowns, and generally squeeze much more performance out of your application. There's no single "silver bullet" that can fix all possible problems, but applying what we have seen here, you are on your way to a far more responsive application.

## 15

Deploying Your Application

This chapter explores the final steps in your development process: how to compile and deploy your application, how to create your own shareable modules, and how to reduce the load time for your application by splitting the code.

In the past chapters, we have been dealing with ways to write efficient, streamlined, modern Internet applications, but it happens there still are some ways to squeeze out yet a bit more of speed and get a faster page load, so we need to look into that. And, obviously, if you cannot deploy your application, all your work will have been for naught; let's also see how to "finish the job" and set up your page for production.

Compilation

With standard GWT development techniques, you won't have to compile your program until you actually want to publish it. Because of how deferred binding works, several different versions of the final JavaScript code will be produced: the number of supported browsers (currently, six, but the number may change from GWT version to version) times the number of supported locales (in our case, four: see Chapter 12, "Internationalization and Localization"). See Figure 15.1.

You can use many compiler options to speed up compilation, to enhance the quality of the produced code, or just to inspect what kind of code is generated; let's turn to this now.

Plenty of compiler options aren't that well documented, so let's give a glance at least to the most important ones, meaning those you are likely to use.

- **-compileReport** creates the Story of Your Compile report; we'll be using this for code splitting. This option used to read **-soyc** but the name was quickly changed.

- **-draftCompile** enables a faster, but with fewer optimizations, compilation process. You should use this option while developing, but leave it out when producing the definitive, production code.

- **-ea** enables assert checks; otherwise, **assert** statements would be ignored.

- **-extra** *aDirectory* allows you to specify to which directory should extra files (not meant to be deployed) be written.

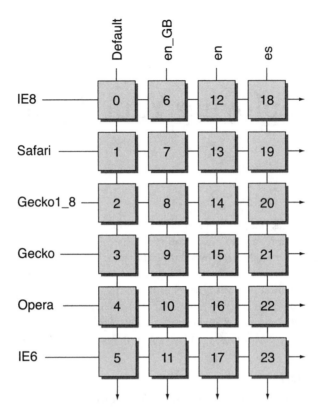

Figure 15.1 The GWT compile process produces a distinct permutation for each combination of browser type and locale. The numbers match those shown in Figure 15.2 but might change from compile to compile.

- **-localWorkers** *someNumber* lets you specify how many local workers (i.e., compiling processes) to run at the same time; by default, it's just one. You should experiment a bit with this; depending on the number of CPUs in your machine, you could get faster compiles by setting it to a higher value.

- **-logLevel** lets you set the level of messages (**ALL**, **DEBUG**, **ERROR**, **INFO**, **SPAM**, **TRACE**, or **WARN**) you will get when compiling.

- **-module** *someModules* lets you specify which module(s) to compile.

- **-out** *aDirectory* lets you specify to which directory to write output files.

- **-style** *outputStyle* lets you set the output JavaScript style to **DETAILED**, **OBF** (obfuscated, the default value), or **PRETTY**.

- **-treeLogger** produces log output in a graphical tree form.

- **-validateOnly** performs a complete validation of all source code, without actually compiling anything. You could use it as a fast check before a long compile.

- **-war** *aDirectory* lets you set to which directory should deployable output files be written; by default, it is "war".

- **-workDir** *aDirectory* allows you to specify which directory should be used by the compiler for internal use; by default, it is the system's temporary directory, and in any case, it should be writeable.

- **-XdisableAggressiveOptimization** disables aggressive optimizations.

- **-XdisableCastChecking** foregoes checking if a cast operation—as in **(someCast)anObject.someMethod(...)**—can throw a **ClassCastException**, thus speeding method calls.

- **-XdisableClassMetadata** disables the usage of the **getName(...)** method but allows reducing the final code size because GWT doesn't have to include any class information within the produced JavaScript code.

- **-XdisableRunAsync** disables code splitting. (We'll be studying this in more detail.)

Adding compiler options with Eclipse just requires clicking the red Google Compile box, and then clicking Advanced, and entering the desired options in the Additional Compiler Arguments box.

If you want to compile your code in the fastest way, you should experiment by using **-draftCompile -localWorkers** *someNumber* **-XdisableAggressiveOptimization** and also add in your application's **gwt.xml** file lines such as the following, so only one code version will be produced.[1]

```
<set-property name="user.agent" value="gecko"/>
<set-property name="locale" value="en" />
```

On the other hand, if you care for the final produced code performance, you should rather consider including **-XdisableCastChecking -XdisableClassMetadata -style OBF** so that your code will be as compact as possible.

Modules

While developing an application, it's a given that you will develop classes (tools, widgets, whatever) that you will want to reuse in other applications. GWT lets you package your classes as modules for future reuse, but there are some particularities that you need to be aware of.

---

1. The default suggestion for implementing this was creating a new module that inherited your original module (i.e., the one defined in the gwt.xml file), adding the <set-property...> elements to it, changing your host HTML file so it would refer to this new module, and compiling it instead of the original one... but I do think the method shown in the text is easier. We saw this briefly in Chapter 3, but see "Renaming Modules" at http://code.google.com/webtoolkit/doc/latest/DevGuideOrganizingProjects.html#DevGuideModuleXml for more on it.

The main problem here is that you won't be able to produce a jar file and simply reuse it as you were used to with common Java development, because GWT requires the actual source code of your class to compile it into JavaScript. (Of course, for server packages, this doesn't apply, and you can use your standard, run-of-the-mill jar files without further ado.) To test this out, let's create a separate module for the `KeyValueMap` class that we wrote in Chapter 4, "Working with Browsers".

1. First, create a new empty project: `KeyValueMap` is a good name, and the package can be `com.kereki.keyvaluemap`. Edit its `gwt.xml` file to remove the `<entry-point...>` element. (Actually, you could have an entry point, if your class implemented the `EntryPoint` interface. When you load a project including two or more entry points, the code from all the `onModuleLoad(...)` methods gets executed before anything else.)

2. Move the `KeyValueMap.java` file from the original project to the client directory in our new project. (Red error marks should pop up all over your original project, showing that the `KeyValueMap` class is now missing.)

3. Compile the new project, so it will generate a `class` file in the war output directory. We will require this file for our module, together with its source file.

4. Create a temporary directory somewhere in your machine, and copy both the source and class files to it:

```
md /tmp/newmodule
cd /tmp/newmodule
cp -R /home/fkereki/workspace/KeyValueMap/src/com/ .
cp -R /home/fkereki/workspace/KeyValueMap/war/WEB-INF/classes/com/ .
```

5. Create a `jar` file for your module by doing

```
jar -cvf KeyValuemap.jar .
added manifest
adding: com/(in = 0) (out= 0)(stored 0%)
adding: com/kereki/(in = 0) (out= 0)(stored 0%)
adding: com/kereki/keyvaluemap/(in = 0) (out= 0)(stored 0%)
adding: com/kereki/keyvaluemap/client/(in = 0) (out= 0)(stored 0%)
adding: com/kereki/keyvaluemap/client/KeyValueMap.java(in = 1627)
    (out= 714)(deflated 56%)
adding: com/kereki/keyvaluemap/client/KeyValueMap.class(in = 2108)
    (out= 1145)(deflated 45%)
adding: com/kereki/keyvaluemap/shared/(in = 0) (out= 0)(stored 0%)
adding: com/kereki/keyvaluemap/server/(in = 0) (out= 0)(stored 0%)
adding: com/kereki/keyvaluemap/KeyValueMap.gwt.xml(in = 947)
    (out= 398)(deflated 57%)
```

6. Add a `modules` directory to your old project at the same level as `src`, and copy the newly created jar file to it. You would use this directory for all modules you add to a project.

7. Add an `<inherits name='com.kereki.keyvaluemap.KeyValueMap'/>` line to the `gwt.xml` file in your old project.

8. Add the new jar to the classpath of your old project. (The red error marks should now disappear.) You are done!

If you study step 7, you will notice that this is exactly the same way GWT requires that you include `com.google.gwt.user.User` and other modules for your application!

Code Splitting

If your application grows (and that's a tendency hard breaking off from!) the initial download will become large enough to become too noticeable, and the user will not appreciate it. Since version 2, GWT provides Dead For Now (DFN) code splitting, which lets you download first only what you need, and then get the rest on demand, if and when it is needed. Of course, if you require the same code a second time, no further downloads will be required, because the code will already be in memory; there will be a trade-off between a shorter initial download time and small future extra downloads, but the cost will be paid only once per code split.[2]

To split your code, you'll just use the `GWT.runAsync(...)` method. This will call the server, download the required code, and then `onSuccess(...)` execute it.[3] The standard pattern will then be

```
GWT.runAsync(new RunAsyncCallback() {
  @Override
  public void onFailure(Throwable caught) {
    // ...warn about the download failure...
  }

  @Override
  public void onSuccess() {
    // ...this is where the original code goes...
  }
});
```

You may have scope problems, because your original code will now be running in the `RunAsyncCallback` object scope, but they are usually simple to solve. Let's try some actual experiments with the Environment menu handling code; given that it's highly likely that not all menu functions will be used (at least, in the same session) by a user, it

---

2. You can read more of the official word on Code Splitting at http://code.google.com/webtoolkit/doc/latest/DevGuideCodeSplitting.html.

3. A not minor point: You should plan for failure—onFailure(...)—because the code download might fail. There is, frankly, little than you can do, but at least you should explain to the user why he isn't getting the form he expected.

stands to reason that these code splits will help.[4] A part of the menu code (see Chapter 4) used to read:

```
...} else if (token.equals(CitiesBrowserPresenter.PLACE)) {
  panel.add(new CitiesBrowserPresenter(args,
    new CitiesBrowserView(), this).getDisplay().asWidget());
} ...
```

We could split off the Cities Browsing code, by rewriting the `else` as

```
...} else if (token.equals(CitiesBrowserPresenter.PLACE)) {
  final Panel myPanel = panel;
  final String myArgs = args;

  GWT.runAsync(new RunAsyncCallback() {
    @Override
    public void onFailure(final Throwable reason) {
      Environment.this
          .showAlert("Couldn't run the Cities Browser code!");
    }

    public void onSuccess() {
      myPanel.add(new CitiesBrowserPresenter(myArgs,
          new CitiesBrowserView(), Environment.this).getDisplay()
          .asWidget());
    }
  });
}...
```

We had to add some final attributes to get at the `panel` and `args` variables, but other than that, the transition is simple; we also had to change the `this` reference to `Environment.this` because of closure problems.

We could even do some refactoring to simplify splitting off more parts of the code. First, we could extend the `RunAsyncCallback(...)` interface by writing:[5]

```
abstract class MyRunAsyncCallback
    implements RunAsyncCallback {
```

Let's have a few attributes to store the arguments that are required for the code. We'll pass the said arguments to our new constructor.

---

4. And, if you feel it will be quite likely that a certain piece of code will get used, but didn't want to load it right at the beginning because of download time reasons, you could apply a variation of the prefetching pattern we used earlier in the book: Do a `GWT.runAsync(...)` call with an empty `onSuccess(...)` method, and thus use background time to get the code loaded in advance of its being required.

5. Yes, and I admit the `MyRunAsyncCallback` name is kind of lame...

```
String myOwnArgs;
Panel myOwnPanel;
Environment myOwnEnvironment;
String myOwnErrorMessage;

public MyRunAsyncCallback(
    final String args,
    final Panel panel,
    final Environment environment,
    final String errorMessage) {

  myOwnArgs = args;
  myOwnPanel = panel;
  myOwnEnvironment = environment;
  myOwnErrorMessage = errorMessage;
}
```

The onFailure(...) method is now trivial.

```
@Override
public void onFailure(final Throwable reason) {
  myOwnEnvironment.showAlert(myOwnErrorMessage);
}
}
```

Using this code requires writing the onSuccess(...) method. For example, we might split off the Cities Creator form, by means of

```
...} else if (token.equals(CityCreatorPresenter.PLACE)) {

GWT.runAsync(new MyRunAsyncCallback(args, panel, this,
    "Couldn't load the cities browser code") {

  @Override
  public void onSuccess() {
    myOwnPanel.add(new CityCreatorPresenter(myOwnArgs,
        new CityCreatorView(), myOwnEnvironment)
      .getDisplay().asWidget());
  }
});
}...
```

If you compile both versions of the code (with and without the code split) you will notice that some files get smaller, but several more files are produced. In these examples, because the Cities Browsing and Creation classes aren't used elsewhere, all their code will be removed from the initial download, reducing its size. But how can you know for sure? Let's analyze an important tool, the Compile Reports, which for a short while were known as Story Of Your Compile, or SOYC—and this will also help understand the compile process.

Turning on the Compile Reports option will produce a directory with a set of HTML files, which comprise the required report. These reports will give you a graphical representation of the results of the compile process and provide you information to find possible code reduction hints to analyze code splitting problems and to let you work out further code optimizations.[6]

The Compile Report is a group of static HTML pages and can be found at the extras directory (in my case, at my home directory, at `workspace/mvpproject/extras`) in the `mvpproject/soycReport` directory; you can examine it by opening the `index.html` file that is situated there. (See Figure 15.2.) In our case, because we were creating code

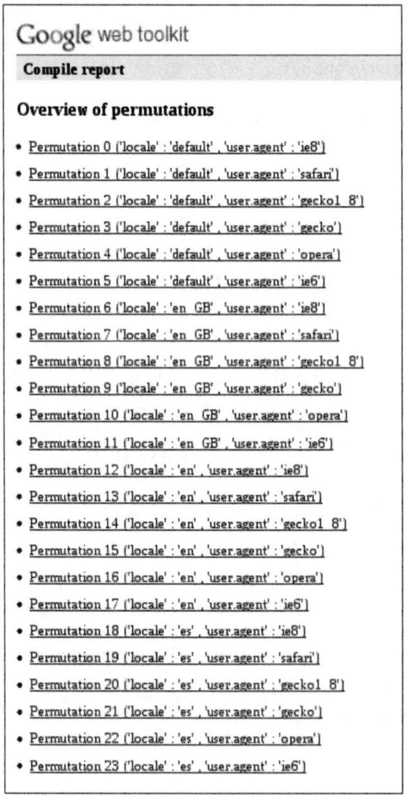

Figure 15.2 The basic compile report shows all permutations that were
generated by the compilation process. The permutation numbers match
those shown in Figure 15.1 but might vary.

---

6. Official usage notes on Compile Reports can be found at http://code.google.com/webtoolkit/
doc/latest/DevGuideCompileReport.html.

for four locales (the default one, plus the three ones we defined in Chapter 12), and GWT always produces code for six browser types, we should get 24 permutations, numbered 0 to 23.

If we click on a specific permutation, we can see its size details. (See Figure 15.3.)

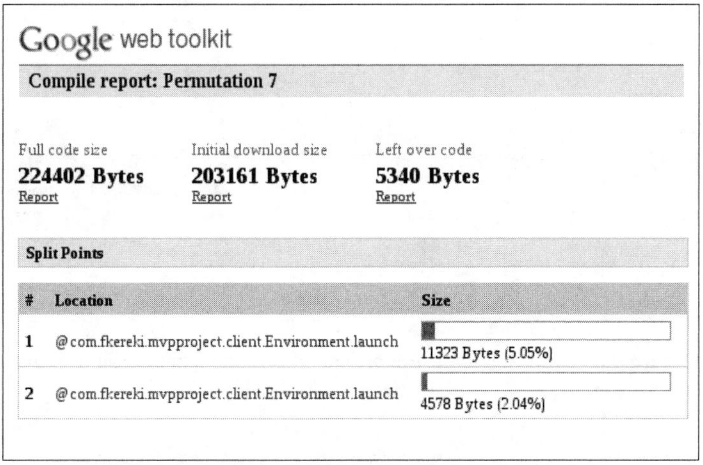

Figure 15.3 Each permutation report shows the full code size (without any splits), the initial download size, and more data on each split.

The Full code size value represents the total size of the code: 224,402 bytes in this case. You can see that the initial download size, given the two code splits we made, would be 203,161 bytes, representing about a 9% reduction in size; not bad for such a small change! The rest of the code is comprised of two code splits (at 11,323 and 4,578 bytes), plus a "left over" split (5,340 bytes) with some general code, not associated specifically with any split; you can check that the sum works out. By clicking on a "report" link, you can get (see Figures 15.4 and 15.5) further reports showing in more detail how the code size is achieved.

By clicking on the package links, you can eventually get to see why a specific class is included; this is a good help in case something unexpected happens, and you don't get the size savings you hoped for.

If sizes do not match your expectation (you tried to create a separate fragment for a specific part of the code, but GWT insists on downloading it from the beginning) examining the dependencies will let you find why you failed in separating it. (The most common reason is that, somehow, you use a class that you wanted to split, from an unsplit part of the code.) You'll have to reorder or reorganize part of your code so this won't happen, and there isn't any specific technique for this, but hopefully you'll work it out.

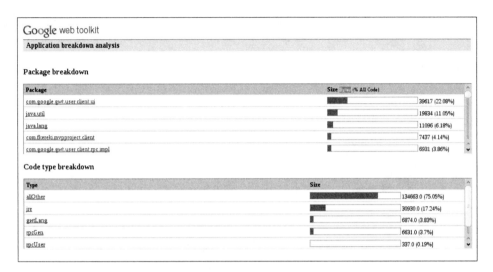

Figure 15.4 Clicking on a Report link shows in higher detail how the code size is divided.

Figure 15.5 An analysis of a specific code split. In this case, all the present code comes from a single class, which we wanted to split, so we got what we wanted.

You should get used to studying the Compile Report; even if your code is in tip-top shape, some new programmer might introduce a change that disrupts your splits. Before distributing an updated version of your application, check that the code downloads are still what they used to be; a perfectly valid statement might go so far as to pull up all of your splits into "initial download country," and while the program would still work the same, the user would feel a throwback to worse performance.

Deployment

After all we did earlier in this chapter, deploying your application is trivially easy. The compiler produces code files following the WAR rules, which makes it simple to deploy. Whether you are working with GWT only for client-side coding, or you are going the "Java way" with server-side code, getting your application on the web will require copying only a few directories and files.[7] Let's start with the simpler case first.[8]

Working with Client-Only GWT

If you don't have Java-based server-side coding (as with a web service-based architecture) you can easily deploy the HTML and JavaScript files that are produced by the GWT compiler to a web server such as Apache, though the details would be similar for other programs.

By default, in Linux you can usually find Apache's pages at /srv/www/htdocs (for OpenSUSE) or /var/www/html, and you can actually set it to store its pages at any other place; check the configuration files. If you do not have any remote servlets, you'll just have to copy the files in the output war directory to the correct location for your home page, and you'll be set.

Working with Client-Plus-Server GWT

If you are going to have servlets (i.e, Java server-side coding) you will need an appropriate web container. GWT produces a standard deployment configuration, so even though in this section we will be working with Tomcat (version 6.0.20) as a web container, changing to other container wouldn't be much of a problem.[9] We won't be covering how to set up that part of the software stack, but there's plenty of documentation everywhere for that. Of course, if your application depends on web services, Enterprise Java Beans, or any other such technology, you'll also have to set them up.

Working with OpenSUSE, Tomcat stores the web pages at /srv/tomcat6/webapps; other Linux distributions, and of course Windows and Mac versions, may store them at different locations. All we have to do is copy (and surely rename; I chose mvpproject) the war directory in our project to a directory in the Tomcat directory. To run the

---

7. You could also work with the generated Ant scripts to build or deploy your application; in my case, I prefer working exclusively within Eclipse.

8. While I'm not an Ant user, it should be said that you can automate both compilation and deployment with it, and there are many GWT developers who swear by it!

9. See http://tomcat.apache.org/ for more on Tomcat.

application, you'll have to navigate to http://yourOwnServer:8080/mvpproject/
Mvpproject.html and you will get something like Figure 15.6.[10]

Figure 15.6 Running our Tomcat-deployed application on Linux-based
Google Chrome shows our deployment was successful.

Of course you could configure Tomcat to find the host HTML page anywhere on
your web server, but mind that all resources should be placed so as to mirror the project
paths, because references to them are relative.

If you are using servlets, GWT will automatically deploy them to the WEB-INF/
classes directory. In our example, you could do

```
# cd /srv/tomcat6/webapps/mvpproject/
# cd WEB-INF/classes/com/fkereki/mvpproject/server
# ls -ld *
-rw-r--r-- 1 root root 3847 2010-03-12 05:16 FileProcess.class
-rw-r--r-- 1 root root 1611 2010-03-12 05:16 FileProduce.class
-rw-r--r-- 1 root root 3458 2010-03-12 05:16 LoginServiceImpl.class
-rw-r--r-- 1 root root 3182 2010-03-12 05:16 Security.class
-rw-r--r-- 1 root root 1642 2010-03-12 05:16 ServerCityData.class
-rw-r--r-- 1 root root 7620 2010-03-12 05:16 WorldServiceImpl.class
-rw-r--r-- 1 root root 2986 2010-03-12 05:16 XhrProxyImpl.class
```

and check that all remote servlet code is present and up to date. If you required any
other server-side classes, you would also place them in this directory. The web.xml file
(which we created with the GWT project; see Chapter 2, "Getting Started with GWT 2")

10. A slight detail: with the current version of the Eclipse plugin, the war directory is both used as
input and output, but this is expected to be fixed soon.

will have to provide all necessary definitions and mappings. Its final version for our application could be as follows.[11]

```xml
<?xml version="1.0" encoding="UTF-8"?>
<!DOCTYPE web-app
    PUBLIC "-//Sun Microsystems, Inc.//DTD Web Application 2.3//EN"
    "http://java.sun.com/dtd/web-app_2_3.dtd">

<web-app>
  <servlet>
    <servlet-name>loginServlet</servlet-name>
    <servlet-class>com.fkereki.mvpproject.server.LoginServiceImpl
    </servlet-class>
  </servlet>
  <servlet-mapping>
    <servlet-name>loginServlet</servlet-name>
    <url-pattern>/mvpproject/login</url-pattern>
  </servlet-mapping>

  <servlet>
    <servlet-name>worldServlet</servlet-name>
    <servlet-class>com.fkereki.mvpproject.server.WorldServiceImpl
    </servlet-class>
  </servlet>
  <servlet-mapping>
    <servlet-name>worldServlet</servlet-name>
    <url-pattern>/mvpproject/world</url-pattern>
  </servlet-mapping>

  <servlet>
    <servlet-name>xhrProxyServlet</servlet-name>
    <servlet-class>com.fkereki.mvpproject.server.XhrProxyImpl
    </servlet-class>
  </servlet>
  <servlet-mapping>
    <servlet-name>xhrProxyServlet</servlet-name>
    <url-pattern>/mvpproject/xhrproxy</url-pattern>
  </servlet-mapping>

  <servlet>
    <servlet-name>fileProcess</servlet-name>
    <servlet-class>com.fkereki.mvpproject.server.FileProcess
    </servlet-class>
  </servlet>
```

11. Note that with previous versions of GWT, you had to do this in the application `gwt.xml` file.

```
<servlet-mapping>
  <servlet-name>fileProcess</servlet-name>
  <url-pattern>/mvpproject/fileprocess</url-pattern>
</servlet-mapping>

<servlet>
  <servlet-name>fileProduce</servlet-name>
  <servlet-class>com.fkereki.mvpproject.server.FileProduce
  </servlet-class>
</servlet>
<servlet-mapping>
  <servlet-name>fileProduce</servlet-name>
  <url-pattern>/mvpproject/fileproduce</url-pattern>
</servlet-mapping>

<!-- Default page to serve -->
<welcome-file-list>
  <welcome-file>Mvpproject.html</welcome-file>
</welcome-file-list>
</web-app>
```

Finally, note that if your application uses RPC, GWT will take care of copying the `gwt-servlet.jar` file to the WEB-INF/lib directory, but if you require any other jars, you'll have to copy them by yourself.

Summary

In this chapter we have finished the complete application development cycle, by actually compiling and deploying our code. We have also seen a method for optimizing the application download code, by means of splitting it into significant parts, and also for analyzing and fixing any situations that might lead to worse-than-expected reductions in size. By combining this method with the previously seen techniques, you will make true the promise of web applications that feel so responsive as if they were actually deployed and installed on the user's PC, rather than downloaded from the Internet and executed on a client-server basis.

Index

P

Q–R

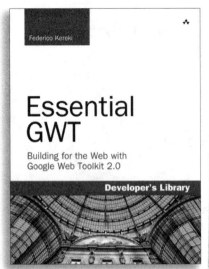

FREE Online Edition

Your purchase of **Essential GWT** includes access to a free online edition for 45 days through the Safari Books Online subscription service. Nearly every Addison-Wesley Professional book is available online through Safari Books Online, along with more than 5,000 other technical books and videos from publishers such as Cisco Press, Exam Cram, IBM Press, O'Reilly, Prentice Hall, Que, and Sams.

SAFARI BOOKS ONLINE allows you to search for a specific answer, cut and paste code, download chapters, and stay current with emerging technologies.

Activate your FREE Online Edition at
www.informit.com/safarifree

> **STEP 1:** Enter the coupon code: RKMAHAA.

> **STEP 2:** New Safari users, complete the brief registration form.
> Safari subscribers, just log in.

If you have difficulty registering on Safari or accessing the online edition,
please e-mail customer-service@safaribooksonline.com